The Movable Garden

The Movable Garden

*How to use potted plants indoors and out
to create a carefree year-round garden*

by Ruth Shaw Ernst

The Globe Pequot Press

CHESTER, CONNECTICUT

Illustrations on pages xii, 6, 8, 19, 26, 29, 36, 38, 41–46, 48, 51–52, 56, 59, 75, 79, 80, and 83 by Joy Stampes
All other illustrations by Mauro Magellan

Library of Congress Cataloging-in-Publication Data

Ernst, Ruth Shaw.
  The movable garden: how to use potted plants indoors and out to create a carefree year-round garden / by Ruth Shaw Ernst. — 1st ed.
      p.   cm.
  Includes bibliographical references and index.
  ISBN 0-87106-304-2
  1. Container gardening.   I. Title.
SB418.E76   1991
635.9'86—dc20   90-26617
                                                                                  CIP

Manufactured in the United States of America
First Edition/Second Printing

Contents

PART II
Decorating with Your Movable Garden

PART III:
Plants for Your Movable Garden

Acknowledgments

Nancy Cook, horticultural consultant, Agricultural Division of Cornell Cooperative Extension in White Plains, New York, has been most helpful in providing information on various horticultural subjects. Valuable aid was generously given by Leonard Marino, manager of the Propagation Range, The New York Botanical Garden, on container culture of bulbs and tropical forest plants. My thanks also to Dave Anderson, senior staff horticulturist, Wayside Gardens, for helpful information on bulbs and plants suitable for growing in containers. Special thanks and appreciation go to the staff of the Scarsdale Library for their assistance.

Introduction

I like to think that long before the dawn of recorded history a cavewoman, pleased at the sight of a pretty flower, pulled up the plant to admire it more closely. Soon it died. Puzzled but still interested, she tried again, this time setting another pretty plant in a hollow of a decaying log near the cave. Rain dampened the earth that clug to the plant's roots, and the plant thrived in the rotting cavity of the wood. Maybe that's when container gardening began.

Actual evidence of container gardening goes back as far as the ancient Egyptian, Babylonian, Roman, and Oriental civilizations, which delighted in growing shrubs and flowering, fruiting plants and trees in pots and tubs outdoors. In later centuries, travelers brought new and strange species to Europe and America from all over the world. But it wasn't until the nineteenth century—more specifically, the early Victorian era—that people began to welcome botanicals into the home and to think of them as necessary components of their environments. As the interest in container gardening grew apace, spreading from the dim recesses of the Victorian parlor to other, brighter rooms and spilling outdoors again, botanists and breeders turned their efforts to creating hybrids and cultivars, or cultivated varieties, more varied than species taken from the wild. The new plants were more diverse in shape, size, and color of leaf and flower and more adaptable to various indoor and outdoor environments and climates, than the original species forms. In many cases, they were also longer-lived and easier to tend. Today the range of plants that can be container-grown is enormous and constantly increasing, to the joy and benefit of potted-plant aficionados, whose number is rapidly growing.

Taking care of gardens has been described by some as a constant battle against pests, disease, the elements, and muscle fatigue. I can't quite agree with this assessment, but there is no doubt that container gardening involves far fewer battles. Healthy plants in pots rarely fall prey to serious infestations of insects, weeds, or other ailments, and rarely is the work back-breaking, unless you count lugging home clay pots and bags of soil. The container gardener can work and enjoy the results of that labor in all seasons of the year. Neither rain nor snow, heat of summer nor cold of winter need keep the container gardener from this pleasurable pastime. Whether indoors on shelf, table, pedestal, or windowsill, or outdoors on patio, deck, balcony or in window box or hanging basket, containers bring viewing and maintenance conveniently close to the hand and the eye.

For the older or physically handicapped person not able or willing to do strenuous garden chores, container gardening is fulfilling and therapeutic. A happy solution for those who love growing things, it takes less time, space, and energy than a larger garden. The experienced container gardener and all others who become hopelessly hooked will continue to propagate new plants from old even when there isn't an inch of space for one more pot, and will be constantly on the lookout for new and different varieties to add to their collections. Youngsters can also experience the joy of growing their own plants, taking pride in seeing leaves emerge and buds form and burst into bloom. The Guide includes many plants that are especially fun for kids to grow themselves.

The Movable Garden

Container-grown plants are never rooted to the spot, merely rooted in the pot. Therein lies the beauty of *movable* gardening. At almost any time, potted plants can be moved, resettled, and replaced for an endless variety of effects. Whole gardens can be created indoors on waterproof trays on floors or tables near a source of light, with eclectic assortments of tall, short, bushy, climbing, or trailing plants with a varied display of foliage and flowers. Any plant past its peak or not thriving can be removed, and a new plant can be put in its place. A tropical jungle group or a desert cactus and succulent garden are intriguing possibilities. A brilliantly colored croton or ti plant that usually basks by a sunny window can be briefly displayed in a less bright spot for a beautiful effect along with poinsettia, Christmas cactus, and other blooming plants. Large green foliage plants can fill corners, serve as room dividers, or present splendid "architectural" effects as single specimens. On a pedestal or Victorian plant stand, large ferns look as handsome as they did when they were the favorites in the Victorian parlor. If you tire of looking at the fern, place it elsewhere and substitute a big bowl of mixed green plants, some upright, some trailing, some variegated for interesting contasts.

Outdoors the situation is as rich with possibilities. Your terrace, patio, deck, or balcony isn't merely a place for furniture, however stylish it may be; just as important are the pots and planters of foliage and flowering plants, without which it would be a stark and uninviting place.

I had always put a few potted plants on the terrace during the summer months and noted how they flourished and seemed to enjoy the fresh air, increased light, and humidity. Well, why not *all* the plants, except the few tender, soft-leaved types that would not stand up to gusty winds, summer storms, and sudden temperature changes? Why not, indeed! I discovered that the possibilities for effective displays are infinite and it's great fun to try them out. Instead of merely carrying my collection of plants outdoors and plunking them down in their preferred bright or shady locations, I found that I could keep them just as happy and healthy grouping them in interesting and exciting ways for decorative effects.

A sunny corner is a fine spot for flowering and variegated foliage plants in pots of different sizes on different levels, a mélange of vivid colors and contrasts. A large tub or planter can become an outdoor garden for three seasons—four, in warm and frost-free regions—with plants that also grow indoors such as coleus, zebrina, blood-leaf, wax begonia, impatiens, and dwarf geranium. Seasonal annuals and perennials from spring-blooming bulbs to late-season chrysanthemums may be added for additional bloom. Large green foliage plants, palms, and ferns that were handsome accents indoors can move out to filtered sun or shade, and the bold, brilliant croton and ti plants to bright sun. Shrimp plant, lantana, gardenia, geranium, and hibiscus will respond with luxuriant blossoms to fresh air and sunshine. Vertical gardening offers even more room for display outdoors on walls, railings, posts, and branches. Hanging baskets look wonderful brimming with ivy geranium, trailing lantana and coleus, tuberous begonia and wandering Jew. Donkey's tail and other trailing succulents will cascade luxuriantly in full sun. Tender tropicals can be combined with green foliage plants, both earthbound and in baskets or hangers, to create a cool, serene, and restful retreat in leafy shade.

Giving Your Plants a Summer Vacation

The truly movable garden goes outdoors in warm weather and comes back inside when temperatures cool down. In the Northeast and other cooler regions, warm weather comes late, and nights reach the 50–60 degree Fahrenheit range only in early June. That's when the botanical exodus should begin—after all danger of frost is well past. The right timing for your area depends on climate and local weather conditions. Here in lower New York state and New England, we need to be alert to sudden dips in temperature in September, so most plants in containers have at best three and a half months of summer vacation. Even in that brief time, though, the plants thrive on the change. Round trips for plants are discussed in Seasonal Changes. In frost-free climates, many plants can stay outdoors year-round.

How to Use This Book

In Part I, all the essentials of container plant culture and maintenance are thoroughly explained. You will learn how to help plants adapt to seasonal changes, when to cut plants back and why, and how to propagate your favorites.

In Part II, you will learn how to decorate with potted plants both indoors and out. Suggestions for creating architectural effects such as using large plants as room dividers accompany ideas for window boxes, hanging baskets, and windowsill gardens. A section on regional favorites will help you choose varieties that will flourish most profusely in your area.

In Part III, you will find fully detailed listings and descriptions of foliage and flowering plants, vines, and bulbs perfectly suited to movable gardening. The Guide tells you what type of soil they prefer, how much water and fertilizer they need, what light levels will make them flourish, and how best to maintain them indoors and outdoors under various conditions. Also included are the best methods of propagation for each plant, storage of bulbs, helpful tips, new varieties to watch for, and remarks based on personal experience.

Bulbs and plants with dazzling blooms get in-depth treatment in The Guide so that you will be able to bring into flower, maintain, and rebloom flowering maple, amaryllis, poinsettia, hibiscus, calla lily, hoya, Thanksgiving, Christmas, and Easter cacti, and the even more exotic Amazon lily, forest lily, and African corn lily. Special attention is given also to delicate moisture-and-shade-needy jungle dwellers like maranta, calathea, anthurium, and many ferns. These are the exciting challenges you will meet.

Everything need not be a challenge, however, and the sturdy reliables like Chinese evergreen, cast-iron plant, snake plant, philodendron, jade plant, figs, dracaena, and others that are the backbone of many a collection of movable container plants are not neglected in these pages.

The resurgence of interest in the greening and preservation of the environment is partly responsible for the vastly increased interest in container planting. The human spirit delights in the presence of green, growing things, and responds joyfully to their vitality and beauty. For an added bonus, plants help to remove pollutants and certain toxic fumes from the air, while releasing oxygen and humidity, making your home a healthier place. Movable gardening is a creative, challenging, useful, and soul-satisfying activity. In these pages you will discover how to make the most of it.

Tools of the Trade

PART I

Movable Gardening Basics

Buying Plants
for Your
Movable Garden

The best time to buy new plants is late spring or summer, when the climate and environment both inside and outside of your home are most like the greenhouse or nursery. Plants will adjust most easily to the change at this time. But don't lock them up in the trunk of your car on a steamy summer day for very long. If you buy in winter, see that any plants you buy are very well wrapped and closed up snugly at the top before you take them out. A chilled plant could end up a dead plant.

Oft-repeated good advice: Buy only from a reputable source where you know plants are well taken care of, and where you can get advice if you need it. I don't entirely rule out the occasional supermarket offerings *if* you check them out in a highly critical manner. Young plants fresh from the greenhouse or nursery are often good buys—and good bargains. Pass by any that are standing in a blast of hot or cold air. They may still look good, but they don't feel good and they may not last.

Perhaps you are just looking for something new and attractive to add to your plant collection; you have plenty of space and light and you can be imaginative. But if you have special requirements—if you need a plant to spruce up a dim corner or to flower in full sun, for example—you need to know in advance which kinds of plants will work best for you. It helps to do a bit of research beforehand (see The Guide, starting on page 105) and to visit greenhouses, nurseries, garden centers, and even the glass house in your local botanical garden to browse around. Such "field research" is enlightening and enjoyable. Besides, it smells wonderful and keeps you in touch with the ever-expanding potted plant scene.

Looking for Trouble

Some danger signals are obvious. A wary buyer's eye can detect others. Fall in love only with a healthy plant.

Don't buy if:
- The soil is very dry or very soggy.
- The leaves are wilted, yellow, brown, or discolored.
- Some leaves have tiny holes in them, or are stunted or malformed.
- You can see tiny insects. Run! And shun other plants nearby.
- Stems are broken.
- The plant is tall and lanky, without full, thick foliage.
- A flowering plant has few stems and few buds.
- A flowering plant is in full flower with no closed buds.
- The surface of the soil or the sides of a clay pot have a white or green crust or scummy appearance.
- A number of roots are emerging from the drainage hole or are visible on top of the soil.

Period of Adjustment

Your carefully chosen plants now have to be kept happy as well as healthy in their new home. First, spray and wash their foliage and water them until water flows freely out of the drainage holes. This process will flush out the excess toxic salts that result from over-fertilizing, which many growers are prone to do. Keep the plants isolated from other plants for a few days to make sure no problems develop. New plants should not be placed in full sun unless they are one of the very sun-needy kinds. Don't move them around; they've had enough movement and change for a while. Hold the fertilizer for several weeks, and don't transplant unless you discover that your new plants are very potbound after all. A few leaves may yellow and drop as the plants cast a wary eye on their new environment. Misting will help them feel comfortable. If you haven't done so already, consult The Guide for details of care and maintenance, so that you can love your new plants in December as much as you did in May.

Containers
Plain and Fancy

A plant will grow in almost anything, given the proper care. Practically speaking, a plain clay or plastic pot with one or more holes at the bottom for drainage is all that is needed. But part of the joy of movable gardening is choosing from the infinite variety of attractive and unusual containers. If they don't have the necessary drainage, it can be provided, or the plant can be placed, already potted, on top of a layer of gravel within the chosen container.

The Pros and Cons of Clay and Plastic

Simple clay pots were in use for centuries before plastic appeared on the scene, and they are still the primary choice of many gardeners. Clay is porous. It lets moisture in and out, which helps roots breathe. Soil is not likely to become waterlogged in a clay pot with good drainage. After baking in the sun, a plant's roots will cool off more quickly in a clay pot than in a plastic one. Clay pots are sturdier for large plants and less likely to be knocked over accidentally or blown over by strong winds outdoors. Clay is also available in shallow half-pots, suitable for shallow-rooted plants and for propagation.

Moreover, the "natural" look of the traditional terra cotta, or earthenware, is pleasing to the eye and blends well with any environment. For a more distinctive look, beautifully decorated and sculpted unglazed terra cotta pots are splendid

Decorative Containers: *A, wall half-pot; **B,** wooden tub; **C,** dolly; **D,** trough or planter; **E,** Regency-style urn and pedestal (reconstituted stone or concrete); **F,** clay pot; **G,** decorative terra cotta pot; **H,** metal cauldron-type pot; **I,** clay pot; **J,** carved-out log (real log or reconstituted stone); **K,** terra cotta saucer; **L,** wooden half-barrel; **M,** glazed earthenware pot; **N,** square plastic pot; **O,** round wooden tub; **P,** large plastic or clay pot.*

on decks and patios. But don't leave them or any clay pot outdoors in winter, as they may crack or flake in freezing weather. The ornate terra cotta pots can be very expensive, so it is worthwhile to protect them.

Plastic is nonporous. More water-retentive than clay, it holds moisture longer, which is a plus unless the soil is too wet and the plant becomes water-logged. But most plastic pots have four or more holes for drainage, so with care-ful watering you should have no problem. Plastic is lighter, cheaper, more durable, and less subject to cracking or breaking than clay. All to the good. You can choose from a variety of colors in plastic pots, but beware of dark colors as they absorb heat, and of colors unsuitable to the plant to be potted and its sur-roundings. Finally, plastic is easier to clean than clay.

I am inclined to use plastic for small plants and for certain tropicals that re-quire a constant, even supply of moisture. I use clay for most other plants, in-cluding the largest ones. Always soak a clay pot in water for ten or fifteen minutes before using it. You can actually hear it sucking in the water. This will keep it from absorbing moisture from the potting soil—and the roots of the plant that will go in it—at least for a while.

Wood and Paper

Wood pots and paper pulp pots are porous. Like clay, they permit good drainage and circulation of air to plant roots. Wood has a pleasing natural look and is often used for window boxes (although those of plastic or metal are more durable), for large tubs and planters for citrus, shrubby, or other large plants, and for handsome six- or eight-sided containers bound in brass. Half whiskey barrels, usually made of oak, are excellent planters, especially picturesque for a mixed flower garden planting. Redwood and cedar are the most rot-resistant woods, but the interior of all wood tubs should be painted with a preservative containing copper sulfate; Cuprinol is a commonly used brand. Never use cre-osote—it's toxic to plants.

Paper pulp pots made of compressed, recycled paper are usually medium-brown in color, lightweight, and not subject to breakage. Their life expectancy, however, is limited to a few years. If lifted by the rims when very wet, these pots may tear easily.

Unusual Containers

Your movable garden will also be quite happy in a whole range of more offbeat containers. Choose from among glazed earthenware or ceramic cachepots and bowls, or pots, jugs, vases, and bowls of brass, copper, and glass; elegant stone or concrete urns and lightweight fiberglass or reconstituted stone urns masquerading as elegant real stone urns; a dazzling variety of woven baskets, to be used with waterproof liners. Use an old kettle or casserole, or the soufflé dish that might look better with a plant than the soufflé (unless you're still trying); a coffee mug or conch shell for a small plant; an old wheelbarrow for a group of upright and trailing plants by the back steps. Or ask in gourmet and specialty food shops for wooden cheese boxes and other containers.

If no drainage holes are present, you can provide drainage with a 1- to 1½-inch layer of pebbles, gravel, clay pot shards, and a few bits of charcoal as a "sweetener" on the bottom of the container before adding the soil and the plant. The alternative is double potting, whereby the potted plant with a drain hole is placed on a layer of pebbles in a larger container with damp peat or sphagnum moss filling in the space between inner and outer pots. Generally, the latter method works better, as the potted plant can be easily removed and replaced, and it gets the benefit of added humidity.

More Decorative Containers: *A, ceramic cachepot; B, Greek-style formal urn; C, classic white Versailles wooden tub.*

Let There Be Light

All plants need light in order to manufacture their food through the process of photosynthesis. Light, acting upon the green pigment or chlorophyll in leaves and stems, converts carbon dioxide from the air and water from the soil into sugars and starches, or carbohydrates, that nourish the plant. During this process, oxygen is released as a waste product. At night, or in the absence of light, these functions cease.

Different plants have different light requirements, but no plant grows in the dark. Many plants do well in low to medium light and require somewhat less water, less fertilizer, and less warmth than plants needing bright light. Low-light plants are generally all green. Plants with variegated or colored leaves must have more sunlight to compensate for their lack of the green chlorophyll and to keep their colors bright. Desert plants, flowering plants, and plants with highly colorful foliage crave lots of light, including several hours of direct sunlight every day, but even these prefer some protection or slight shade from the hottest rays of the midday and afternoon sun, which can scorch and burn them.

While most plants contend quite amiably with the vagaries of sunlight and clouds, others have strictly defined preferences. Shady ladies from the rain forest, such as anthurium and maranta, will swoon and die if they are exposed to the blazing sun. True sun worshippers like crown of thorns, burro's tail, and ti plant will pine away in the shade. Refer to The Guide for the light requirements of individual plants.

Windows on the World

Indoors, you can quite accurately monitor and control the quantity and quality of water, humidity, fertilizer, and soil your plants receive. Regulating light is much trickier because light itself is so variable. The amount (number of hours) and the quality (direct or indirect sunlight, bright light, filtered or dappled light, medium or low light) vary from morning to afternoon, from one exposure to another, from one season to another. Outdoors, where your movable plants will spend the summer, clouds, rain, smog, haze, and deep or dappled shade cast by trees or shrubs all have a bearing upon the light that plants receive. Outdoor conditions are far more unpredictable than the conditions usually present indoors. The following will help you place your container plants in the best of the four exposures inside your home.

The South Window

The sunny, warm, south-facing window, if unobstructed by buildings, walls, dense trees, or shrubbery, gets approximately six hours of direct sun each day. If east or west windows are nearby, they will contribute a few hours of direct sun in the morning or afternoon. It is interesting to note that in winter, when the sun is lower in the sky, the south window gets far more light than in summer, when the sun is higher in the sky. If deciduous trees are close, even more light will fall upon the indoor plants in winter when the branches are bare. In the summer, leafy trees will create filtered or even heavy shade indoors, but by that time, you will have moved most of your sun-loving plants outdoors, where even light shade is stronger in quality of light than bright light indoors. A south window is the place for desert cacti, succulents, citrus, most flowering plants, and plants with brightly colored leaves, such as croton, coleus, and ti plant. A caveat: On especially hot sunny days, unobstructed sun in the middle of the day can scorch the foliage of even the sun worshipers; if you're at home during the day, you might want to draw a light curtain or blinds for an hour or two.

The East Window

An east window unobstructed by buildings, trees, or shrubs usually gets direct morning sun from first light. If somewhat obstructed, this is a fine exposure for plants that tolerate some shade or partial light. The sunlight may be dappled through tree leaves or filtered through a sheer curtain or fine blinds. Morning sun gives a good, bright light that is not too harsh or hot. It suits most foliage plants and some flowering plants.

The West Window

An unobstructed west window gets afternoon sun starting shortly after noon. It provides about the same amount of sun that enters an east window, but the quality of light is different. The sun has become hotter and continues to be hotter, stronger, and harsher than morning sun. Later in the day as the sun descends, its strength weakens and the light is gentler. Foliage plants that thrive in an east window will do as well in a west window, and flowering plants flourish better there. The west window is second to the south window in intensity of light.

The North Window

An unobstructed north window gets the least light of all indoor exposures. Although it gets no direct sun, it's a mistake to think that this is a poor place to grow plants. The light is of a uniform intensity and has an even, medium brightness. It can't scald foliage; nor will it require you to draw curtains or blinds against the glare. Soil does not dry out so quickly in a northern exposure. This exposure is well suited to low- to medium-light plants, including tropical forest plants such as fern and caladium, as well as Chinese evergreen, philodendron, dracaena, some palms and figs, and a great many others.

Low-Light Areas

A position 5 or more feet from a window, in a dim corner, or in the shadows cast by an outside structure such as a wall or other building will cause low to poor light levels. Outdoors, partial to full shade is never as dark as interior dimness because outdoor light surrounds and penetrates all vegetation. Outdoor light is more intense than indoor light, so indoor plants must be gradually acclimated to sunlight or even dappled light or partial shade when brought outdoors. Plants that grow well in low light or poor light include old reliables like the rubber plant, snake plant, dracaena, bird's nest fern, cast iron plant, dieffenbachia, and several others. (They would all prefer better light if they could get it.)

A Place in the Sun

Just as the sun's rays are both beneficial and harmful to humans, so are they to plants in containers.

Too much strong sunlight can sear plant tissues and overheat and dry out pots, soil, and plant roots. Too little sunlight deprives the plant of the ability to manufacture sufficient food for itself and to remain sturdy and healthy.

Too Much Light

Distress signals from a plant that is getting a glut of light can be seen in wilted or scorched-looking leaves. Look also for leaves with yellow, brown, or dried-out patches. Even if the soil is wet, a plant can broil in the midday sun that streams through a south-facing, unobstructed window or that blasts it with those powerful early afternoon rays on the terrace or deck. The injury is compounded if the container is nonporous and retains heat. Sun-needy plants such as most succulents, croton, geraniums, amaryllis, gardenia, and setcreasea can withstand several hours of full sun each day. Still, it's a wise precaution to close the blinds or draw a light curtain at a south window in the middle of a brilliantly sunny day, mist the plants an extra time, and perhaps ventilate the room a bit for more circulation of air. A slightly wilted plant will soon perk up if removed from the sun.

Outdoor plants have the advantage of the movement of air and breezes around them. Even in partial shade outdoors, however, plants are bathed in far more light than bright light indoors, even at a south-facing window. Thus, when you move your container plants outside for the summer months, expose them very gradually to greater light. Ideally, try to provide some shelter from the strong rays of the summer sun with a latticed or lath roof overhead, a roof overhang, shadows from a nearby shrub or two, or, best of all, a big leafy tree that casts dappled sun and shade and that can bear on its sturdy branches a display of hanging baskets. I have a large, wide-spread sugar maple that, obligingly, does all that, keeping both plants and people on the terrace from getting sunburned and overheated.

Too Little Light

As damaging as too much light can be, the misery of a light-starved plant is also plain to see. As it cranes its neck toward the source of light, which, obviously, is too far away, its stem grows tall and lanky and its leaves become smaller, sparser, and lighter in color due to the lack of chlorophyll. The leaves may even drop off, usually starting at the bottom. If the plant isn't too far gone it can be saved. Move it to a spot where it gets better light, but not full sun. Have no qualms about pruning it rather severely; this will improve its appearance, ease the workload of the roots, and motivate the plant to send out fresh shoots. Water and fertilize regularly, gradually providing more sun according to the particular plant's requirements.

For short-term decorative purposes, perhaps a week or two at most, foliage plants will stoically endure a shift to a dim or poorly lit spot without ill effects. Part of the fun of a movable garden is in showing off a specimen plant or a group of plants for an eye-catching effect. Just be sure to return them to their original location as soon as possible. Flowering plants, however, will start to sulk soon after being taken from sunlight and will definitely decline in health and appearance after a week or so.

Plants with variegated or highly colored foliage (croton, coleus, polka dot plant, or purple passion) must be exposed to consistently good light to maintain their color. If any such plant is given insufficient light, it will gradually lose its bright colors—and its charm—and will revert to plain green. If the plant is returned to its preferred sunny or well-lit spot, it will regain its colors.

Conversely, plants growing contentedly in low light or partial shade (ferns, caladium, syngonium, and many other favorite container plants of tropical or semi-tropical origin) should never be exposed to intense sunlight. In their native habitat they live partly shaded in warm, humid jungles and rain forests. While greenhouses have the facilities to simulate these conditions, most homes do not. It is important that gardeners of movable plants learn the light needs and other requirements of the individual plants in their collections. These needs are outlined in The Guide starting on page 105. Fortunately, most plants are tolerant of slight variations in the light they receive, and those that are ideally suited to one level of light can usually manage nicely in another closely linked one. If the conditions are too drastically different from the plant's needs, the plant will let you know it.

Phototropism

Almost all green growing things have a natural tendency to seek light, turning their stems and leaves toward the source of light in a phenomenon called phototropism. Indoor plants left in one position tend to develop a one-sided look no matter how much light they are getting. Outdoor plants are far less likely to develop this look since the containers are more or less surrounded by light, but even these plants have a natural tendency to lean toward the sun. To avoid a lopsided, unattractive look, give your container plants a quarter or a third turn once or twice a week, always in the same direction. Budded or flowering plants should be turned infrequently with exceptional care; touchy plants may react by dropping their buds or blossoms.

Supplementing Natural Light

It is possible to grow plants in dim rooms, dark hallways, or other places where sunlight is insufficient or even nonexistent, as in a cellar. Artificial light can supplement or replace natural light, and fluorescent bulbs are ideal for this purpose since they produce high-intensity light without heat.

Fluorescent-light fixtures can be suspended from the ceiling, attached to the underside of a shelf above plants, or mounted on plant stands or carts. Designed to take the place of sunlight, the fluorescent bulbs are available in straight or ringed tubes of various lengths and wattages. A good combination for maintaining growth is one cool-white tube, which has mostly the red coloring of the spectrum, and one daylight tube, which has mostly blue. The red light stimulates root growth and flower production; the blue light works for stem and leaf growth. Growth lights, which provide wide-spectrum light, combine all the necessary elements for plant growth in one straight or ring-shaped bulb. The round tubes are particularly useful for spotlighting a single large specimen plant or a group of small plants.

Automatic timers can be attached to the fixtures and set for the length of exposure desired. The recommended average exposure to light for foliage plants is 12 to 14 hours; flowering plants need 16 to 18 hours of light.

For type, length, wattage of tubes, suitable distance from surface of pots, and details on the light-and-dark schedules of specific plants, consult The Indoor Light Gardening Society of America or your local botanic garden. Nursery or garden supply store managers may also be helpful, and your library may include books on artificial lighting in the gardening section.

Light Requirements Of Plants

Many plants thrive in more than one location or one category of light. In the following lists of light requirements, a number of plants appear in two groups of light levels. Barring those with strictly limited and specific needs, a great majority of container plants are quite adaptable to deviations from their preferred environments, if the changes are not too abrupt or too drastic.

Bright or Filtered Sun

Botanical Name	Common Name	Botanical Name	Common Name
Achimenes	Cupid's bower, magic flower	*Maranta*	
Anthurium	Pigtail flower, flamingo flower	*Nematanthus*	Goldfish plant
		Palm	
Asparagus	Asparagus fern	*Peperomia*	Watermelon begonia
Begonia			
Brassaia (Schefflera)		*Philodendron*	
Calathea		*Pilea*	Aluminum plant
Caladium		*Plectranthus*	Swedish ivy
Chlorophytum	Spider plant	*Sansevieria*	Snake plant
Cissus	Grape ivy, kangaroo vine	*Saxifraga*	Strawberry begonia, strawberry geranium
Crossandra	Firecracker flower	*Scindapsus*	Pothos
Cyclamen		*Spathiphyllum*	Peace lily
Dieffenbachia	Dumb cane	*Syngonium*	Arrowhead plant, arrowhead vine
Dracaena			
Eucharis grandiflora	Amazon lily	*Tolmiea*	Piggyback plant, mother-of-thousands
Euphorbia pulcherrima	Poinsettia	*Tradescantia*	Wandering Jew, inch plant
Ficus	Fig		
Fittonia		*Veltheimia*	Forest lily
Fuchsia		*Zebrina*	Wandering Jew, inch plant
Hedera helix	English ivy		
Impatiens			

Note: *Although the plants on this list prefer bright light, many perform satisfactorily under other conditions, tolerating less bright or medium light. Keep in mind, however, that those with variegated foliage tend to become predominantly green in medium or low light.*

Medium to Low Light or Partial Shade

Botanical Name	Common Name
Aglaonema	Chinese evergreen
Aspidistra	Cast iron plant
Fern	

Caladium, Calathea, Dracaena, Dieffenbachia, and *Maranta* are among the tropical plants that also do well in medium as well as filtered light. Consult The Guide for individual plants.

Direct Sun: Full sun half a day, or four to six hours.

Botanical Name	Common Name	Botanical Name	Common Name
Abutilon	Flowering maple	*Hippeastrum*	Amaryllis
Agapanthus	Lily-of-the-Nile	*Hoya*	Wax plant
Aphelandra	Zebra plant, saffron spike	*Hypoestes*	Freckle face, polka dot plant
Aloe		*Iresine*	Bloodleaf
Alstroemeria	Lily-of-the-Incas, Peruvian lily	*Ixia*	African corn lily
Ceropegia woodii	Rosary vine, string of hearts	*Justicia brandegeana*	Shrimp plant
		Kalanchoe	
Citrus	Orange, lemon, lime, kumquat	*Lantana*	
		Lilium	Lily
Clerodendron	Bleeding heart vine, glory bower	*Pelargonium*	Geranium
		Rhipsalidopsis	Easter cactus
Clivia	Kaffir lily	*Schlumbergera*	Thanksgiving cactus, Christmas cactus
Codiaeum	Croton		
Coleus		*Sedum*	Donkey's tail, burro's tail
Cordyline	Ti plant		
Crassula	Jade plant	*Senecio rowleyanus*	String-of-beads, string-of-pearls
Euphorbia milii	Crown of thorns		
Freesia		*Setcreasea*	Purple heart
Gardenia		*Vallota*	Scarborough lily
Gynura	Purple passion plant	*Yucca*	
Hibiscus	Chinese hibiscus, rose of China	*Zantedeschia*	Calla lily

Water

Of all movable gardening tasks, pouring on the water seems to be the favorite. To many gardeners it has an irresistible attraction, and to those less experienced it brings a glow of satisfaction at a job well done. Alas, overwatering, however well-intentioned, will result in waterlogged soil, limp or mushy yellow or brown-tipped leaves, weak or rotting leaves and stems, rotted roots, and, eventually, the demise of cherished plants.

Dryness, usually a result of neglect rather than overattention, can also kill a plant. When delicate roots are dried out, they cannot deliver water and nutrients to stems and leaves. Wilted leaves and yellow or brown foliage indicate dryness.

If your plant becomes exceedingly limp or collapses entirely, check its other symptoms and the conditions of the soil to determine whether the cause of the plant's distress is over- or underwatering. If the damage is not too far gone, the plant will recover when an adjustment in its watering schedule is made.

How to Tell if a Plant Needs Water

All of your container plants cannot be watered on the same schedule. Many factors affect the water requirements of different plants. The kind of container, the amount of soil in the container, and the degree of drainage the container provides will affect the amount of water a plant can absorb. In addition, temperature, humidity, and exposure to sunlight influence water demands, as do the plant's rate of growth, amount of foliage or blooms, and its usual seasonal pattern of growth and inactivity. Lastly, but significantly, the origin of the species (jungle, desert, or other) will determine its watering requirements.

For all of its influencing factors, watering is actually a simple matter. A look and a touch will tell you what you need to do. Dry soil is lighter in color than moist soil. Rub your finger over it, and if it feels dry, poke your finger a half-inch or so into the soil. If you encounter no moisture, the plant needs water. A thirsty plant is also likely to have a slight droop to its leaves.

Flowering plants and most foliage plants like their soil to be slightly moist, never completely dried out. Some dryness should occur between waterings, however; limit this dryness to the surface of the soil (less than an inch deep). Plants native to tropical forest regions need to be kept constantly moist and humid in order to thrive. Succulents and desert cacti store water in their leaves, stems, and even roots, just as they do in the dry areas of their natural home; they can survive in dry soil for a long time. When thoroughly dry, however, their leaves will shrivel, as they begin to draw on their reserves. Avoid allowing them to become dry to that extent.

Many of the most beautiful tropical forest plants such as maranta, calathea, anthurium, and ferns need a constant supply of moisture in their soil, as well as frequent mistings. A favorite tropical of mine is the handsome red-veined fittonia, a heavy drinker that flops and appears comatose if its soil becomes dry. Fortunately, a thorough soaking revives it quickly. Almost any slightly wilted plant on the verge of dryness will perk up after a good watering. Still, it's best not to let this happen too often. A plant that is frequently allowed to dry out becomes stressed and does not flourish. Prevent this by getting to know your plants and their individual needs, as specified in The Guide.

How To and How Much

Roots get a nasty shock when doused with cold water. Use only tepid or room temperature water. After watering, refill the watering can and let the water warm up to room temperature, saving it until the next time you need to water. This also gives the chlorine in the water a chance to evaporate. For a large collection of plants (or for very large plants), I like to use lightweight plastic half-gallon jugs with handles (the kind that juices or distilled water come in); they are comfortable to hold, and the water line is visible.

When you water, do it thoroughly; no daily dribbles or surface-only sprinkles. Pour the water on the soil slowly and let it work down until you see water seeping out of the drainage holes into the saucer. Every indoor pot, including hanging baskets, must have a saucer to protect furniture and floors from drips and rings. Outdoor pots should not have saucers; rainwater collects in them and the roots will become waterlogged and begin to rot.

Water requirements are greater for large plants in large pots, rapidly growing plants, flowering plants, plants in full sun, and plants with a great deal of fo-

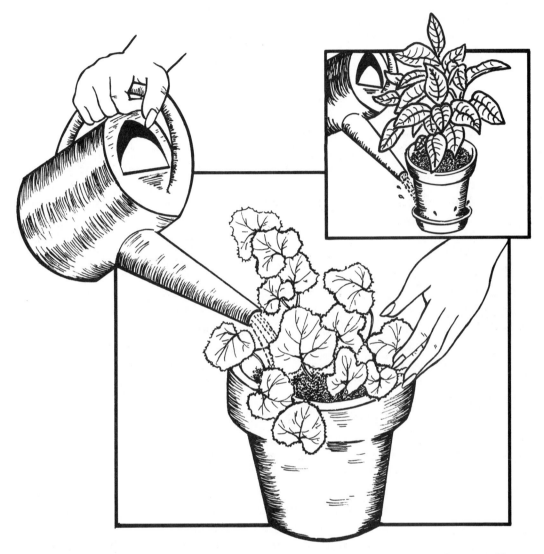

Watering. *Top watering: Water from the top until a trickle appears in the saucer.* **Bottom watering** *(inset): Water goes directly to the roots. This method may require filling the saucer more than once and therefore may not be practical for a large plant that needs a big drink.*

liage. In addition, all plants in clay pots will get thirstier faster than those in plastic. Mulching helps retain moisture, as does double potting and mossing (see following section).

If the water drains quickly from the bottom of the pot, the soil may still not be well saturated. Sometimes a very dry root ball doesn't "grab" the water immediately. Dry soil shrinks, causing spaces between the root ball and the sides of the pot, and the water runs down those spaces and out. Wait fifteen minutes and take a look at the saucer. If the plant has now absorbed the water, pour on a little more and check the saucer again later. A few drops still there will not be harmful, but any more than that should be discarded. Plants, like babies, shouldn't sit around for long with wet bottoms. Don't re-water until the soil again feels dry.

Double Potting

Double potting allows you to put a humble pot within a handsome container that you enjoy displaying in your home. Assuming the waterproof, outer container is drainless, place a 1½- to 2-inch layer of pebbles or gravel in the bottom of this decorative pot. When you water, any excess drains down into the pebbles so that the plant doesn't sit in water. Evaporation brings moisture back up into the foliage. Moisture-needy plants in clay pots are greatly benefited by double potting, especially when long-fibered sphagnum moss is packed loosely between the two pots. Well-moistened moss will keep the clay pot from drying out and prevent it from drawing moisture from the soil. Allow an inch or two of space between the inner and outer pot. First, water the plant well. Moisten the moss and keep it very moist, applying future waterings to the moss, not the soil. This method permits a constant release of moisture to the pot and its contents.

When to Give Little or No Water

Most plants have active and inactive periods of growth. The active growing period is generally from late February or early March to early or mid-autumn. A few plants continue growing and some, such as the wax begonia and the crown of thorns, even continue flowering intermittently all year round. Most plants, however, require a winter rest. Plants that have summered outdoors and have grown vigorously need to quiet down and take it easy. Some bulbs and tubers go completely dormant and require no more water until spring. The others need water to stay alive and healthy, but their winter requirements are reduced. See Winter Rest on page 53, and check individual entries in The Guide.

Bottom Watering

Watering from the bottom of the container is a sure way to convey moisture to the lower soil and the roots, but you may need to refill the saucer several times before the plant has enough. When the surface of the soil becomes well moistened, you can be sure that enough water has been absorbed. If excess water remains in the saucer, dump it out. Don't leave a plant sitting in water, but make sure you have allowed it time to absorb a sufficient amount through the drainage holes.

Problems and Puzzlements

What if a plant is too heavy or unwieldy to lift in order to empty its saucer? Soak up the excess water with crumpled paper towels, newspaper, or a sponge.

What if there is no drainage hole to let the excess water out? With large drainless containers, err a trifle on the moderate side when watering. Get to know about how much water your big plant needs before the soil becomes dry to the touch. If the leaves were slightly droopy, check back in a while after watering to see if they have become perky and upright. If not, give a little more water. Instruments called moisture meters can measure the moisture present in soil and are useful for deep containers where your finger cannot probe too far. Since the readings may not always be accurate, make your final judgment on the appearance of the plant and the look and feel of the soil both before and after watering.

What to do if you don't enjoy climbing ladders with a watering can to water your hanging baskets? If a long-spouted watering can doesn't reach far enough, take the basket down and water it, outside or in the kitchen sink. Let it drain on the kitchen drainboard or on the ground outdoors, depending on the season. If the plant is quite dry, give it a thorough soaking by immersion in tepid water. Place the plant in the kitchen sink or in a large pail and let the water cover the container just over the rim. When air bubbles stop rising, the plant is well saturated. Let it drain before putting it back in place. This method should revive almost any overly dry plant, hanging or not. Immersion is welcomed now and then by a great many plants, especially during warm weather. Outdoors, an angled extender to the garden hose can deliver drinks high up. For easiest access, a pulley attached to a hanging basket will raise or lower it for watering, fertilizing, or grooming.

Can a waterlogged plant in obvious distress be saved? Yes, if a few healthy leaves remain. When leaves turn yellow or brown, get droopy and soft, or drop off without changing color, the plant is calling for help. Perhaps the roots are rotting in heavy soil without adequate drainage. Without air in the soil, the roots cannot take up nutrients and deliver them to stems and leaves. Drastic action is needed if the plant is to survive. Sadly, there are no guarantees.

Carefully lift the plant out of the pot and remove the wet soil around the roots. Remove dead or overlong roots. Repot with fresh soil according to the plant's needs, using a pot just large enough to accommodate the roots. (It may be slightly smaller than the old pot.) Water only enough to settle the roots in the new soil. Do not fertilize. Food is not what this plant needs now, or for weeks to come. It does need a pruning to ease the roots' workload. Cut back the top and side branches by about a third. Assuming the patient survives, don't water again until the soil feels quite dry. A successful recovery has occurred if new stems and leaves appear, indicating fresh root growth and perhaps the survival of some old roots. This process may take some time.

What to do to save a dried-out plant? Use the immersion method, as described above. Prune back a third or more. Again, no guarantees.

Other Ways to Retain Water

The estimable practice of mulching garden beds to retain moisture, keep temperatures even outdoors, and discourage weeds can be extended to container plants and large pots. Though container plants are unlikely to get many weeds, they can reap the other benefits of mulch.

If you have mulching materials on hand for an outdoor garden, you can also use the finely shredded bark chips, wood chips, or cocoa bean shells on your potted plants. Mulching materials and bagged pebbles, gravel, or volcanic stone are available at garden centers and greenhouses. Otherwise, you can make your own mulch from mixtures of peat moss, pebbles, gravel, bits of twigs, or small shards of pottery. For a decorative touch, top it off with colorful sea shells or stones. Tropicals, however, still prefer damp sphagnum.

Mulching is particularly good for outdoor pots with a large soil surface. Applied a half-inch to 1-inch deep on top of the soil, mulch cuts down the need for watering, keeps roots cooler in warm weather, and helps counter the effects of drought and drying winds. Do not use peat alone; it will dry, bake, cake, and become impermeable.

Self-Watering Planters or Pots

Pots with clear plastic reservoirs attached are a boon for the forgetful waterer. Water is drawn up into the soil through capillary action. Some self-waterers have a wick that delivers water up into the soil via the drainage hole of the pot. The reservoirs are easily refillable, and hold enough water to last from two to four weeks, depending upon the size of the reservoir, the size of the planter, and the needs of the plant. Self-watering pots are also available with chains and ring or hook attached so that they may be hung. All of these systems are great for the vacationing gardener. (See When You're Away, p. 55, for more on self-watering.)

Hydrogels

Research into ways to save water in times of drought and to enable soils to hold water longer has resulted in some interesting products called hydrogels, or polymeric crystals.

Mixed well into the soil and watered heavily, the tiny crystals or granules quickly expand and act as a water reservoir, releasing water to plant roots as the plant requires.

In my experience, if the crystals aren't buried deeply at potting or repotting time, they rise in the soil as they swell with water and may work their way to the surface. Use them sparingly and bury them deeply.

Humidity

Many popular container plants have their origin in tropical climates such as the jungles and rain forests of South and Central America, where rains are frequent and often heavy and the air is constantly humid. They are not at all tolerant of the dry, heated air found inside the average home. Favorites such as succulents and desert cacti don't mind these conditions, since they come from dry regions where there is little humidity and are able to store water in their thick leaves, stems, and roots.

Adding humidity to the air benefits most container plants and is vital to those of tropical origin. A room humidifier placed near plants will increase the moisture content of the air. Other less costly but effective ways to do this are described in the following sections. Incidentally, plants originating from dry regions will not suffer from the extra moisture on their foliage, when grouped with or set close to moisture-lovers, as the humidity level in most homes is extremely low.

Misting

A pint- or quart-sized mister filled with room temperature water surrounds plants with a fine spray that covers both sides of the leaves. This cloud of moisture also helps keep foliage clean and tends to discourage insects from taking up residence in your plants.

Lush foliage plants introduced into your home from a greenhouse, where the humidity is as high as 70 or 80 percent, may suffer initially at the sudden lack of moisture in the air. Misting twice a day helps them readjust. Later on, regular daily misting is good, but continuing the twice-a-day spray is better. Potted plants set outside in summer are most grateful for a fine spray from the garden hose in hot, dry weather. To avoid possible mildew or mold, apply spray early in the day so that the foliage is dry by nightfall.

Humidity Trays

A waterproof tray, pan, or saucer can be filled with one-half inch to an inch of pebbles or gravel. Add water to just below the top of the pebbles and set the pots on the pebbles. As the water evaporates, add more water to the tray, always making certain that the level of the water is just below the bottoms of the pots. Moisture-needy jungle plants like ferns, spathiphyllum, calathea, fittonia, and many others will respond positively to this treatment.

Grouping Plants

In the process of transpiration, water is drawn up into a plant and evaporates from the foliage. When plants are massed closely together on humidity trays, this process creates a humid microclimate that is very beneficial. Leave enough space between the plants so that some circulation of air is possible and the likelihood of mold and mildew formation is reduced. A group of plants set on humidity trays benefits from the moisture in the atmosphere and presents pleasing visual effects when attractively arranged on a shelf, table, floor, or porch. For more ideas, see section on decorating with plants, page 61.

Double Potting

In double potting, a clay pot is placed within a waterproof, drainless container on top of a layer of shards or pebbles. The space between the pots is loosely filled with moist peat or sphagnum moss, thereby increasing water retention and humidity, and exhibiting a nice plant in a plain pot within a handsome or unique cachepot. The technique of double potting is discussed in more detail in the chapter on watering container plants. See page 17.

Choice Locations

During the time of the year they spend indoors, if plants could choose their setting, a great many would like to call the kitchen or bathroom home. They love the moisture and warmth produced by hot water and steam. Any space near the washing machine or dryer would be a favorite spot, too. A shelf or corner in the kitchen or bathroom that gets filtered or indirect light is a fine place for ferns, palms, and trailing plants such as pothos, arrowhead vine, and philodendron.

On the windowsill over my kitchen sink, small pots of rooted cuttings and cuttings rooting in water flourish happily until they get too big and must be shifted into larger pots and moved elsewhere. On cold winter nights, I remove them from the window when the glass gets too cold for comfort, returning them to the sill in the warmth of day. The greenery is a delightful addition to the room, and as these youngsters move on to new containers, I always have more ready to take their places.

Humidity. A. *Double potting provides constant moisture from damp peat moss between the two pots.* **B.** *With a hand-held mister, spray plant from all sides.* **C.** *A humidity tray, or pebble tray, supplies moisture evaporating from wet pebbles into foliage.*

Good Earth

Good potting soil is of vital importance to plants in containers, even more so than to garden plants, because they must survive and be healthy and happy in confined spaces under conditions of light, air circulation, moisture, and heat that are often far from ideal and different from those prevailing in their native habitats. Container gardeners can mix their own soil or buy packaged or pre-mixed soils from nurseries and garden centers. This chapter explores the best choices for a movable garden of various species.

Packaged Sterile Potting Soil

Bags of weed-, insect-, and disease-free (sterile) potting soil can be purchased at garden centers, nurseries, supermarkets, and some hardware stores. They contain varying amounts of soil, perlite, or vermiculite, which absorb and retain moisture and aerate the soil, a small amount of nutrients and minerals, and peat moss, which retains water and nutrients in the soil for release to plant roots. Some all-purpose bagged soils are dense and heavy; as they become dry, these soils harden and become impervious to water, leaving a plant's roots thirsty and without air. Look for soils with added lighteners, preferably perlite, vermiculite (perlite is usually preferred for pot culture), or sand, and additional peat for moisture-loving plants. If the soil doesn't have much perlite or vermiculite, add some. Bagged sterile potting soils are also available in formulas designed for desert cacti, acid-loving plants like gardenia, and other special groups.

Sterile Soilless Mixes

Bagged sterile soilless mixes contain perlite and vermiculite and peat moss, and sometimes a slight amount of fertilizer. Clean, lightweight, and easy to handle, they are excellent starters for tip and stem cuttings, bulbs, and seeds. They are especially well-suited for use in hanging baskets together with other materials. Most commercial growers use a soilless medium with a dash of fertilizer to nourish a young plant for a couple of months. This accounts for the lightweight feeling of the small plant you buy at the nursery or supermarket. Unless it is transferred soon to a pot with a soil-based mixture, it will need fertilizing quite often.

A soilless mix may be used to lighten and aerate potting soil; conversely, some good potting soil may be added to soilless mixtures to give them extra nutrients.

Making Your Own Soil Mixes

Greenhouses, garden centers, and garden supply stores can supply you with all the mix-your-own ingredients you need to create a basic potting medium that can be easily altered to suit different kinds of plants.

Happily, most plants thrive on a well-balanced, all-purpose potting soil, which is designated here and in The Guide by the words "Basic Soil Mix." It consists of equal parts of sterilized bagged potting soil, perlite or sand (builder's sand, not sea sand), and peat moss (slightly dampened or it will fly about).

Some desert plants, such as crown of thorns, donkey's tail, and other succulents with fat leaves that store water, prefer a lighter soil that is more porous and well-drained. To the basic mixture, then, add more sand or perlite.

For tropical forest plants like ferns, caladium, spathiphyllum, Christmas cactus, and certain others, a richer, more moisture-retentive mix is needed. The Basic Soil Mix becomes "Peaty Basic" for them, which means that you add more peat to the recipe. You can also add an organic substance such as leaf mold, fine tree bark or fir bark chips, sphagnum peat moss, or a combination of any or all of these substances.

A Glossary of Ingredients

Peat moss is absorbent, partly decomposed organic matter dug from peat bogs.

Sphagnum moss is a highly absorbent, fibrous bog moss, useful in mixtures for jungle plants and other moisture addicts, excellent for moisture retention on the surface of pots holding these plants, for double potting, and as a liner of wire and plastic openwork hanging baskets.

Leaf mold is composed of partially decayed, richly organic leaves.

Fine fir bark or wood chips, like peat, help retain water and improve the quality of the soil by providing a loose, porous texture.

Perlite is a light, sterile, absorbent material from ground volcanic rock that aerates the soil and retains the water and nutrients to be delivered to plant roots.

Vermiculite, a sterile mica product, serves much the same purpose as perlite. These materials can be used together or alone with peat moss to start cuttings and seeds. Perlite is generally preferred to give porosity to soil mixes and to lighten heavy soil.

Compost. Completely sterile compost is very difficult to obtain and very expensive. If you are fortunate enough to live where you can maintain a compost pile of leaves and garden waste plus fruit and vegetable waste from the kitchen, this wonderful stuff, when thoroughly decomposed, contains few injurious organisms and absolutely teems with nutrients. A small amount added to any soil mix makes it richly organic.

Humus is a term used broadly to include any and all decayed or decomposed organic (vegetable) matter.

Organic fertilizers added to the soil at potting or repotting time include bone-meal or superphosphate for strong roots and production of flowers, and dehydrated or dried cow manure, which is exceedingly rich in nutrients and gratefully received in very small amounts by almost all growing things. See the discussion of fertilizer on p. 31.

Ingredients for Potting Soil Mix

Mix Mastery

Once you have assembled the ingredients for your homemade soil, you will need a large container in which to blend them together and a measuring cup or small kitchen pot to scoop up the soil, perlite or sand, and peat for a Basic Soil Mix. Measurements do not have to be exact; just dump more or less equal parts into the larger container. Blend the elements together and keep a fair amount always ready to use. You will definitely use the Basic Soil Mix often. A 16-ounce measuring cup or kitchen pot holds about the right amount of mix for a 6-inch pot.

Keep supplies of perlite, sand, peat, bonemeal, and other organic substances on hand. When a lighter, more porous soil is needed, or a richer, peatier soil, just add some of the necessary substances to some Basic Soil Mix, and blend them in thoroughly. The best quality bagged potting soil that contains peat and perlite or vermiculite in small amounts may be used instead of a homemade Basic Soil Mix; adjust its suitability to different kinds of plants by adding more lighteners or more peat or humus. Each plant entry in The Guide specifies the appropriate soil.

When mixing your own potting soil medium, it's best not to use garden soil. While some garden soils may be excellent, even the best garden soil may contain weed seeds, insects or their eggs, and harmful bacteria. I suggest that you do not use it for container plants.

Fertilizer

Kinds of Fertilizers

Plant food comes in many forms. Water-soluble liquids or powders diluted in water are the most convenient to use. Pellets or granules dissolve in the soil with watering, as do slow-release spikes and pills pressed into the soil.

The water-soluble forms to be poured on the soil are generally preferred because they are easy to apply and are absorbed quickly by the roots. The common, all-purpose plant food is a 5-10-5 formula (see Fertilizer Formulas in this chapter). It is called "Dilute liquid fertilizer" in The Guide and is appropriate nourishment for most plants. Use it every two or three weeks in the active growing season—from early spring when new growth appears until fall when growth slows down. Plants have individual needs, however, and variations are specified in The Guide. Bear in mind that soilless mixes contain few or no nutrients, and plants in this medium will need more frequent fertilizing.

Timed-release spikes or pills must be used with great care. When pushed down deep into the soil close to plant roots, they may deliver a very strong dose of nutrients to the roots, which may burn them. In addition, the continuous supply of these nutrients cannot be cut off when the plant's resting period arrives.

Carefully placed, slow-release solids work to nourish a plant over a period of several months. If you use them, keep a record of the dates you apply each group of spikes or pills.

Organic Fertilizers

When repotting or topdressing a plant, restore some organic matter to the soil in the form of small amounts of bonemeal or superphosphate, which work toward strong roots and flower production; dehydrated or dried manure, which is rich in many nutrients; and possibly some form of humus, which is decayed vegetable matter, or finely ground leaf mold, which is partially decomposed leaves. Other organic substances that may be delivered in small amounts are fish emulsion and liquefied forms of seaweed and kelp, rich in nitrogen and potash.

Foliar Feeding

Occasionally a few drops of liquid plant food or special foliar feeds may be diluted and sprayed on leaves. The nutrients in the spray are quickly absorbed. This form of feeding is a booster and a tonic, not a replacement for regular fertilizing into the soil.

Fertilizer Formulas

Certain essential elements are always present in varying proportions in plant fertilizers. The big three nutrients are nitrogen, phosphorus, and potash (potassium). The proportions are always stated on the bag, box, or bottle in that order. N-P-K are the chemical symbols.

- Nitrogen (N) encourages the growth of stems and leaves.
- Phosphorus (P) promotes the growth of strong roots, encourages flower buds, and stimulates colored foliage.
- Potash (K) increases the production of flowers and promotes sturdy growth and resistance to disease.

The common or standard house plant fertilizer labelled 5-10-5 contains 5 percent nitrogen, 10 percent phosphorus, and 5 percent potash. A 10-20-10 formula has the same proportions in a stronger concentration and should be diluted twice as much. Most foliage plants thrive on 5-10-5. Flowering plants and bulbs also benefit from this formula, but when flower stalks and signs of buds appear, production of flowers will be stimulated by switching to a formula lower in nitrogen and higher in phosphorus and potash, such as 10-30-20, 10-20-15, or 5-10-10. After flowering, many bulbs appreciate a high potash formula, to be applied until their leaves begin to yellow. This helps build strength toward next season's flowering.

Plant foods also contain small amounts of trace elements needed for plant health: boron, calcium, copper, iron, manganese, molybdenum, sulphur, and zinc.

How Much and How Often

The amount recommended on the box or bottle of plant food and the advice on when to apply it should be viewed with skepticism. Feeding a plant a strong dose of fertilizer every time you water, or even once a week (certain flowering bulbs and plants excepted, as specified in The Guide), is an overzealous approach that overworks the plant. Feed your plants a water-soluble, all-purpose plant food about every two to three weeks during their active growing period, generally from March to October in most areas. Use about half the amount recommended on the label. An alternative would be to use one-fourth the amount recommended every time you water, or once a week. Different plants have different needs; consult The Guide for specific fertilizing recommendations.

The Perils of Overfeeding

Although the restricted area of container plants and their soil mandates regular fertilizing, too much of a good thing can be perilous. Overfeeding results in general lack of sturdiness, weak stems, and an excess of leaves, some of which may get brown spots or fall off. Overfertilized flowering plants may produce fewer blossoms (this may also occur with underfeeding), and consistently overfed plants will soon have a buildup of white, chalky, or crusty deposits (fertilizer salts) on the pots or soil surfaces. Eventual death is the most dire result. Here's how to avoid such catastrophes:

Don't feed
- when the soil is bone dry and leaves droop. Fertilize when the soil is damp.
- a plant that is sick or diseased. Isolate it, try to ascertain its problem, and treat it accordingly. Food is not a cure-all.
- a newly purchased plant. It was probably fertilized at the nursery, perhaps even heavily. Wait two months or more before feeding.

- when a plant is not actively growing, is in a resting period, semi-dormant or dormant, unless otherwise stated in The Guide. This period is usually in winter, from late October to March.
- a plant that has been recently transplanted or repotted in good soil. It will not need feeding for six to eight weeks.
- fertilizer at a higher dosage or more frequently than specified on the label in the mistaken belief that more is better. Less is better. The manufacturers would like you to use their products generously and buy more. Generally, half the prescribed amount is sufficient to keep the plant well nourished.

Potting, Repotting, and Topdressing

Spring marks the start of a plant's active growing season, after it has had its winter rest and before it puts forth new growth. It is the perfect time to repot or topdress a plant in need of these procedures. But how can you tell when a potted plant is needy? Let us list the ways.

- Roots have grown out of the drainage hole and have perhaps also appeared on the surface of the soil.
- The soil dries out quickly and the plant tends to wilt before the next watering.
- Growth is slow, new leaves are scant or small, and the plant doesn't look as vigorous or healthy as it once did.
- The plant is top-heavy and has grown much bigger than its pot.
- The plant has cracked the (clay) pot. Mayday!

To find out what is going on inside the pot, you have to remove the plant. Some plants can be turned out by merely pushing up against the shard or piece of clay pot that rests above the drainage hole. If this doesn't work easily, place your hand on the surface with the stem or main stems between your fingers, tap the rim of the pot against a hard surface and rap the bottom of the pot smartly. To eject really stubborn subjects, run a sharp knife around the inside of the pot, and start again—something has to give.

Once out of the pot, the condition of the roots will be revealed. If the roots form a dense ball or coil around the base of the pot, repotting may be indicated, but not necessarily so. Sometimes the soil above the root coil is not filled with roots; in this case you merely cut off the coil and return the plant to its pot with a little additional soil. Some plants flower best when potbound and should not be repotted too readily; clivia and many other flowering bulbs, gardenia, hoya, and most palms dislike having their roots disturbed unless it's absolutely necessary (for instance, when roots appear on the surface or crack the pot).

Return to the Same Pot

If the plant doesn't have a very heavy root ball, it may merely need a light trimming of any dried, entangled, or overlong roots. Remove some of the old soil from the roots and add some of the recommended soil for that particular plant,

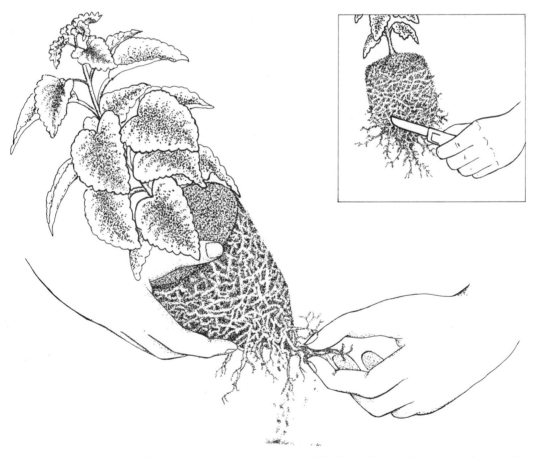

Repotting. *Remove potbound plant from its pot and remove some old soil from the roots. Loosen tangled roots and trim overlong ones. Inset: Prune an especially dense root mass more severely with a sharp knife.*

resetting the plant in the same pot at the same height it had been previously. Press the soil down firmly to eliminate air pockets, but don't pack it hard. You want the surface of the soil to be an inch below the pot rim in a medium-size pot and 1½ to 2 inches below it in a large 10- to 12-inch pot. Water well. If the soil settles a bit, add a small additional amount.

Move on to a Larger Pot

If your plant roots have cracked their container, those roots are yelling for help and absolutely need repotting. The first four symptoms in the list at the beginning of the chapter are also valid reasons for repotting. Individual entries in The Guide indicate whether specific plants should be repotted frequently or infrequently, and provide other pertinent information on the subject.

When you remove the plant from the pot and find a dense and intertwined root mass, in which there are far more roots than soil, it is unquestionably time to repot. Always use only the next larger size pot. Roots should not have a great deal of soil to ramble about in as they search for nutrients. Provide only enough soil to accommodate them comfortably and give them a little extra space in which to grow. Disentangle the thick root mass carefully, using a kitchen fork or pointed stick; trim and replant according to the guidelines given in the previous section. Remember to use only the next larger size pot and rich, organic soil, more or less porous or well drained, according to the plant's needs.

Root Pruning

Perhaps the roots need more than a light trimming and disentangling. In the case of a severely potbound or rootbound plant, the roots are unable to process water and nutrients properly to the growth above and the plant is in decline. With a sharp knife, slice off slabs of the matted roots from all sides as well as the bottom. The poor thing can then be reinstalled in the same pot it was in before, as it will take up much less room, with rich, fresh soil and a thorough watering. Of course, if it had been checked out and repotted well before it arrived at such a calamitous condition, such a drastic step would not have been necessary. The plant, now in a state of shock, will take some time to recover, and it may not produce new roots or shoots for quite a while. It will revive more quickly if you do some top pruning as well. Those battered roots will need a well-earned rest. I suggest that you perform a root prune surgery only if you dearly love the plant, for it will need pampering. Recovery is not a given.

Topdressing

When a plant has reached the largest convenient size pot, a yearly procedure called topdressing will maintain it in good health for a number of years.

Carefully spoon up an inch or two of soil on the surface of the pot. Scratch the exposed surface lightly in any places where it seems especially compacted. If a fine root or two is cut, the plant will not be harmed, but avoid damaging large roots. Now add a rich, nourishing soil mixture with a sprinkle of dried cow manure, bonemeal, and/or other nutritious element. Water thoroughly, and the plant will be revitalized. Subsequent waterings will filter more nutrients to the roots.

After this procedure or any others discussed earlier, keep the plant out of direct sun for a few days while it adjusts to its new state. Sun-needy plants, specified in The Guide, can remain in their usual places. Mist frequently to help the repotted or refurbished plant become well established and produce new growth; the new shoots will appreciate a fine spraying as well.

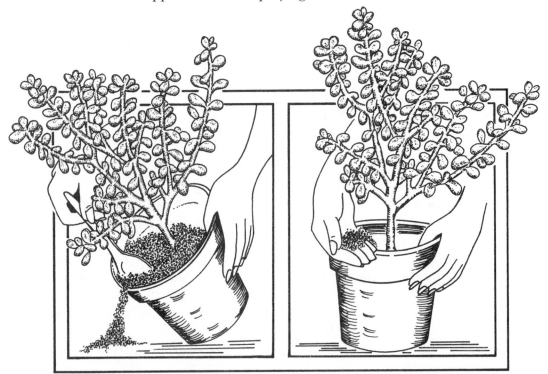

Topdressing. *When a plant is in the largest convenient size container, topdress yearly by removing 1 to 2 inches of soil from the top and adding fresh, rich soil.*

Ready or Not

A small, young plant grown from a tip or stem cutting in moist rooting mix will resist a gentle tug on its stem when its root system is developed enough to warrant potting. A cutting grown in water is ready when its roots are an inch or so long. A section of stem or leaf propagated in a rooting medium produces new leaves when its root system is ready to go. These plantlets can be transferred, with as much moist soil clinging to their roots as possible, to a 2½- to 3-inch pot, larger in some cases, in the recommended soil for the species. Keep them moist, misted, and in filtered light out of direct sun for a few days. You won't believe how fast they grow—pretty soon they will be clamoring for the next size pot.

Propagate and Multiply

One of the most exciting and rewarding activities of container gardening is growing new plants from old. You might even begin to find it hard to resist. When I trim a long trailer or cut back a plant that has grown too large over the summer, I can't bear to throw out those trimmings. Even when windowsills and every inch of space near sunlight are crammed with cuttings or plantlets, the urge to propagate another ti plant from a tall topknot or a shrimp plant from a lengthy stem is irresistible. In time, there are plants to give away, but that is a pleasure, too.

A number of simple methods will increase your collection of plants and replace aging or ailing favorites with vigorous young ones. Sexual reproduction, or growing from seed, is not easy to do with the vast majority of container plants. A plant grown from seed takes a long time to reach maturity and to bloom, and it may not closely resemble its parents since it derives its characteristics from both parents. Seedlings are tender, need careful nurturing, and are subject to devastating diseases that can knock them flat—literally—overnight. If you just want one, two, or three new plants like the one you cherish, why bother to attempt to raise a whole brood?

With vegetative reproduction, using a part or parts of a plant, you soon will have a mature plant that is a clone of its parent. The vegetative reproduction methods described in this chapter will make it easy to expand your movable garden. Refer to The Guide for the best propagation methods for individual plants.

Tip or Stem Cuttings

The most common method of propagating a plant involves taking a 3- to 5-inch cutting from the end of a stem, removing any buds or flowers, and trimming leaves that will be below the surface of the rooting medium. Make the cut just below a node or leaf joint; some plants, including wandering Jew, plectranthus, ivies, and others, may be cut farther down on the stem as well. Cuttings should be taken during a period of active growth in the spring, summer, or early fall. Some overlong stems may be cut and rooted in winter.

Make a hole with a pencil or twig about 1 to 1½ inches deep in a container of moist rooting mix—half peat moss and half sand and perlite (or sand alone or perlite alone). Many cuttings get a quicker start if rooting hormone is applied to the lower end. Insert the cutting in the hole and firm the medium close to

Rooting a Tip Cutting. A. *Make holes in moist rooting medium with a stick or pencil.* **B.** *Insert tip or stem cuttings in holes and firm mixture around them.* **C.** *Cover with plastic and tie around the pot, creating a miniature greenhouse.* **D.** *Well-rooted cuttings can be removed and potted separately.*

the stem. Now cover plant and pot with a plastic sandwich bag or other plastic wrap held up, if necessary, by twigs or sticks; secure it with a rubber band around the pot. This makes a mini-greenhouse that retains moisture and humidity. Keep it warm and in medium to bright light, but not direct sun. Check now and then to make sure the rooting mix is moist, but do not let it become soggy. In two to four weeks (soft-stemmed varieties such as coleus, purple passion, zebrina, and others may take only a week or ten days to root), give a light tug to the stem. If it resists, it has developed a root system and can be carefully transplanted into a pot of the recommended soil. Keep out of bright sunlight for another week or two.

Many cuttings root readily in water and are so indicated in The Guide. Pot them in a lighter, more porous soil mixture—water-grown roots are delicate. The roots should be 1 to 1½ inches long, but no longer than 2 inches. Proceed according to potting directions given for cuttings propagated in rooting mix.

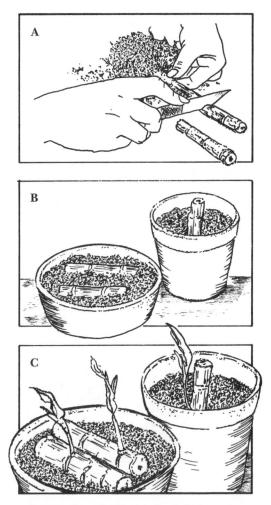

Leaf Cuttings

Individual leaves cut from some species can form new plants in moist rooting mix. Insert the leafstalk at a slight angle. After several weeks, a plantlet will emerge at the base of the stem. Some leaves may root in water. Insert the stem into a hole punched in a piece of plastic secured over a jar of water, and watch for a cluster of roots to appear.

In the rooting mix, baby plantlets will grow at the base and in a few weeks can be moved into small pots of the recommended soil. Two or three attached leaf segments from epiphytic cactus (the Thanksgiving, Christmas, or Easter cactus) inserted in moist rooting mix will take root and grow, as will leaves from succulents such as burro's tail and string-of-beads. A jade leaf will take

Stem or Cane Cutting. A. *Cut a thick stem into sections with one or two nodes on each.* **B.** *Place stem sections in moist rooting medium horizontally, partly exposed, or upright the same way they grew on the plant.* **C.** *Sprouting stem sections.*

hold on almost any soil and in time produce a new plantlet. Certain species of kalanchoe leaves laid or fallen on moist rooting mix or soil will form miniature plantlets along their margins; these plantlets grow tiny rootlets. Some leaves, such as those of the snake plant, can be cut into horizontal segments and planted, soon developing into new plants. The horizontal segments must be planted the way they grew on the leaf (topside up) or they will not take root. The piggy-back plant, which bears babies on its leaves, readily forms new plantlets when a leafstalk is inserted in rooting mix up to the base of the leaf. These interesting and less common methods of propagation are slow, but produce good results.

Stem or Cane Sections

Cut down a tall and rather bare-stemmed dracaena or ti plant and slice up 2- to 3-inch pieces with at least one growth node on each. Place these in damp rooting medium either horizontally with nodes just above the surface, or vertically in the same way they grew on the plant, with 1 or more nodes buried. Leaves will sprout from the nodes. The old plant will make new growth and the severed topknot will root in water.

Plantlets

Some plants, such as the spider plant and saxifraga, or strawberry begonia, create miniature replicas of themselves at the ends of runners or stolons, sometimes with tiny rootlets. Placed in firm contact with rooting mix or even light potting soil, they will take root and become sturdy little plants in a short time. The runners can be severed, and the youngsters will soon be sending out their own.

Plantlets. *Some species such as the spider plant produce miniature plantlets that will root when placed in rooting mixture or potting soil.*

Division

In dividing a plant you immediately have two or more plants from the original one merely by pulling it apart. Some give way easily. Tight, dense clumps of roots or thick rhizomes that are resistant may have to be parted with a sharp knife, with roots and some leaves on each section. This sometimes becomes necessary with a large, potbound plant after a certain number of years. This rough treatment is usually well-received by a tough plant, which will recover and be much happier split up into separate pots with good, fresh soil. Spathiphyllum, Boston fern, asparagus fern, cast iron plant, and maranta are some of the plants that can be propagated by division. Keep them moist and out of direct sun, and they will soon be flourishing.

Division. *Pull apart sections of a plant, here a snake plant, each with suffieicient roots and leaves for becoming a separate plant.*

Offsets

Offsets may be in the form of side-shoots, or suckers, from the base or stem of the parent, or bulblets from the mother bulb near the base. Sometimes they have grown their own rootlets. They should remain where they are until they have reached a size roughly one fourth that of the parent—tiny offsets don't take root easily. The succulent aloe produces rosettes that are easily detached and potted in the recommended soil. Caladium, tuberous begonia, Scarborough lily, other lilies, and most bulbs develop bulblets. The birds' nest fern grows bulbils, tiny bulbs that develop into fernlets on their fronds; these are easily detached and can be propagated. Offsets of the anthurium grow rootlets down to the surface of the soil and can be removed and potted separately at repotting time.

Offset. *A new young plant such as this clivia can be detached from the parent and planted separately in a small pot.*

Layering

Most climbing and trailing plants can be propagated by layering. If a stem is partially buried or placed in close contact with rooting mixture in a pot nearby, it will lay down roots at that point, and new leaves will shoot up. This works well with ivies, cissus, plectranthus, fittonia, wandering Jew, and others. When a firmly rooted plantlet is established, cut it free from its mother plant.

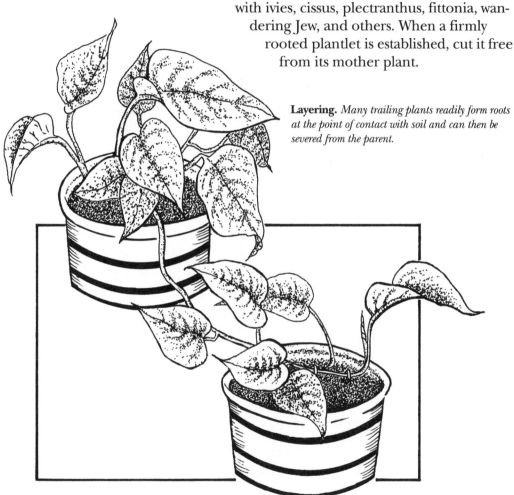

Layering. *Many trailing plants readily form roots at the point of contact with soil and can then be severed from the parent.*

Air Layering

This procedure is performed on a large or woody plant with a thick stem. Either you want a replica, or the stem has become bare and unattractive. Here's how: Make a slanting upward cut partway through the stem a few inches below some healthy leaves. Insert a toothpick or tiny twig to keep the cut open. Or cut two rings around the stem about half an inch apart and strip off the bark between them. Dust the area lightly with hormone rooting powder. Wrap a chunk of damp sphagnum moss around the cut and cover the moss with plastic. Tie at the top and the bottom, making the bundle airtight and keeping the cut moist. Roots will develop, and in a month or two you will see them poking through the moss. A new plant is born. Cut the stem below the root ball, remove the plastic, and pot the new plant, moss and all, in the recommended soil for the species. The parent plant will usually sprout new growth near the cut area, but if the stem is still too tall and bare, you may wish to cut it down farther. It will still feel strongly impelled to send forth new shoots. Use this method of propagation on some of the dracaenas, schefflera, rubber plant, and others. Pieces of the stem, or cane, can be cut into sections with nodes and propagated in damp peat or rooting mix.

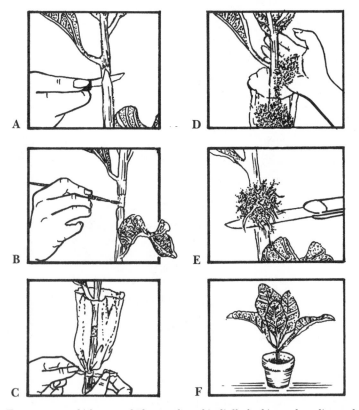

Air Layering. A. *To propagate a thick-stemmed plant such as this dieffenbachia, make a diagonal slash or score two rings around the stem and remove the bark between them.* **B.** *Dust the cut area with hormone rooting powder.* **C.** *Place plastic in a cuplike fashion around the stem and tie firmly at the bottom.* **D.** *Fill the "cup" with moistened sphagnum moss and tie at the top.* **E.** *When a mass of roots appears through the moss, remove plastic and cut through the stem below the roots.* **F.** *Pot the newly rooted plant in appropriate potting soil.*

Cutting Back

Even within their limited space, container plants grow quickly enough so that from time to time that growth needs to be controlled or directed by judicious trimming. Careful pruning keeps the size of your movable garden within reasonable bounds and results in more shapely and productive plants. Early spring is the best time of year to prune, just as a plant is getting ready to make new growth. During the active growth period, continue to pinch back growing tips if stems become too long and straggly. Plants that summer outdoors often grow so vigorously that they need pruning before making the return trip.

When you pinch a growing tip, or terminal point of a stem, the plant's growth at the point is halted; this procedure is often called "stopping." Instead, the plant turns its energy to side-branching, producing more leaf buds lower down on the main stem. As these side branches emerge and grow, they may in turn need pinching back. The result: a bushier, more compact plant with more foliage and flowers, far more attractive than a skinny, lanky one.

The Art of Pinching and Pruning

Pinch back a growing tip of tender or soft-stemmed plants with thumbnail against forefinger, just above an emerging pair of leaves or a leaf node. The "pinch" need not be more than half an inch long. If you want to shape a plant and shorten stems that have grown too long, take a longer 3- to 5-inch pinch that can be used for propagation. A large, old plant that has outgrown its youthful, full look can be perpetuated by pinching all healthy growth for cuttings and discarding the tired remainder.

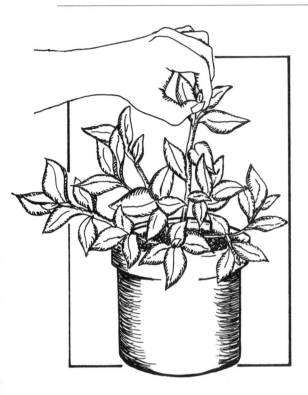

Stems that are thick, tough, or woody must be cut back with a sharp knife or pruning shears above a node, or growth bud. A big plant shooting toward the ceiling can be cut back 1 or 2 feet, not just a couple of inches. Never fear—it will branch out in time.

Plants climbing on or supported by stakes, trellises, mossed poles, or bark may also need occasional pruning. Cutting back main stems will divert energy to side growth. Long, dangling stems or unwanted aerial roots can be trimmed at any time of the year.

Pinching and Pruning. *Pinching off the growing tip or point of a stem above a node encourages side branching and bushiness, stopping lanky growth.*

Summertime Expansion

The surge of growth in spring and summer is particularly strong in plants luxuriating in the benefits of fresh air, sunshine, and dew. Some large plants vacationing outdoors may need rather severe pruning in the fall in order to return to their usual places inside the house. Smaller, soft-stemmed plants that have flourished and spread despite continued pinching back may need to have crowded stems cut close to the base or greatly shortened. Such clippings are very suitable for propagation indoors during the winter.

Top Pruning

When a severely potbound plant needs to have a root prune (see section on repotting on page 35), this drastic procedure should be accompanied by top pruning. The height and width of a root-pruned plant must be decreased if the plant is to survive the shock, or else the strain on the reduced root ball will not be tolerated. As the plant struggles to develop new roots, it should not be expected to nourish an overload of stems, branches, and foliage. Prune all lanky growth and cut back side branches to within a few inches of the main stem.

Seasonal Changes

The needs of a movable garden fluctuate as the seasons pass, and a container gardener is wise to use the cues of weather to schedule the regular care the potted garden requires. Your plants will benefit from special care meted according to nature's calendar, and you will enjoy the continuing health and beauty of a well-tended collection.

Spring Forward!

When the weather has warmed up and all danger of frost is past, it's time to move your container plants outdoors. Before you bring them out, inspect them closely. Steel yourself to dispose of any plants that are in poor condition or unattractive. They are not worth saving, and you have vigorous young plants that were propagated from tip and stem cuttings to take their place. Repot any large plants that have clearly outgrown their pots or topdress those in maximum convenient size pots. Trim straggly ends and remove yellow or brown leaves and dead flowers from all plants.

If you have only a few plants, take them to the kitchen sink and wash foliage and stems and the outsides of the pots; a sprayer works well for this purpose. If you have a sizeable collection and a hose in the backyard, give plants and pots a thorough shower outdoors. The fuzzy, soft, and tender-leaved gesneriads and other similar plants should not be included in the community bath, nor should they be subjected to winds and storms outdoors.

If your five foot croton is unmanageably large and heavy, and not on a dolly, you might want to leave it indoors where it will continue basking contentedly in a sunny south window, but bring out the pots of caladiums, lilies, callas, and other bulbs and tubers that have started into growth. Hanging baskets of tuberous begonias, ivy geranium, and rabbit's-foot fern can also come out at this time. A trip to the greenhouse might be rewarding if you wish to enhance the ambience of your outdoor living area with something new.

Start off all plants, including those that are kept in full sun when indoors, in semi-shade or dappled shade for a few days. Even desert plants that have their origin in hot regions with a blazing sun must not be subjected to direct sun the moment they are brought outside. Container plants are exposed to far more intense light from all sides outdoors than indoors, even in a sun-drenched south window. Move the sun-lovers gradually into filtered sunlight; after a few more days, some of them, including donkey's tail, geraniums, crown of thorns, jade, ti plant, and others, can be moved into full sun.

Exposure to sun, wind, and air causes pots and soil to dry out faster than when indoors, and anything suspended in the air, particularly a moss-lined basket, requires careful attention to watering. Some containers may need water every day in a warm, dry spell. Check plants frequently and treat them to a gentle but thorough drenching from the garden hose. This will wash off foliage as well as soaking the soil. An opportune summer rain may do the job for you, but don't depend on it.

If you like the look of a group of flowering plants in pots on the ground near your steps or patio, set them on a layer of gravel, pebbles, shards, or sand to keep the roots from growing through the drainage hole into the soil below. Give the pots a half-turn every week or so as an added precaution. Containers on patio floors or outdoor tables will get better air circulation and drainage if placed on wood blocks, bricks, stones, or other support.

A prolonged hot spell can be debilitating to many plants, and even several hours of searing midday sun can be harmful to all but the most ardent sun-worshippers. Remember that morning sun is less powerful than early to mid-afternoon sun and try to arrange your plants accordingly. When you spray, do so in the morning and/or early afternoon. Do your watering fairly early in the day as well. If foliage has a chance to dry before nightfall, it is less likely to become moldy or mildewed.

Summer Maintenance

All summer long you will give your outdoor plants a daily checkup. Remove yellow, sickly, or dead leaves and spent blossoms and snip off brown leaf tips with scissors. Feed your container plants regularly and water whenever a plant feels or appears dry. Be careful, though, because too much water or rain will cause soft stems and roots of tender young plants to rot, and they may have to be discarded. If they are part of a container planting, they can be replaced. Waterlogging is bad for almost every plant but calla lilies, which love it.

After a severe storm, heavy rainfall, or violent winds, check your collection for possible damage. Cut off broken stems and torn leaves, and move plants in puddles to a drier area.

Insects can be picked off by hand or removed by a rather forceful spray of plain water. If the infestation is too tenacious, move the affected plant away from others temporarily and use an insecticidal spray .

If one of the plants in your mixed container garden fails to survive a soggy early summer, garden centers and nurseries carry a vast assortment of flowering and foliage plants up to at least mid-July. Replace lost plants with a flowering wax begonia, sweet alyssum, lobelia, impatiens, or verbena that will add color and charm to your patio, balcony, or deck. (See chapter on decorating with plants outdoors, p. 61.)

Summer Maintenance. *Snip off dead flowers to keep plants looking their best and to encourage more blooms.*

Fall Back!

In late summer, perhaps around Labor Day, at any rate a couple of weeks before an early frost might arrive and well before the heat is turned on in the cooler regions, plants vacationing outdoors must be readied for the return trip. It's a busy time, fraught with sadness for the northern gardener who is now contemplating the long, cold winter. Container plants that luxuriated in the summer sunlight and air will need some help in adjusting once more to a different lifestyle indoors. Many of them have grown considerably and are more colorful and vigorous than they were before their summer exodus. The period of adjustment to the indoor life is stressful for your movable garden, just as it is for those of us who have spent delightful hours on terrace or balcony amidst a profusion of foliage and flowers.

Begin by reversing the spring procedure of gradually adjusting the plants' exposure to light. Move the sun-worshippers into filtered shade over a week or so in early fall or late summer. Give all plants a cleansing shower, making sure to dispatch any pests such as aphids or spider mites that arrived during the summer. Direct the spray at the lower as well as the upper sides of the leaves and clean the sides of the pots. Inspect drainage holes and pot bottoms for little critters that will not be welcome in your home.

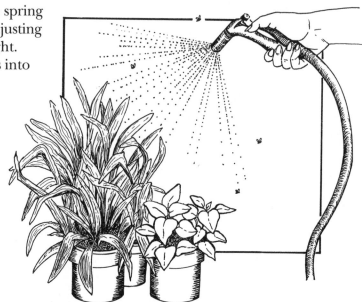

Hose Spraying. *A garden hose spray of medium force to clean foliage and pots and to rout insects should be applied before and after a plant's sojourn outdoors; frequent light spraying is also welcomed by plants, especially during hot, dry weather.*

If a plant has a serious insect infestation, spray with a teaspoonful of mild liquid detergent in a quart of tepid water. If this doesn't eliminate the problem, use an insecticidal spray. If that fails, consider chucking the plant. It may well transmit its problems to others in close proximity indoors. Snip off yellow leaves and dead flowers and trim overgrown trailers and overlong stems. Repot and cut back a plant only if its roots have filled the pot and are pushing out of the drainage hole, or if its top growth is very heavy; otherwise wait until early spring, as plants will soon enter the winter rest period of little growth or dormancy.

Before bringing the plants indoors, decide where you want to place them. Those that were doing well where they were in winter should return to those places. The most sun-needy again deserve front row center seats. All but the most tender and well-shaded tropicals will be seeking as much light as they can get. To help them all readjust, mist frequently and provide some ventilation, particularly in regions where the heat goes on during nights that are becoming chilly. Expect some leaf drop at this time due to the drier, hotter air indoors.

Continue light fertilizing up to mid-October and then withhold until late February or early March, whenever it is late winter or early spring in your climate. Plants that flower during the winter may still be fertilized according to the guidelines in their individual entries in The Guide.

In areas that are not frost-free, flowering plants in window boxes, tubs, or planters can be dug up and potted. Water them well, trim them, keep them in shade or part shade for a week or two outdoors, and then bring them inside to a sunny window. With plenty of moisture and light and frequent liquid feeding, the plant may continue to bloom for several weeks. Some, such as wax begonia, impatiens, New Guinea impatiens, shrimp plant, lantana, and browallia, may keep on blooming quite a while. I have found that the wax begonia, both kinds of impatiens, torenia, and shrimp plant are the best bets, but it's fun to experiment with a number of summer-blooming annuals, provided you have a sunny indoor location. (For geranium survival, see *Pelargonium* in The Guide.) If a flowering annual plant is large and bushy, it has less chance of success and takes up too much space indoors; take cuttings instead. Include coleus, wandering Jew, arrowhead vine, and other long trailing foliage plants or vines. Cuttings will become thriving plants that, in turn, provide you with more cuttings. (See section on propagation, page 40.) By next spring, you will have a good supply of husky clones of your favorite plants to set outdoors.

In the fall before the first frost, bulbs and tubers that summered outside need proper winter storage in frost-free locations. Consult individual entries in The Guide for information on bulb storage.

The jungle cacti—the Thanksgiving, Christmas, and Easter cactus—and the jade plant set flower buds outdoors as the temperatures cool down, nights get nippy, and days grow shorter. Let them have a taste of fall on your terrace or deck, with plenty of sun. Leave them outside longer than any other plants, but be alert to predicted frost or very cold nights; although they enjoy cool weather, a serious chill will harm them. Take no chances with citrus, tender tropicals, or ferns; they also find chilly weather hazardous to their health.

Winter Rest

After a long period of vigorous activity from early spring to fall, most potted plants need a rest. Even evergreen foliage plants and evergreen plants with flowers produce little or no growth, with a few exceptions. Nearly all the requirements of most plants slow down. They need less water and fewer nutrients, and most are content with less light and warmth. Many plants prefer cooler temperatures, especially at night, but humidity should be kept high to offset dry, heated air (see section on increasing humidity, p. 24).

Final fertilizing should be finished by mid-October. Don't stimulate plants with more food. Many bulbs go completely dormant and need only to be properly stored over winter. Flowering plants cease making buds, with a few delightful exceptions such as crown of thorns, nematanthus, crossandra, wax begonia, spathiphyllum, and sometimes hibiscus. These should be watered and fed as usual (consult The Guide). Tender tropicals must not be allowed to dry out, and plants with colored foliage will continue to need bright light. Sun-lovers will enjoy liberal misting.

In late winter or early spring, new growth and renewed vigor indicate that the winter rest has ended. It's a joyous time for the gardener and the plant as new sprouts, leaves, and buds eagerly arise.

When You're Away

How can you make sure your plants will survive your absence when you go on vacation? If it's only for a few days, water them all well and take them out of direct sunlight. In summer and in all warm climates, move the patio plants to a sheltered, rather shady area. But for more than a week, you will need to make further preparations, unless you are fortunate enough to secure the services of a reliable plant sitter.

Survival Strategies

Indoors, remove the plants from full sunlight, but keep them near a source of indirect light. Water them liberally. In winter or in a cold climate, protect the plants from temperature extremes. Make certain none are left on windowsills or near a source of heat, and turn the thermostat to 62–65° F. Less sun and less heat add up to less need for water. Inside a clear dry cleaning bag or other plastic bag, group small or medium plants close together but not touching. Use a larger bag for a large plant. If the bag rests on the foliage, insert sticks or narrow stakes into the pots in several places so that the plastic is raised. Damp peat moss packed around the pots is an extra moisture aid. Close all bags snugly with twist-ties. In this way, moisture is retained and recirculated, creating a greenhouse effect.

For moisture-needy tropicals, the capillary action method may be the best solution. Place well-watered plants on a capillary mat next to the kitchen sink, with the end of the mat hanging down into the water-filled sink. Plants will soak up water from the mat as it is needed. Check out drain and faucet for leaks or drips.

You can also keep soil moist by using wicks that convey water by capillary action from jars of water to plants placed at a lower level than the jar. This is ideal for clay pots, which are too thick to absorb water from a capillary mat. The wick watering method also works well with the wick pushed up through the drainage hole from a well of water beneath the pot.

Succulents and desert cacti, which store water, will be fine if they are well watered before you leave. They do not require a source of constant moisture.

Safeguarded by these precautionary measures, your collection should survive your absence in good condition. Container plants summering outdoors have the added boon of a possible rain shower, but even they, if well watered before you leave, may not even miss you.

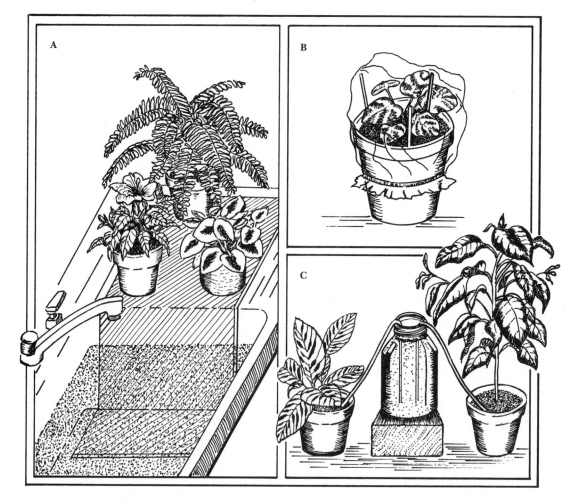

Vacation Watering. A. *A capillary mat with one end in a water-filled kitchen sink draws moisture to plants above.* **B.** *Enclose one or more pots in plastic wrap. Prop up with sticks or twigs if necessary and tie snugly around bottom.* **C.** *Water travels by capillary action down wicks from water-filled jar to plants at a lower level.*

Pests and Problems

Healthy container plants grown with the proper care are seldom troubled by insects or disease. Occasionally, however, a pest is brought in unnoticed on a greenhouse plant or a couple of aphids get a free ride into the house on your sleeve or pants. A plant that is oversprayed or left standing in water invites fungus disease. You may be at a loss to explain why your plant is ailing, but explanations are usually found after a careful examination.

Cleanliness Is Next to Healthiness

The bottom line for plant health is: Keep it clean. Wash large leaves of large plants with a sponge or cloth and give smaller plants with small leaves a thorough spraying in the sink. This simple method removes dust and traces of pollution, which varies according to the geographical and industrial location, and also removes insects or insect eggs that may be present. Frequent misting helps in the same way, and the extra moisture is appreciated by most plants. Isolate a sick plant until it recovers or dies, so that other plants don't get infested or infected. Lastly, groom your container plants by picking off sickly, yellow, or dead leaves and spent flowers.

The Six Most Pernicious Pests

Aphid. Usually green or yellow and sometimes black or red, these small insects like to suck the juices out of the tips of new growth of many soft and tender plants. They can cause stunted growth and deformed leaves and buds. The sticky substance they exude is sooty mold, a fungus disease. Remove affected parts, wash or spray foliage, and if aphids return, apply an insecticidal spray such as Safer's.

Cyclamen Mite. These critters are bad news. You can't even see them, but you can see the harm they do. Leaves and stems are stunted, curled, and unhealthy-looking, and buds wither. Although the mites often affect cyclamen, they are attracted to many other plants as well. Destroy infected parts at once. Isolate the plant and apply insecticide, but be aware that mites may be an incurable problem and you may need to sacrifice the plant before the infestation spreads.

Mealy Bug. A cottony mass on a stem or leaf axil is a mess of mealy bugs sucking the sap out of a plant. Apply a Q-tip soaked in alcohol to the cluster. Spray and wash. The mealy bug can attack a variety of plants.

Red Spider Mite. So tiny you can't see them, red spider mites cluster on the undersides of leaves and suck the plant's juices. Symptoms are tiny holes in leaves, curled and yellowing leaves, stunted new growth, blasted buds. You may see fine, threadlike webs near the joints of leaves and stems. Use a soapy spray or insecticidal spray for control of mites. Ivy and cissus are particularly susceptible if the air is hot and dry.

Scale. These round, brown lumps, usually on stems but sometimes elsewhere, enclose sluggish insects that are sucking out the life of the plant. You can scratch or scrape them off. Keep the plant clean and spray with insecticidal soap.

Whitefly. You may not realize they are present, but if you touch a plant and a swarm of tiny white insects flies up and about, you've got whitefly. They reproduce and spread with horrifying speed, so don't neglect them. Soapy spray may not give enough control. Before they suck the foliage juiceless and yellow, try this simple remedy. It is known that certain insects are attracted to the color yellow. Take any yellow-colored plastic or paper and coat it with a greasy or oily substance. Place several pieces close to the affected plants. Soon these surfaces will be dotted with whiteflies. Discard the papers and do it again. I've tried this and it works! One remedy I haven't tried: suck whiteflies into a hand-held vacuum cleaner with moth balls inside. Do this every few days until you don't see any more whiteflies. I suggest caution around tender-leaved or flowering plants, but try it!

Fungus Diseases

Plants placed fairly close together benefit by shared moisture, but if they touch, poor air circulation may result, which invites mold. Fungus diseases are usually manifested by different kinds and colors of molds. Black sooty mold comes from sap-sucking insects that exude a sticky honeydew. Remove the sticky residue with a damp cloth and go after the insects that caused the problem. Powdery mildew shows up as white powdery patches on leaves. Removing the affected leaves should quickly solve the problem. Gray mold appears as gray, fluffy patches also known as botrytis (another form is blackleg, or black stem rot). Cut off affected parts, and don't mist this plant. If botrytis spreads, it can be a killer and the badly infected plant should be discarded.

In fact, any seriously infected or infested plant should be discarded if you cannot control the problem with a soapy spray or the appropriate insecticide or fungicide.

Good air circulation outdoors in summer averts fungus problems. Heavy rains may cause some tender stems and leaves to rot and fall, but mold and mildew seldom occur even with a great deal of extra moisture. You might want to check outdoor containers for plump, little gray pillbugs and sowbugs. They hide under pots and enter drain holes snacking on roots but not causing any serious damage. You will still want to remove them before returning pots to the house.

Grooming. A. *Sponge off top and bottom surfaces of large leaves with tepid water.* **B.** *Cut off dried leaf tips.* **C.** *Periodically spray plants in the kitchen sink to remove dust and deter insects.*

PART II

Decorating with Your Movable Garden

Enhancing Indoor and Outdoor Living Areas

Plants have texture and form as well as color and scent. They can be integrated into the decor of a home, displayed singly or as an attractive group. A striking specimen tree or shrubby plant lends a note of drama to an entrance hall inside or a patio door outside. A garden grouping with splashes of color in leaf and flower brighten the sunroom or den in winter or the deck in summer. A desert garden or a jungle garden can be created indoors or out. Exotic or unusual flowering bulbs and plants can be prominently displayed when at their peak bloom. The possibilities are endless. Every container garden can be moved or changed—for more or less light, for better compatibility of size, shape, and color with surroundings, or for more visual impact where and when you want it. These changes can be made easily and spontaneously. And always, of course, there is the sheer joy of seeing your plants grow, bud, and flower, inside and outside your home as the seasons change.

Dressing Up

A glazed ceramic cachepot or jardinière, a woven basket with a waterproof liner or saucer, a handthrown pottery urn, or a bright copper kettle add immeasurably to the overall appearance of a plant growing in a plain clay or plastic pot. A handsome plant deserves a handsome container, which has the dual virtue of retaining moisture and combatting dry, hot air, especially when damp peat moss or sphagnum moss is placed between inner and outer pot. Once you have your plants well dressed, show them off indoors as well as out.

Indoor Accents

Large, imposing tree-like plants or bushy plants can be displayed as solitary features indoors in an empty corner, against a wall, in a foyer, or in sets of two or more as room dividers in a living-dining area. The ficus family is excellent for this purpose, in particular the weeping fig, the fiddle-leaf fig, and the rubber plant. Philodendrons, both tall vining or climbing types and the shorter, broader self-heading types are also useful as architectural or sculptural accents. Brassaia, aspidistra (the cast iron plant), dieffenbachia, some of the palms and dracaena, and Chinese evergreen are other plants of substantial size that can be grouped in decorative "poses" that add color and drama to the room. By and large, these are plants that tolerate low-to-medium light and humidity levels. They will grow slowly in low or poor light, an advantage to the gardener who will not often need to prune them back. But occasionally give these plants a treat for a week or two by switching them to a brighter spot.

An imposing plant with striking, multicolored foliage such as croton, ti plant, or corn plant can be taken out of its sunny location to enliven a corner of the dining room, entrance hall, or living room. Use them to add bright, vivid color to any all-green group, bearing in mind that they cannot be considered permanent members of the group but are only special-occasion guests. Without plenty of good, bright light those handsome leaves will soon lose their colors and tend to revert to green.

Impressive plants of lesser size that are not in need of a great deal of sun can be featured prominently on a pedestal, plant stand, or table. Among these are Boston fern and Dallas fern, grape ivy and kangaroo ivy, Chinese evergreen, pothos, heartleaf philodendron, piggyback plant, spider plant, and asparagus fern. The jungle cacti—the Thanksgiving, Christmas, and Easter cactus—are spectacular when in bloom. All of these plants are highly suitable for hanging baskets as well. See section on hanging baskets, page 74.

Also on a pedestal or Victorian plant stand, a large bowl of upright and trailing plants that grow harmoniously together in medium light looks splendid. I like the interesting contrasts that can be achieved with all-green and variegated foliage with touches of cream, yellow, and white. Use combinations of arrowhead vine, pothos, English ivies, aluminum plant, peperomia, and wandering Jew. Cascading stems lend a graceful note. As a variation of this display, place a handsome Chinese evergreen or dracaena of medium size in the center and surround it with small pots of trailing plants, such as Swedish ivy and heartleaf philodendron. Contrasts in heights and shapes in close proximity are very pleasing, and plants in individual pots are easily moved about or replaced by others. The mantelpiece is also a good setting for an attractive trailing plant.

Blooming Beauties

Pride of place must surely be granted to those pampered aristocrats of container plant society, the flowering bulbs. Those few that bloom in winter or early spring—the resplendent amaryllis, fragrant freesia, exotic veltheimia, and Amazon lily—should be shown off where they will get the most admiration. So bump the fern off its pedestal and substitute a blooming beauty. Many more of the bulbs you have tenderly nurtured indoors, such as lilies, agapanthus, alstroemeria, ixia, and Scarborough lily, will be ready to bloom outdoors starting in mid-spring and continuing until midsummer. Clivia, though it may have finished blooming before the warm weather, goes outside too. All these flowering bulbs like sunny spots or at least part sun on terrace, deck, or patio. Choose a bright corner for a splendid summer show of color. Those that finish blooming can be retired to a less conspicuous—but still partly or mostly sunny—location; remove spent blooms, but not stems and leaves, which are needed to nourish the bulb. Shift other sun lovers into their places. For details on storage and winter care of bulbs, see Winter Rest, page 53, and individual entries in The Guide.

The Tropical Forest on a Pebble Tray

In a low-to-medium light area indoors you can create a fascinating jungle of tropical, moisture-loving plants. Place a two- or three-inch high waterproof tray (available in many sizes) on the floor or table where it can receive a moderate amount of light. Fill it with an inch or so of pebbles or gravel. As with any pebble or humidity tray, add water up to the top of the pebbles. This is the proper indoor setting for a large number of moisture-loving plants with modest light requirements. Suitable plants, all potted individually, include calathea, ferns, maranta, peperomia, pilea, heartleaf philodendron, creeping fig, and for blooms, anthurium and spathiphyllum, if they're contented enough to bloom. A caladium adds a lovely touch of color. Place the smallest pots in front and larger ones to the rear; if there is room, set snake plant, dracaena, dieffenbachia, or a vining philodendron on bark or pole in the back. Different sizes and heights add depth and dimension.

Because water vapor is constantly arising from the wet pebbles, and the moisture in the air is increased by liberal use of the hand mister, these jungle plants are surrounded by the humidity they crave. You will have to water them, too, of course; give just enough to keep the soil constantly moist. In the winter, when they are not in active growth, water them less, but don't neglect the misting. The heated atmosphere in winter in cold climates tends to make the air less humid.

Some of these exotic and less common plants present real challenges to the gardener, but the challenge is exciting. It's a thrill to see a delicate calathea put forth a new leaf or an anthurium send up its odd orange-red flowers. Bring your tropical forest outdoors in summer or mild climates; the plants will flourish if they are kept shaded, moist, and misted. A pebble tray is not needed, but a gentle hosing when the weather is hot and dry is most appreciated.

The Foliage and Flower Garden Indoors

One of the best ways to create a foliage and flower garden indoors is on a large pebble tray or several smaller ones. You can group plants quite closely and they will benefit from one another's transpiration (the release of moisture through their leaves into the air) and from frequent misting of the foliage. Since this garden is meant for a sunny spot, give careful attention to its moisture needs.

Choose a sun-soaked table, plant stand, or a spot south-facing (or southeast or southwest) bay window or broad windowsill, or near a doorway opening to a sun-filled courtyard or patio. Foliage plants can include coleus, bloodleaf, purple passion, zebrina, variegated English ivy, 'Golden Hahnii' snake plant, and young croton and ti plants. Good choices for flowering plants are wax begonia, impatiens, kalanchoe, dwarf geranium, Rieger begonia, crown of thorns, and young lantana and shrimp plants. To this collection, add recently propagated plantlets that need bright light. You can also create a colorful mini-garden of rooted cuttings and young plants placed directly into the soil of a shallow 10- or 12-inch pot.

All of your flowering plants are not likely to bloom at the same time or all season long; if you have a variety of bloomers, though, you will probably have some flowering even in the fall and winter. Include the jungle cacti—Thanksgiving, Christmas, and Easter—when budded, after their rest period in the dark. If they are too large to join the group, give them a place in the sun elsewhere, as you must do with a mature hibiscus, yucca, or any other large foliage or flowering plant.

If you wish to move such a garden come spring, fill tubs and planters with attractive combinations of the same foliage and flowering plants. Keep plants in their pots and place them inside a larger container so that they may be shifted about or replaced later on if desired. New plants, and plants removed from their pots, should go into a rich, well-drained potting medium inside your outdoor planters, generally to stay the season.

Northern Lights

A north exposure, often judged wrongly to be a poor place for plants, actually gets good to medium light and sometimes quite bright light (if not obstructed by trees, shrubs, or a wall) without direct sun or glare and is an excellent place for a group of all-green plants and some with lightly variegated foliage. In my north-facing bay window, dracaena, dieffenbachia, Chinese evergreen, and a variety of philodendrons live long, happy lives. Plants that grow too tall for the windowsill are switched to the floor below the window. All these plants can be rearranged with others in low and medium light on tables, stands and pedestals, or the floor. A Boston fern is lovely suspended overhead in a north window.

Making the Transition

All large foliage plants can be distinctive outdoors as well as indoors. Of course, you may wish to retain some of them in the home all year round so that you are not totally bereft of greenery when you step inside the door. It's true, however, that all plants will benefit from the brighter, fresher, airier, and generally more humid atmosphere outdoors and will happily put forth new growth. The green and lightly variegated foliage plants of considerable size—brassaia, fig, palm, dieffenbachia, and others—can be individual accents on the terrace or deck by a door, steps, an entranceway, in a shady corner, or grouped in shade or semi-shade. They can also serve as an impressive backdrop for the shorter foliage plants that don't require bright light.

Sizable sun-needy plants such as croton, ti plant, agapanthus, clivia, yucca, hibiscus, and, in particular, citrus trees will eagerly welcome as much sun as they can get and will be spectacular eyecatchers outdoors, standing by themselves or grouped with other sun-loving plants.

Outdoor Ornamental Container Displays

A single imposing plant, or a few full, bright, blooming plants in an ornamental urn or sculptured terra cotta pot can make a strong impact by steps, path, bird bath, pool, or fountain. In such a prominent position and in a handsome, decorative container, you can show off a specimen palm or fern or highlight a harmonious color combination of, perhaps, red, pink, and white lilies, geraniums, and petunias, with green and white variegated ivy cascading over the sides. A simple, pleasing color scheme here is more effective than a mixed bouquet, which is better displayed in tubs, planters, and hanging baskets closer to the eye.

The North-Facing Window. *This group of plants suited to a northern indoor exposure includes, (hanging) Boston fern; (on sill, from left) prayer plant, cast iron plant, dieffenbachia; (on table) philodendron 'Burgundy'; (on floor) dracaena marginata, rubber plant.*

The Flowering Container Garden Outdoors

A flowering container garden can be a showpiece in four seasons in warm-winter regions and in three seasons in cooler regions. The ideal container is a large, round pot or tub, 16 to 18 inches across and a foot or more deep, with good drainage. Use rich soil with added bonemeal. Start in autumn by placing spring-blooming bulbs such as tulip, narcissus, grape hyacinths, or any other at their proper depth. Cover the bulbs with soil. In warm-winter regions you can proceed with more planting; in cold regions, don't plant until spring, but mulch to protect the bulbs.

For the early spring season, a tall green perennial foliage plant, perhaps a philodendron on a pole in its pot, can be placed in the center. Surround it with wax begonias, impatiens, forget-me-not, white, rose, or purple sweet alyssum, pansies, and primroses. As the season progresses, add geranium, dwarf marigolds, verbenas, and petunias; trailing plants such as variegated ivy, zebrina, and lobelia; blooming perennials such as shasta daisy, penstemon, coreopsis, gaillardia, and marguerite; and perennials with silvery-gray foliage such as dusty miller, lamb's ears, and snow-in-summer. Buy dwarf or miniature varieties if at all possible. Remove early-blooming annuals and any plant past its peak bloom or not performing as well as you would like; lift bulbs with sprawling foliage and plant them in your garden. If you can't get at the bulbs without disturbing other plants, cut off the bulb foliage; you need the space it occupies for new plants, and messy foliage will spoil the beauty of the flowering garden.

The idea is to keep the tub always full to overflowing with prolific, exuberant flowers and foliage. To that end, replace faded plants, feed lightly and often, and groom meticulously. Let no faded flower or yellowing leaf escape your clippers. The color scheme can be a rainbow riot of glorious color or a simple, stunning combination of yellow, orange, and white or yellow, blue, purple, and white. If chrysanthemums are available in your area, tuck in a cushion 'mum, low-growing and small-flowered, for fall color and bloom.

If you sacrifice a bulb or a plant now and then, so be it. Display is the name of this game, and it is constantly subject to change for the better. In warm regions, some plants may survive to bloom another season, and if you love them, that's a plus; otherwise, don't bother to save them. The plants mentioned are generally available in most regions and adapt well to containers, but there are a great many other choices. Find out which annuals and perennials are available as transplants in your local nurseries and garden centers and in catalogs where sun and shade preferences and tolerance for hot or cold and moist or dry conditions are indicated. Know the season and duration of bloom—then indulge your fancy!

For anyone with a limited outdoor living area, this kind of garden is highly desirable and easily managed. It can be adapted to a rectangular box or planter

of large size, possibly set against the wall of the house. With this kind of place-
ment, taller plants should be set to the rear of the container rather than in its
center.

When the temperature starts to dip, you can pot some of these plants and
take them indoors. Those that will survive the winter inside the home will be the
ones you grew there and then planted out—the geranium, impatiens, wax begonia, ivies, and others. Most flowering annuals and perennials will not survive
indoors for long, but they will brighten the home for a short while if you have a
sunny spot for them. See the chapter on seasonal changes for more details.

Since many of the survivables have grown too large or lanky for potting, I
like to take cuttings in the fall and propagate them for my indoor winter garden.

The Outdoor Cluster Garden

You can create a dazzling picture with colorful foliage and flowering plants clustered in a sunny or partly sunny corner of a deck or patio. Place different kinds
and sizes of plants and pots at different heights. Rocks, bricks, or chunks of
wood or concrete placed under some of the pots will provide more contrast in
heights and levels. Bright mounds of color can come from geraniums; use both
zonals and large-flowered regals (Martha Washingtons). Encircle one or two
sturdy New Guinea impatiens with rambling wandering Jew, which becomes
beautifully colored in the sunlight. Tuck in a pot of wine-red iresine and a pink-
splashed polka-dot plant. The floriferous wax begonia and the exuberant coleus
must be included. Add a pot of variegated cream and green English ivy. Low in
front, set a spreading purple heart setcreasea, and up at a touch-and-sniff level,
at least one of the scented geraniums. Add, if desired, flowering annuals such as
trailing lobelia, sweet alyssum, browallia, and torenia. Voilà! A sensational scene,
and all of its components can be moved, removed, or replaced for maximum
impact at any time.

You can have a color scheme if you like, perhaps shades of pink, rose, and
purple with touches of white; but I think a vivid potpourri of color is ideal for
this kind of grouping. Clay pots are best, as they draw the least attention to
themselves, and they let roots "breathe" better than plastic will in sunlight and
hot weather.

The Potted Desert Garden

In the warm, or hot, and dry climates of the Southwest, parts of California and
Texas, and southern Florida, pots and planters are often filled with cacti and
succulents that are heat- and drought-tolerant or resistant; succulents such as

Outdoor Cluster Garden. *Thriving in a sunny location, this group includes (on rail) common geranium, zonal geranium; (on deck, from left) Calamondin orange, hibiscus, variegated English ivy, bloodleaf, impatiens.*

aloe, jade plant, string-of-beads, burro's tail (look for 'Burrito', a dwarf), crown of thorns, other sedums, kalanchoe and agave, and desert cacti of many odd and intriguing shapes that bear vivid, beautiful flowers. Well-stocked greenhouses carry dozens of these varieties. Use them outdoors, grouped in their individual pots or planted in shallow bowls or other containers. Small or miniature varieties can be pleasingly arranged on a table or tray. Indoors, give them the sunniest window in a warm room, and they will be quite comfortable in the average warm and dry home environment. In cool climates, wait until temperatures warm up before setting them outdoors.

Indoors or out, they are easy to care for. Provide sandy, gritty soil, water only when the soil is dry, and fertilize only once or twice during the active growing period. With ample sun and warmth, low humidity and good drainage, cacti and succulents need not be confined to hot, dry regions of the country. In colder, less sunny, or moist coastal areas, many of these plants are most successfully grown indoors in a southern exposure.

I like to see a desertscape in a shallow terra cotta bowl or large plant saucer; avoid fancy or brightly colored containers that may detract from the often curious and bizarre appearance of the occupants. A pottery casserole or baked bean pot make fine containers, as do bonsai pots. If drainage is needed, place a layer of pebbles or gravel and a few charcoal chips at the bottom. Very young forms of succulents and cacti create an effective sunny dish garden. Top it off with small pebbles, stone chips, bits of wood, a sprinkle of sand, tiny chips of clay shards, or any combination thereof. A good-looking stone or rock can be added to an uncrowded desertscape. Skip the bleached bones and, please, no gnomes.

Place this container on patio or deck where it will get the most sun all summer long and you can almost forget about its care. One caveat: Try to rescue an outdoor desert garden from a heavy downpour before it turns into a bog garden.

Moving Shade-Lovers Outside

Plants that shun the direct rays of the sun have their own distinctive charms. They include most of the green-leaved foliage plants, palms, ferns, vines, the tropical forest dwellers, and others with lightly variegated foliage such as pothos, arrowhead vine, Chinese evergreen, some of the English ivies, and all others that spent the winter in low or medium-to-bright light indoors. Filtered shade cast by a leafy tree on terrace or deck suits them perfectly. Gleams of early morning or late afternoon sun will not harm them. In semi-shade these plants will thrive and make new growth over the summer.

Ideal for pots of tropicals, forest cacti, ferns, pilea, and other sun-shunners are containers that hook over or straddle a railing or fence. Ivies, maranta, calathea, anthurium, fittonia, and rabbit's foot and pteris ferns luxuriate in such hangers on my terrace railing beneath a big maple. (These planter frames of vinyl-coated wire or wood are fine for sunny spots, too.) Beneath them are grouped the foliage plants that spent the winter in low-light exposures on plant stands, pedestals, the north window, and the like.

Perhaps the most spectacular shade plant is the caladium, which is started indoors from tubers in early spring. They bear huge yet delicate leaves up to a foot long in a variety of lovely color combinations: green and white; green, red, and white; pink, white, and green; and more, all elegantly veined, patterned, or mottled. New leaves keep coming up all summer and into fall. Back indoors when cold weather threatens, they will continue to leaf out for several weeks, adding a charming note to your tropical forest garden or any convenient spot out of the sun. Keep them moist and misted as they continue to grow; when leafing stops they are beginning their winter rest period and should get no more water. Remove dry leaves and store over the winter. (See The Guide for instructions on storage.)

For another colorful note where the shade is not dense, use the versatile and richly variegated coleus. It really prefers bright light or direct sun, but will still glow exuberantly in semi-sun or dappled shade. It's reliably decorative almost everywhere, as is the cheery and bright-blossomed impatiens.

If you have the space outdoors, try something a little bit different. A flat-topped rock, up-ended sturdy log, or level chunk of wood are perfect sites for a particularly handsome specimen of Swedish ivy or grape ivy, piggyback plant, asparagus fern or other foliage plant that likes to spread and sprawl in shade or filtered shady places. Such displays are especially picturesque under a tree, next to a bench, at the foot of steps, or near a bird bath, pool, or fountain.

Somewhere among the vacationing leafy green plants that climb, spread, and trail in the shady realm of your outdoor living space is where you, too, will find a cool and tranquil setting away from the sun's rays. Relax, and take delight in the scene that you have created.

Hanging Baskets

A hanging garden is a delightful form of container planting, especially useful when space is at a premium. Handsome foliage and flowering plants that trail, cascade, or billow from a container are superbly ornamental and are displayed to best advantage in pots or baskets suspended from the ceiling or attached to a wall. Indoor hanging plants can be moved outdoors as climate and weather permit, and beautifully decorative effects can be created when you suspend the baskets from eaves, posts, railings, fences, and tree branches. Easy to move and pleasing to the eye, hanging baskets are an important element of a movable garden.

Kinds of Baskets

Common, serviceable, and not terribly attractive, white or green plastic baskets are available in various sizes with drip-tray or saucer attached and wires and hook ready for hanging. Of course, you can place them within a more aesthetically pleasing macramé, rattan, or other attractive holder. Brackets or pot-holders for one to three pots can be hung from a railing on a terrace or deck, a solution particularly useful where it's not feasible to install wall brackets. A true openwork basket of wire, plastic, or wood is the most attractive option, but it is best suited to the outdoors, as it is liable to leak a bit.

Preparing an Openwork Hanging Basket

Use sheets or pieces of unmilled sphagnum moss, available at garden centers, nurseries, and florists, to line your baskets. Remove the hangers of the basket first to make the work easier. Soak the sphagnum moss well, then squeeze out the excess water and line the basket with overlapping pieces to make a layer about 2 inches thick. At the top, let the moss extend just over the rim all around. Have the soil ready; a light, well-drained basic formula (described on page 90 of The Guide) suits most plants. If you use a soil-less mix, add some good potting soil to provide nutrients for a start. Consult The Guide for the individual plant's special needs, if any. Fill the container with soil about two-thirds full and place the plant or plants in it. Add more soil to within an inch of the top, then firm it gently around roots and stems. Water it very thoroughly. For a sunny or partly sunny spot, keep the basket somewhat shaded for a few days, then gradually give more light before hanging it in its permanent place.

It's a great temptation to buy a hanging basket fully loaded with colorful blooms for an instant lush, splashy display. But if you do buy a ready-to-hang basket, pick one that's not in full bloom, one with more buds than open flowers. Then you can have the pleasure of seeing them open. Furthermore, an extravagantly blooming basket may have no more buds, or none for a long time. Keep that warning in mind as you inspect these entrancing plants, looking also for signs of insects, disease, and weak or rotted stems.

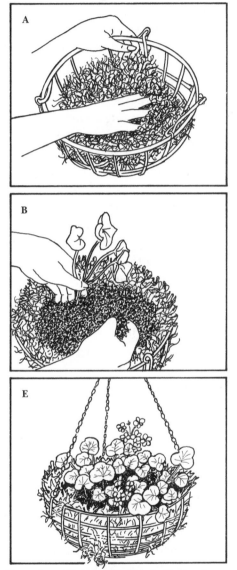

Preparing a Hanging Basket. A. *Line a wire or plastic openwork basket with overlapping sheets of damp sphagnum moss.* **B.** *Fill partway with light soil mixture. Arrange plants. Place vines next to the rim so they can trail over the sides. Taller plants should go in the center.* **C.** *Fill with soil mixture up to about an inch below the rim and press soil firmly around stems of plants. Water well. Hang basket.*

Choosing Your Plants

You can choose from a host of splendid flowering plants for hanging baskets, but remember that flowering plants with few exceptions need bright and sunny locations. Among the best choices are ivy geranium, trailing lantana, hoya, glory bower, trailing flowering maple, and pendent tuberous begonia. Fuchsia, achimenes, and nematanthus (goldfish plant) prefer light or filtered shade. Many annuals that flower profusely in sunny places may also be added to hanging baskets for an extra splash of color. Try sweet alyssum, lobelia, petunia, nasturtium, impatiens, and wax begonia.

Sun-worshipping foliage plants include the succulents string-of-beads (string-of-pearls), string-of-hearts (rosary vine), and burro's tail (donkey's tail), all capable of storing water and all exhibiting odd and interesting trailing stems and leaves. Purple heart setcreasea and purple passion vine are vibrant in full sun. Other brightly hued foliage plants for sunny places are trailing coleus, some variegated English ivies, zebrina, and the tricolor strawberry begonia (saxifraga). Foliage plants that prefer light shade or filtered light are mostly all green; among the most popular choices for hanging baskets are Swedish ivy, heartleaf philodendron, pothos, asparagus fern, grape ivy, and spider plant.

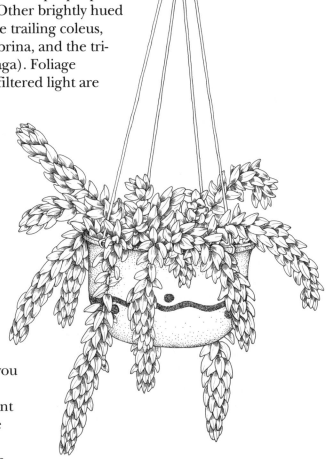

A number of plants that are not specifically categorized as hanging basket plants tend to spread out, dip, and spill over the sides of a pot and may be used in baskets. Among these are the piggyback plant, some of the peperomias, and fittonia.

Before you choose a plant to hang, use The Guide to help you anticipate its needs and give it a good start. Feel free to experiment with many varieties beyond those suggested here. Just remember, whatever goes up can come down again—that's part of the fun of movable gardening!

Burro's tail *(Sedum morganianum) is a good choice for a hanging basket in a sunny spot.*

Care and Maintenance

Fertilizer: As with any container plant, use an all-purpose liquid houseplant food for foliage plants and a blossom-boosting, low-nitrogen food for flowering plants. Plants in soilless mixes need extra nourishment and water, so add a few drops of liquid fertilizer every time you water (one to three times a week, sometimes more).

Water: Never let the soil in a basket dry out. Check hanging plants daily, as wind and sun outdoors in summer and heat that rises indoors in winter tend to dry out the soil very quickly.

Grooming: Whether indoors or out, hanging plants are particularly visible, often from all sides, so keep them impeccably well groomed. Remove faded or dead blossoms and leaves; trim straggly stems and trailers; turn the baskets occasionally so that an even distribution of light produces a full, overall mass of foliage and flowers.

Weathering a Storm

If the weather takes an unseasonably cold turn or becomes very windy and stormy, try to rescue the most exposed basket plants from the elements. Shove them unceremoniously into the nearest shelter—under a table or bench, in the porch or garage, inside an entranceway, or beneath a broad overhang—and take them out again as soon as the weather becomes pleasant. The nuisance factor is high, but so is the value of the plants you are protecting. When it's time to move the plants into the warm, dry, and less bright environment of the house, treat hanging plants as you would earthbound plants, as discussed in the chapter on seasonal changes.

Window Box Gardening

Window box gardening is an easy and rewarding way of gardening when you don't have much ground space outdoors. Even if you have a large patio or deck, window boxes are an attractive addition to your home. Before you choose the plants for your window box, consider its exposure: Will it be in a sunny, partly sunny, or shady spot? Choose from the flowering and foliage plants most suitable for that exposure. Consult the light requirements list on page 15 for quick reference. The Guide has more complete light recommendations for each plant.

Kinds of Window Boxes

Window boxes can be wood, plastic, or metal. Wood has the advantage of porosity, which allows the roots to breathe, and insulating properties, which protect roots against the summer heat. Cedar, redwood, and pressure-treated pine are the most durable woods for window boxes. If you are building the boxes at home, choose thick boards to increase the insulation factor. A window box of any length should be about a foot deep and 10 inches wide. Be sure it is strong enough and well-supported enough to bear the weight of plants and soil and remain firmly attached. Drainage holes at the bottom of the box should be covered with fine wire mesh or screening.

Preparing a Window Box

For the planting medium, ready-made, bagged soilless mixes are best; they are light, clean, and sterile, and they drain well. A small amount of good, rich potting soil mixed into the soilless medium will add nutrients. Plants in soilless containers need fairly frequent fertilizing, so provide a very light application of an all-purpose plant food every time you water (once or twice a week, possibly more in very hot weather).

Before planting, moisten the soil well and add more soil if the initial amount settles more than an inch below the rim. For a lively, full effect, set the plants quite close together, leaving a bit of elbow room for future growth. Between the upright plants, add some trailing plants that will cascade gracefully over the side of the box. It is important to mulch the surface with pebbles and/or bark chips to help retain moisture. You can also mix the mulching material with grass clippings, dried seaweed, or compost.

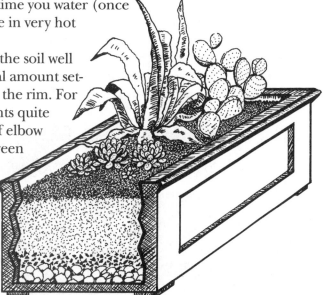

Cross Section of Window Box. *Cover drainage holes with screening or wire mesh. Layer pebbles or coarse gravel on the bottom, then some charcoal chips, and finally well-drained soil mixture. When plants are in place, add a mulch of small pebbles, bark, or wood chips.*

Choosing Your Plants

For bright masses of color in a sunny or partly sunny exposure, include flowering annuals such as blue and white trailing lobelia, petunia, miniature zinnia, annual vinca, variegated English ivy, lantana, and nasturtium. These will make a lovely display in between your own pot-grown wax begonias, geraniums, ivy, coleus, or wandering Jew. For a semi-shady or shady location, you might use caladium, grape ivy, zebrina, arrowhead plant, Swedish ivy and other trailing plants, with impatiens, and wax begonia. As with hanging baskets, use The Guide and the list of light requirements for plants (p. 15) to help you make a choice of varieties best suited to your exposure.

The "Movable" Window Box

The alternative to planting directly into the soil of your window box is to place pots with well-grown plants directly into the empty box. Set pots with short plants on a layer of pebbles or sand thick enough to bring the plant into full view. Fine screening below the pots will keep roots from growing out of the drainage holes.

When you have arranged the plants in a pleasing display, add peat, perlite, or sand to the box; moisten this material each time you water so that the pots remain moist. A window box with potted plants offers a wide range of possibilities, for the contents are all movable. During the season, you may want to make a substitution or addition, or even change the entire color scheme.

Window Box. *For a sunny or partly sunny exposure, select colorful flowering and foliage plants such as geranium, New Guinea impatiens, and coleus. Here, annual vinca vines add a graceful note.*

Care and Maintenance

Have no qualms about chucking out any plant that doesn't perform well, whether in soil or in a pot. Replace castoffs with something better-looking; these little gardens are charming only when filled to capacity and spilling over with healthy, happy, colorful plants in top-notch condition. As with any container plants, pinch off faded blossoms, yellowed or dead leaves, and unkempt or over-long stems and trailers.

In winter, the window box need not be a disaster area. After you bring your ivy or geraniums back indoors for the cold season, decorate your window box with evergreen branches and pine cones, sprigs of bittersweet with orange berries, dried gourds, or any dried plant material with attractive berries or seed pods.

The Windowsill
Water Garden

Cuttings from a surprisingly large number of plants will readily grow roots in water, and with them you can create a lovely miniature garden especially suited to a sunny windowsill. The rooted cuttings can remain in their water-filled containers or can be transferred to small pots. You can choose plain or colored glass, ceramic, or plastic containers; almost anything that holds water will work. Clear or light-colored glass lets you see the delicate tendrils of roots as they form. Tinted glass and opaque substances filter the light to varying degrees and tend to discourage the growth of algae; these containers may be more attractive as decorative objects if you plan to keep the plants in water for a long time.

Making the Cut

A good time to take cuttings is when you plan to prune or trim your plants, usually in spring or fall. Many plants will provide you with plenty of loose ends during the winter, too; this is a good way to keep them down in size and shape. Coleus, ti plant, jade, and wandering Jew are perfect for starting a windowsill water garden. Take a 4- to 6-inch tip or mid-section of a stem just below a node (the bump on the stem where a leaf or side shoot arises), and remove any lower leaves, which may rot under water. Place the cutting in the container with tepid water; set it in medium to bright light, but not full sun. A few bits of charcoal in the water keep it sweet and fresh. As long as there is plenty of water in the jar, you have no worries about watering needs. Change the water every few weeks, always making sure it is room temperature, never cold, and gently rinse off stems and roots before replacing the cuttings. As the roots grow, plants in medium or good light can be exposed to bright light. Turn the jar or vase now and then for even exposure. Feed with a very weak solution of standard house-plant fertilizer once a month if you plan to keep cuttings in water. Never add fertilizer to water that already has fertilizer in it; this causes a build-up of too many nutrients.

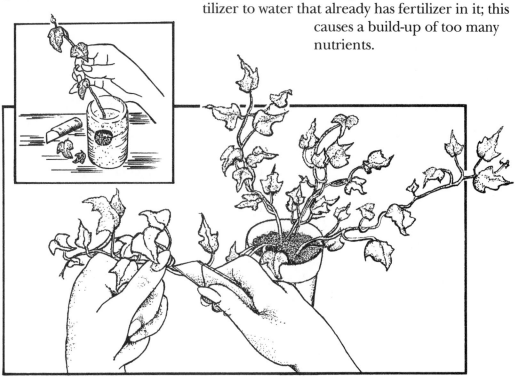

Tip Cuttings for a Windowsill Water Garden. *Take a tip cutting below a node, strip off lower leaves, and place cutting in water.*

A caveat: Hours of exposure to strong sunlight will heat the water in the container. Test the water with your finger to find out if the tender roots are in danger of getting boiled and, if so, remove the vessel to a less intensely sunny spot.

Propagating Water-Rooted Cuttings

Potting up well-rooted young water-grown cuttings is a wonderfully simple way to add to your plant collection. When several roots on a cutting are ¾ to 1 inch long, plant the cutting in light Basic Soil Mix in a small pot. Keep it moist and out of direct sun as the young plant adjusts to its new medium. Water-grown roots tend to be slightly brittle, so handle and plant with care. As it becomes firmly established, treat the rooted cutting as you would the mature plant, according to instructions in The Guide.

Choice Cuts

Cuttings from these plants can be rooted in water:

Arrowhead plant	Hoya	Pothos
Bloodleaf	Jade plant	Purple passion
Brassaia	Kalanchoe	Setcreasea
Chinese evergreen	Kangaroo ivy	Shrimp plant
Coleus	Impatiens	Swedish ivy
Dieffenbachia	Lantana	Piggyback plant
Dracaena	Peperomia	Ti plant
English ivy	Pilea	Wandering Jew
Fittonia	Philodendron	Wax begonia
Grape ivy	Polka dot plant	

The cut ends of thick or woody stems of dracaena, ti plant, Chinese evergreen, and dieffenbachia should be allowed to dry for a day before placing in water.

PART III

Plants for Your Movable Garden

Introduction to
The Guide

The Guide is composed of a selection of foliage and flowering plants that can be grown in containers indoors and outdoors. The natural varieties, which grow in the wild, and their cultivated varieties (cultivars), were chosen for their beauty and adaptability to container life. Entries are presented alphabetically by genus name. The common name is also given, and for easy reference the Index has both.

Each entry, clearly defined, provides cultural directions for optimum conditions of light, soil, moisture, fertilizer, care, propagation, and storage of dormant and semidormant bulbs. Remarks and recommendations are presented with the average home in mind. Between the ideal greenhouse climate (not good for people) and the ideal people's environment (not good for most plants), an atmosphere can be created that can suit both, if the gardener understands the basic needs of the chosen container plants. That information is exactly what I wish to impart to the reader, along with a big dollop of enthusiasm for the wonderful world of container-grown plants.

The range of plants that can be grown in pots is so enormous that any book on this subject is necessarily limited in scope. I have therefore chosen to present only a selection of attractive and appealing plants that are hardy and predictable or unusual and rare. Some species are excluded because they are not suited to the vagaries of sun, wind, and weather of outdoor life, or because they are generally believed to be too delicate or too difficult to grow and maintain in containers. Of the scores of included varieties, there are choices that will suit both novice and veteran gardeners. All methods of increasing your collection are explored with one exception: growing by seed. This method is slow and tricky, resulting either in many fewer or far greater a number of plantlets than you desire.

Here you will find challenges: wintering an exotic bulb and bringing it to bloom again; successfully nurturing a tropical forest plant; coaxing a "throwaway" flowering gift plant to live on and flower another season. The rewards are many: A pampered gardenia perfumes the air deliciously; a sturdy new plant arises from a bit of stem or leaf; a Christmas cactus displays its ravishing blossoms year after year.

I urge you to be adventurous. Meet the exciting challenges of growing unusual or exotic foliage or flowering plants in your movable garden, in addition to the familiar favorites.

How Plants Are Named

All plants are named according to a scientific system of classification. Four levels of classification are used in The Guide: family, genus, species, and variety. A **family** is a group of plants with similar characteristics. It is comprised of several **genera** (plural of **genus**). A **species,** as its name implies, is a more specific form of a genus. There are usually several different species within a genus. Each species, in turn, often has one or more different **varieties.** A cultivated variety, or one that did not originate in the wild, is called a **cultivar.**

Following is an example of all four classifications:

Family: Agavaceae

Genus: *Sansevieria (Snake plant)*

Species: *Sansevieria trifasciata* (or *S. trifasciata*)

Cultivated variety: *Sansevieria trifasciata* 'Laurentii' or (*S.t.* 'Laurentii')

Other genera in the Agavaceae family are *Dracaena, Yucca,* and *Cordyline.* Other cultivars of *Sansevieria trifasciata* are *S.t.* 'Hahnii' and *S.t.* 'Golden Hahnii'.

How Plants Are Listed in The Guide

The plants in The Guide are listed alphabetically according to their genus names. (Exceptions are ferns and palms, two major plant groups that each include many different genera.) Beneath the genus name is the family name in Latin and in English. The information that follows gives the plant's common names and briefly describes one or more species as well as selected varieties and cultivars, where applicable.

Explanation of Terms Used in The Guide

Dilute Liquid Fertilizer: A water-soluble all-purpose plant food, dissolved in water, applied every two to three weeks, sometimes more or less often, according to the individual plant. See Fertilizer. Consult Guide entries for appropriate feeding for each plant, and various modifications. Use about half the amount recommended on the label.

Well-Established or Well-Rooted: When a young plant growing in a rooting medium has developed enough of a root system to resist a light, gentle tug, and may also have produced new shoots, it is ready to be lifted and repotted in the recommended soil. A cutting grown in water will have several rootlets about an inch long.

Basic Soil Mix: The formula that suits most potted plants, consisting of equal parts of sterilized packaged potting soil; sand, perlite or vermiculite; and peat moss. To this are often added additional nutrients and/or lighteners for better drainage. Each entry specifies the soil.

Humidity Tray, Pebble Tray: Half an inch to 1 inch of pebbles or gravel on a tray or saucer filled with water up to but not above the top of the pebbles. Plants placed on the pebbles get humidity from the evaporating water, but do not sit in the water.

Double Potting: For added humidity, a plant with a drainage hole is set within a waterproof container with damp peat or sphagnum moss between inner and outer containers, and drainage material at the bottom of the outer container.

Winter Rest Period: A period of slow or no growth (semi-dormancy or dormancy) is experienced by a great many container plants and bulbs after their active growth period in spring, summer, and early fall.

Classification
of Bulbs

The following are all loosely called bulbs and almost always grow underground. Although they differ in many respects, all of them gather and stockpile food for their foliage and flowers. Within this storage structure are the embryo forms of the leaves and often the flowers.

Bulb: A thick, swollen structure that grows underground. Layers of fleshy scales enclose the leaf bud and, usually, embryonic flower buds. The thin, dry, brown outer covering, the tunic, is protective. Bulbs are storage organs for water and nutrients. *Examples:* Amaryllis, Lily.

Rhizome: A fleshy or thickened stem that is usually horizontal, growing below the surface of the soil and, sometimes, on the surface. It produces roots as well as plant growth, and can store food. *Examples:* Spathiphyllum, Fern.

Tuber: A thick, swollen stem that usually grows underground and stores food. Buds, or eyes, on tubers produce plant stems. Roots may grow anywhere on the surface of an underground tuber. A few plants grow tuberous growths on their stems. *Examples:* Caladium, Tuberous begonia. Rosary vine has stem tubers.

Tuberous Root: A thick, fat root that is a storehouse of water and nutrients delivered to it by thin fibrous roots. Like tubers, they have growth buds that send up stems. *Examples:* Spider plant, Alstroemeria.

Corm: A solid, nutrient-packed, underground base of a stem with a dry, scaly protective covering similar to that of a bulb. *Examples:* Freesia, Ixia.

Offsets: How Bulbs Multiply

All of these offsets may be propagated, but the small ones will take two to three years or more to reach the blooming stage.

Bulblet: A baby bulb formed at the base of the parent underground.

Bulbil: Tiny bulblet produced on stems where a leaf joins the stalk (some lilies) or on a fern frond (bird's nest fern).

Cormel or **Cormlet:** Miniature corms that form around the base of the corm during the growing season.

Foliage and Flowering Plants in The Guide

The following charts are a quick reference to all the foliage and flowering plants mentioned in The Guide. For more information on specific plants, consult The Guide.

Flowering Plants

Genus	Species/Variety	Common Name	Form
Abutilon	A. hybridum A. pictum 'Thompsonii' A. megapotamicum A.m. 'Variegata'	*Flowering maple, Chinese lantern	Shrub Trailer, hanging basket plant
Achimenes	A. grandiflora A. longiflora	* Cupid's bower, magic flower	Rhizome, trailer, hang- ing basket plant
Agapanthus	A. 'Peter Pan' A. 'Dwarf White'	* Lily-of-the-Nile, African lily	Tuberous root
Alstroemeria	A. aurantiaca A. ligtu	* Peruvian lily, lily-of-the-Incas	Tuberous root
Anthurium	A. scherzerianum A. andreanum A. crystallinum	* Flamingo flower, pigtail flower Crystal anthurium	Fleshy root
Aphelandra	A. aurantiaca A.a. 'Fiery Spike' A. squarrosa 'Louisae'	* Zebra plant, saffron spike	Flowering plant
Begonia	B. semperflorens-cultorum B. tuberhybrida B. tuberhybrida pendula B. hiemalis; Rieger and Cheimantha hybrids	Wax begonia Tuberous begonia Hanging basket begonia Winter-flowering begonia	Flowering plant Tuber Tuber, trailer Semi-tuberous
Citrus	Consult The Guide	Orange, mandarin, kumquat, lemon, lime	Shrub or tree
Clerodendron	C. thomsoniae	Glory bower, bleeding-heart vine	Climber or trailer
Clivia	C. miniata	Kaffir lily	Bulb
Crossandra	C. infundibuliformis	Firecracker flower	Flowering plant
Cyclamen	C. persicum	Florist's cyclamen	Corm

*Common name(s) for all species and varieties listed in this genus.

Flowering Plants

Genus	Species/Variety	Common Name	Form
Eucharis grandiflora (also called *Eucharis amazonica*)		Amazon lily	Bulb
Euphorbia	*E. milii*	Crown of thorns	Succulent, shrub
Euphorbia	*E. pulcherrima*	Poinsettia	Succulent, shrub
Freesia	*F. armstrongii* *F. alba* *F. refracta*	* Freesia	Corm
Fuchsia	*Fuchsia hybrids*	Lady's ear-drops	Hanging basket plant
Gardenia	*G. jasminoides* *G.j.* 'Veitchii'	* Gardenia	Shrub
Hibiscus	*H. rosa-sinensis* *H. r-s.* 'Cooperi'	* Chinese hibiscus, rose-of-China	Shrub Dwarf form
Hippeastrum	*Hippeastrum* hybrids	Amaryllis	Bulb
Hoya	*H. carnosa* *H.c.* 'Variegata' *H.c.* 'Krinkle Kurl' *H. australis* *H. bella*	* Wax plant	Climbing or trailing basket plant Miniature
Impatiens	*I. wallerana* New Guinea impatiens	* Impatiens	Flowering plant
Ixia	*I. maculata* *I. paniculata*	* African corn lily	Corm
Justicia (formerly *Beleropone guttata*)	*J. brandegeana*	Shrimp plant	Shrubby plant
Kalanchoe	*K. blossfeldiana* *K. tomentosa* *K. fedtschenkoi marginata* *K.f.m.* 'Aurora Borealis'	* Kalanchoe Pussy ears, panda plant	Succulent

*Common name(s) for all species and varieties listed in this genus.

Flowering Plants

Genus	Species/Variety	Common Name	Form
Lantana	*L. camara*	* Lantana, yellow sage	Shrub
	L. montevidensis	Hanging basket lantana	Trailing form
Lilium	*L. candidum*	Madonna lily	Bulb
	L. longiflorum	Easter lily	
	Asiatic hybrids and others		
Nematanthus (formerly *Hypocyrta glabra*)		* Goldfish plant, candy corn plant	Gesneriad
Pelargonium	*P. hortorum* hybrids	Common or bedding geranium, zonal or fancy-leaved geranium	Shrubby plant
	P. domesticum hybrids	Regal, Lady Washington	
	P. peltatum hybrids	Ivy-leaved geranium	Trailing form
	P. fragrans and others	Scented geranium	
Rhipsalidopsis	*R. gaertneri*	* Easter cactus	Jungle cactus, hanging basket plant
	R. rosea		
Schlumbergera	*S. truncata* or *Zygocactus truncatus*	Thanksgiving cactus, crab cactus	Jungle cactus, hanging basket plant
	S. bridgesii	Christmas cactus	
Spathiphyllum	*S.* 'Wallisii'	* Spathe flower, peace lily	Rhizome
	S. 'Clevelandii'		
	S. 'Mauna Loa'		
Vallota	*V. speciosa*	Scarborough lily	Bulb
Veltheimia	*V. capensis*	* Forest lily	Bulb
	V. viridifolia		
Zantedeschia	*Z. aethiopica*	* Calla lily	Rhizome
	Z.a. minor		
	Z. rehmannii		
	Z. elliottiana		
	Z.e. 'Green Goddess'		

*Common name(s) for all species and varieties listed in this genus.

Foliage Plants

Genus	Species/Variety	Common Name	Form
Aglaonema	A. *commutatum* A. *modestum* A. *crispum* 'Silver Queen'	*Chinese evergreen	Foliage plant
Aloe	A. *barbadensis* (A. *vera*) A. *aristata* A. *variegata*	Burn plant, medicine plant Lace aloe Partridge-breasted aloe, pheasant's wings, tiger aloe	Succulent, rosette
Asparagus	A. *densiflorus* 'Sprengeri'	Asparagus fern	Trailer, hanging basket plant
Aspidistra	A. *elatior* A.*e* 'Variegata'	*Cast iron plant	Foliage plant
Brassaia (formerly *Schefflera*)	B. *actinophylla*	Schefflera	Foliage plant
Caladium	C. *hortulanum* hybrids	Fancy-leaved caladium, elephant's ears	Tuber
Calathea	C. *makoyana* C.*ornata* C. o. 'Roseolineata' C. *insignis* C. *zebrina*	Peacock plant Rattlesnake plant Zebra plant	Foliage plant
Ceropegia	C. *woodii*	Rosary vine, hearts entangled, string-of-hearts	Succulent, tuber, trailer, hanging basket plant
Chlorophytum	C. *comosum*	Spider plant	Tuberous root, hanging basket plant
Cissus	C. *antarctica* C.*a.* 'Minima' C. *rhombifolia* C.*r.* 'Ellen Danika' C. *striata*	Kangaroo vine Grape ivy Miniature grape ivy	Climber, trailer, hanging basket plant Miniature Miniature

*Common name(s) for all species and varieties listed in this genus.

Foliage Plants

Genus	Species/Variety	Common Name	Form
Codiaeum	*C. variegatum pictum*	Croton, Joseph's coat	Bushy shrub
Coleus	*C. blumei*	* Coleus, painted nettle	Upright form, foliage plant
	C. pumilus		Trailer, hanging basket plant
Cordyline	*C. terminalis*	Ti plant, tree of kings	Foliage plant
Crassula	*C. arborescens*	Chinese or silver jade	Succulent
	C. argentea	Jade tree	
Dieffenbachia	*D. amoena*	Dumb cane	Foliage plant
	D. maculata		
Dracaena	*D. deremensis* 'Warneckii'	* Dracaena	Variety of forms and shapes
	D.d. 'Janet Craig'		
	D. fragrans 'Massangeana'	Corn plant	
	D. marginata	Dragon tree	
	D.m. 'Tricolor'		
	D. sanderana	Belgian evergreen	
	D. surculosa	Gold-dust dracaena	
Ferns	See end of chart.		
Ficus	*F. benjamina*	Weeping fig	Tree
	F. carica	Fig (edible)	Tree
	F. elastica	Rubber plant, India-rubber tree	Bushy plant
	F. lyrata	Fiddleleaf fig	Bushy plant
	F. pumila	Creeping fig	Creeper or vine, hanging basket plant
	F. p. 'Variegata'		
	F. sagittata	Trailing fig	Creeper or vine, hanging basket plant
	F.s. 'Variegata'		
Fittonia	*F. verschaffeltii*	* Mosaic plant, nerve plant, painted net plant	Creeper, trailer, hanging basket plant
	F.v. argyroneura		
	F.v.a. 'Nana'	Miniature	
Gynura	*G. aurantiaca*	* Velvet plant, purple passion	Upright form, foliage plant
	G. sarmentosa		Trailer, hanging basket plant

*Common name(s) for all species and varieties listed in this genus.

Foliage Plants

Genus	Species/Variety	Common Name	Form
Hedera	*H. helix*	English ivy	Climber, trailer, hanging basket plant
	H.h. 'Glacier' *H.h.* 'Jubilee' *H.h.* 'Manda's Crested' *H.h.* 'Needlepoint' *H.h.* 'Gold Heart' *H.h.* 'California Gold'		
	H. canariensis	Canary or Algerian ivy	
	H.c. 'Variegata' (also called 'Gloire de Marengo')		
Hypoestes	*H. phyllostachya*	Polka dot plant, measles plant, freckle face	Foliage plant
Iresine	*I. herbstii* *I.h.* 'Aureoreticulata'	* Bloodleaf, beefsteak plant	Foliage plant
Maranta	*M. leuconeura* *M.l. erythroneura*	* Prayer plant	Foliage plant
	M.l. 'Kerchoviana'	Rabbit's foot or rabbit's tracks plant	
	M.l. 'Massangeana'		
Palms	See end of chart.		
Peperomia	*P. argyreia*	Watermelon peperomia	Foliage plant
	P. caperata 'Emerald Ripple'		
	P. obtusifolia	Baby rubber plant	
	P.o. 'Variegata'		
Philodendron	*P. bipinnatifidum*	* Philodendron	Bushy plant
	P. bipennifolium	Fiddle-leaf philodendron	Climber
	P. 'Burgundy' (a hybrid)		Climber
	P. erubescens		Climber
	P.e. 'Royal Queen'		
	P. oxycardium or *P. cordatum*	Heartleaf philodendron	Climber, hanging basket plant
	P. radiatum or *P. dubium*		Climber
	P. wendlandii		Bushy plant
	P. selloum		Bushy plant

*Common name(s) for all species and varieties listed in this genus.

Foliage Plants

Genus	Species/Variety	Common Name	Form
Pilea	*P. cadierei*	Aluminum plant, watermelon pilea	Foliage plant
	P.c. 'Minima'		Miniature
	P. involucrata	Panamiga, Pan-American friendship plant	
	P. mollis or *P.* 'Moon Valley'		
	P. depressa	Creeping Jenny	Creeper, trailer, hanging basket plant
	P. nummularifolia	Creeping Charlie	
Plectranthus	*P. oertendahlii*	*Swedish ivy	Creeper, trailer, hanging basket plant
	P. australis		
Sansevieria	*S. trifasciata*	*Snake plant, mother-in-law tongue	Succulent
	S.t. 'Laurentii'		
	S.t. 'Hahnii'		Rosette
	S.t. 'Golden Hahnii'		Rosette
Saxifraga	*S. stolonifera*	*Strawberry begonia, strawberry geranium	Rosette, trailer, hanging basket plant
	S.s. 'Tricolor'		
Scindapsus	*S. aureus*	*Pothos, devil's ivy	Climber or trailer, hanging basket plant
	S.a. 'Golden Queen'		
	S.a. 'Marble Queen'		
	S.a. 'Tricolor'		
	S. pictus 'Argyraeus'		
Setcreasea	*S. pallida* 'Purple Heart'	Purple heart	Trailer, hanging basket plant
Sedum	*S. morganianum*	*Donkey's tail, burro's tail	Succulent, trailer, hanging basket plant
	S.m. 'Burrito'		Miniature
Senecio	*S. rowleyanus*	*String-of-pearls, string-of-beads	Succulent, trailer, hanging basket plant

*Common name(s) for all species and varieties listed in this genus.

Foliage Plants

Genus	Species/Variety	Common Name	Form
Syngonium (formerly *Nephthytis*)	*S. podophyllum* *S.p.* 'Emerald Gem' *S.p.* 'Albolineatum' *S.p.* 'Green Gold' *S.p.* 'Flutterby'	* Arrowhead plant, arrowhead vine	Climber or trailer, hanging basket plant
Tolmeia	*T. menziesii*	* Piggyback plant, youth-on-age	Foliage plant
Tradescantia	*T. fluminensis* *T.f.* 'Quicksilver' *T. blossfeldiana* *T.b.* 'Variegata' *T.b.* 'Rainbow'	*Wandering Jew, inch plant	Trailer, hanging basket plant
Yucca	*Y. aloifolia*	Spanish bayonet, dagger plant	Rosette-form foliage plant, woody stem
	Y. gloriosa	Spanish dagger, Roman candle, palm lily	
	Y. filamentosa	Adam's needle	
Zebrina	*Z. pendula* *Z. p.* 'Quadricolor'	* Wandering Jew, inch plant	Trailer, hanging basket plant

The following two major groups of foliage plants include several different genera.

Ferns

Genus	Species/Variety	Common Name	Form
Adiantum		* Maidenhair fern	Ferns are found in a variety of forms and shapes; most trail and are suitable for hanging baskets. Consult The Guide for specific listings.
	A. capillus-veneris	Venus or southern maidenhair	
	A. hispidulum	Australian maidenhair	
	A. raddianum	Delta maidenhair	
	A. tenerum	Fan maidenhair	

*Common name(s) for all species and varieties listed in this genus.

Ferns—*continued*

Genus	Species/Variety	Common Name	Form
Asplenium	*A. bulbiferum*	Mother fern, hen-and-chicken fern	
	A. daucifolium		
	A. nidus	Bird's nest fern	
Cyrtomium	*C. falcatum*	Holly fern	
Davallia	*D. fejeensis*	Squirrel's foot or rabbit's foot fern	
Nephrolepsis	*N. exaltata* 'Bostoniensis'	Boston fern	
	N.e. 'Dallasii'	Dallas fern	
	N. cordifolia	Southern sword fern	
Pellea	*P. rotundifolia*	Button fern	
	P. viridis	Green cliffbrake	
Pteris	*P. cretica* 'Albolineata'	Table fern, Cretan brake, White ribbon brake	

Palms

Genus	Species/Variety	Common Name	Form
Chamaedorea (formerly *Neanthe bella*)	*C. elegans*	Parlor palm	Potted palms take the form of trees or shrubby plants. Consult The Guide for specific listings.
Chamaerops	*C. humilis*	European fan palm	
Howea	*H. forsteriana*	Paradise or Kentia palm	
	H. belmoreana	Sentry palm	
Rhapis	*R. excelsa*	Lady palm, bamboo palm	

The Old Reliables

All of the following plants are dependable, tolerant, and easy to care for.

Botanical Name	Common Name
Aglaonema modestum	Chinese evergreen
Aloe vera	Burn plant
Asparagus sprengeri	Asparagus fern
Aspidistra elatior	Cast iron plant
Chamaedorea bella (Neanthe bella)	Parlor palm
Chlorophytum comosum	Spider plant
Crassula	Jade plant
Dieffenbachia amoena	Dumb cane
Dracaena	Dracaena
Ficus elastica and other ficus	Rubber plant and other figs
Howeia forsteriana	Kentia or Paradise palm
Peperomia	Peperomia
Philodendron	Philodendron
Plectranthus	Swedish ivy
Rhapis excelsa	Lady palm
Sansevieria trifasciata	Snake plant
Sansevieria trifasciata "Golden Hahnii"	Bird's nest snake plant
Scindapsus	Pothos
Syngonium podophyllum	Arrowhead plant
Tradescantia blossfeldiana	Wandering Jew
Zebrina pendula	Wandering Jew

The Guide

GENUS: *Abutilon*
FAMILY: Malvaceae (Mallow)

Flowering maple, Chinese lantern, bellflower.
Native to tropical South America. This old
favorite appeared in many a Victorian parlor
at a sunny window and was known as the parlor maple. The three- to five-lobed leaves are
maple-shaped and may be green or variegated.
The pendent flowers resemble hollyhocks, to
which they are related. *A. hybridum* exhibits
flowers in shades of pink, rose, yellow, white,
and red. *A. pictum* 'Thompsonii' bears striking
mottled yellow on green foliage and orange or
salmon flowers. *A. megapotamicum* is a trailing
plant suitable for a hanging basket, with bell-
shaped red and yellow flowers. *A.m.* 'Variegata'
has mottled green and yellow leaves. Abutilons

Abutilon pictum 'Thompsonii'

are vigorous shrubs that need to be pruned often to control size. If kept sunny and
moist, they may flower almost continuously.

Light:	Indoors: half a day full sun, bright light. Outdoors: filtered light; some full sun.
Soil:	Basic Soil Mix recommended on page 28.
Moisture:	Water liberally from spring to late autumn. Keep moist; mist.
Fertilizer:	Dilute liquid feeding every two weeks except in winter.
Care:	Flowering maple needs pruning and pinching to keep a bushy shape. It's a fast grower. Cut back hard in fall and spring; prune again to encourage side branching. Remove crowded, skimpy shoots. Light trimming and shaping may be done anytime. Some yellow leaves are to be expected; merely re-move them.

Propagation: Tip cuttings in moist rooting mix.

Remarks: Flowering maple is a big, handsome plant with attractive foliage and exotic, colorful flowers. A fine choice for a sunny spot, indoors and out, and a spectacular hanging basket plant.

GENUS: *Achimenes*
FAMILY: Gesneriaceae (Gesneriad)

Cupid's bower, magic flower, rainbow flower, orchid pansy. Native to tropical regions of South and Central America. A rhizome. With those charming common names, this is a plant certain to have colorful and lovely flowers. It does indeed, and presents them for a long flowering season from early summer to October. The flowers are tubular with flaring petals an inch to 1½ inches wide. *A. longiflora* has stems up to 2 feet long that tend to trail; it has violet-blue flowers. *A. grandiflora* has upright, shorter stems with purple flowers. Hybrids come in shades of red, yellow, rose, pink, salmon, or white, some with contrasting veins, most with white throats. More compact dwarf forms are available.

Achimenes

Light: Indoors: bright or filtered; no direct sun. Outdoors: partial shade.

Soil: Peaty Basic Soil Mix (page 28); add a bit of dried manure.

Moisture: Water plentifully and keep moist. Dry soil and hot, dry air are lethal; the plant likes warmth with humidity. Misting and pebble tray are beneficial.

Fertilizer: Dilute liquid fertilizer every two to three weeks. When buds begin to form, give light feeding of a high phosphorus-potash formula to stimulate flowering.

Care: The scaly rhizomes are small and can be planted shallowly (less than an inch deep) late winter to early spring. Plant three or four to a 4-inch pot, five or six to a 6-inch pot, eight or ten to a larger pot. After growth appears, never let the soil dry out. Pinch back 3- to 4-inch stems to encourage branching, which will produce more bloom As they grow, they may need support on twiggy sticks, unless they are trailing in a hanging basket. As bloom ends in mid-fall, cease fertilizing and reduce watering. Leaves and stems will dry and may be cut off. The rhizomes go dormant.

Storage: Dormant rhizomes may be left in their pots during the winter rest or removed and stored in dry peat, sand, or perlite in a dark, cool (but not cold) place, 50° to 55° F is ideal; not over 60° F if possible.

Propagation: Rhizomes have overlapping sections that can be easily pulled apart or divided. They tend to get crowded. In early spring examine them and replant whole rhizomes or sections of them shallowly and quite closely in fresh soil (some may already have sprouts). Keep moist, and mist young plants frequently.

Remarks: Achimenes, like most gesneriads, can be temperamental if growing conditions are not to its liking. Keep it moist, humid, sheltered from drafts and full sun, and it will reward you with a lavish and long-lasting floral display, particularly pretty in a hanging basket. Look for upright and trailing forms, as well as new large-flowered double forms; they are spectacular. A tip: water all kinds carefully. Like most gesneriads, leaves may spot if wet, especially in sunlight.

GENUS: *Agapanthus*
FAMILY: Liliaceae (Lily)

Lily-of-the-Nile, blue African lily. Native to South Africa, not to the Nile. A fleshy tuberous root. *A. africanus* has numerous arching, glossy, straplike dark green leaves 1 to 2 feet long. Dense round umbels of blue or purplish-blue rise in spring or early summer on stems 1 to 2 feet high. Dwarf forms suitable for container culture are *A.* 'Peter Pan', blue, and *A.* 'Dwarf White'.

Agapanthus africanus

Light: Indoors: full sun. Outdoors: in very hot climate, filtered sun; light shade.

Soil: Basic Soil Mix (page 28), some added sand for drainage; a bit of bonemeal.

Moisture: Water plentifully in spring and summer and keep moist. Taper off watering after flowering, which may last until early fall. Let soil get nearly dry during winter rest period.

Fertilizer: Weekly dilute liquid fertilizer early spring to early fall.

Care: In many respects, care for agapanthus is similar to that for clivia, also native to South Africa. In mild climates both may remain outdoors in sheltered spots. Neither tolerates sudden dips in temperature and in northern regions must be taken indoors if frost or chilly nights are imminent. Winter rest, or semi-dormancy, mandates cool temperatures, around 50° to 55° F, and just enough water to keep the soil from getting completely dry. In early spring they need a warm, bright spot and increased moisture. Agapanthus prefers more direct sun than clivia. As it grows larger, it may need to be transferred from a clay pot to a wood tub—the powerful roots can crack or break the clay. It is best, however, not to move the plant into a larger pot until it becomes very potbound, as the roots dislike being disturbed. Like clivia, too, it flowers profusely when potbound. Give topdressing when maximum convenient size container is reached.

Propagation: Every few years when repotting becomes necessary, lift the plant from the pot in early spring and remove old soil carefully from the roots. Separate or divide the thick rhizomatous roots into pieces with shoots and roots attached. Plant separately in pots just big enough to comfortably accommodate the roots. The top of the rhizome should be just below the surface of the soil, and the soil should be richly organic with enough sand or perlite added to give it good drainage. Keep all divisions in a partly shaded location, water well, and spray occasionally to encourage new growth. Move gradually to bright light.

Remarks: Blue agapanthus is arguably the most glamorous beauty among the large flowering container plants. Bear in mind that it will become a very sizeable plant in time and may need a dolly for portability. Agapanthus is long-lived and has a long season of summer bloom. The big clusters of an intense sky blue are breathtaking.

GENUS: *Aglaonema*
FAMILY: Araceae (Arum)

Chinese evergreen. Native to Southeast Asia, Philippines. A tolerant and long-lived plant that is quite content with less than the best of anything. *A. modestum,* the common Chinese evergreen, has oblong 6- to 8-inch plain green leaves. *A. commutatum,* the most popular variety, has narrower green leaves with pale grey markings. *A. crispum* is gray-green with darker green markings. *A. crispum* 'Silver Queen' has silvery markings. Aglaonemas range from 1 to 3 feet in height, and bear flowers in spring and summer typical of the arum family. A narrow white spathe encloses a greenish spadix that bears the tiny true flowers. These are followed in autumn by clusters of bright red berries that stay on the plant all winter long.

Light: Indoors: medium to low. Outdoors: filtered shade or shade.

Soil: Basic Soil Mix, page 28.

Moisture: Water well; then let soil get quite dry. This is not a water-needy plant.

Fertilizer: Dilute liquid feeding once a month is sufficient.

Care: Very little. These old stand-bys thrive in low light and low humidity. Very tall canes may need staking.

Propagation: Leafy tops with some stem will take root in water, where they can live for years. Pieces of stem with one or two nodes will root when placed shallowly in moist peat or sand.

Aglaonema crispum

Remarks: Chinese evergreen is a toughy, thriving in low light or a north window and not giving any trouble. You will have it for many years. I like it when it is orna-mented gaily with clusters of scarlet berries during the winter months. In early summer the small, pretty, calla lily–type flowers are always a pleasing sight.

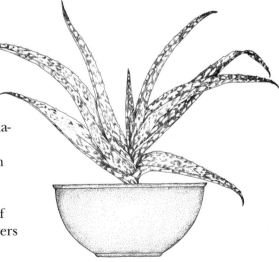

GENUS: *Aloe*
FAMILY: Liliaceae (Lily)

Native to tropical South Africa and Mada-gascar. A succulent. The hundreds of species and varieties of the aloe range in size from windowsill dwarfs to tree-size giants. Most aloes grow their leaves in rosette formations and produce stalks of tubular-shaped pink, red, or yellow flowers in late winter or early spring.

Aloe barbadensis

A. barbadensis. Barbados aloe, *A. vera.* Medicine plant, burn plant. The discovery of the medicinal virtues of this plant is attributed to the Greek Dioscorides in the first century B.C. The juice, or gel, within its leaves has analgesic and antibacterial properties. Its practical use as a healing agent for burns, sunburn, scalds, insect bites, cuts, scrapes, and sores dates back hundreds of years in many parts of the world. It is also claimed to be a remedy for poison ivy, acne, itching, and dandruff, and a stimulant for sluggish hair follicles. "Aloe vera" is listed among the ingredients of numerous creams and lotions to smooth and nourish the skin and condition the hair. At the very least, the plant by your sunny kitchen window offers you the opportunity to squeeze out a bit of gel from a cut leaf to ease a burn. When mature, the pointed, succulent, gray-green leaves with lightly toothed, pinkish edges may grow over a foot long and will not fit on the windowsill; its rosette-shaped offsets can take the mother's place, however. Yellow flowers cluster densely on a tall spike.

A. aristata. Lace aloe. This nice, neat dwarf grows in a tight rosette of small, dark green, pointed leaves dotted with tubercles, or tiny white bumps. Flowers are orange, appearing in summer. This aloe is ideal for a sunny windowsill and bears many offsets.

A. variegata. Partridge-breasted aloe, pheasant's wing aloe, tiger aloe. One of the most beautifully marked of the miniature forms, this aloe has thick, pointed, spear-shaped, dark green, overlapping leaves 4- to 6-inches long with pronounced white markings. Pinkish-red flowers often bloom on young plants. The partridge-breast does not require the direct sun that the other kinds do, preferring less bright or filtered light. Propagate by offsets.

Light:	Indoors and outdoors: full sun; plenty of bright light.
Soil:	Basic Soil Mix (page 28) with extra sand for good drainage and a bit of bonemeal.
Moisture:	Moderate. Aloes tolerate fairly dry soil, especially in their winter rest period, and dry air as well. Leaves of succulents store water; don't let the soil get bone dry, however.
Fertilizer:	Dilute liquid fertilizer every two to three weeks. Apply more frequently to older, crowded plants.
Care:	No special demands. Repot infrequently, as aloes like being potbound. While they prefer cool temperatures during their rest, they are intolerant of cold temperatures. If plants are outdoors they should be brought inside before nights get chilly.
Propagation:	Offsets form at the base of the parent. Allow them to grow into the rosette shape and begin to form roots of their own before removing and potting them.

Remarks: The dwarf aloes are attractive, easy-to-grow, undemanding small plants and are among the easiest of plants to propagate. They appreciate mild summers outdoors in filtered shade.

GENUS: *Alstroemeria*
FAMILY: Amaryllidaceae (Amaryllis)

Peruvian lily, Lily-of-the-Incas. Native to west coast of South America and Brazil. Not a true bulb or tuber, alstroemeria can best be described as a mass of fleshy, fibrous roots. As a cut flower of remarkable diversity and long-lasting qualities, these relatives of the amaryllis have come into great favor with florists. Stems 3 to 4 feet tall bear umbels of lily-like blossoms from late spring to midsummer. Most are bicolored or have markings or blotches of contrasting colors. *A. aurantiaca* has orange or yellow flowers with red or purplish-brown streaks. *A. ligtu* (St. Martin's flower) and various hybrids are available in yellow, red, salmon, apricot, purple, lavender, and combinations thereof, borne in clusters of twenty to thirty blossoms on shorter stems, 1½ to 2 feet high.

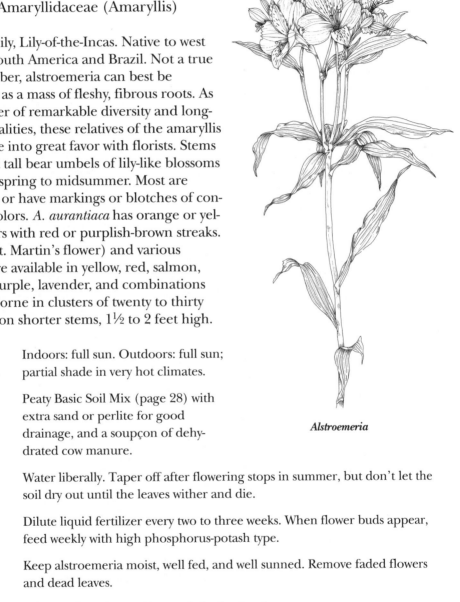

Alstroemeria

Light: Indoors: full sun. Outdoors: full sun; partial shade in very hot climates.

Soil: Peaty Basic Soil Mix (page 28) with extra sand or perlite for good drainage, and a soupçon of dehydrated cow manure.

Moisture: Water liberally. Taper off after flowering stops in summer, but don't let the soil dry out until the leaves wither and die.

Fertilizer: Dilute liquid fertilizer every two to three weeks. When flower buds appear, feed weekly with high phosphorus-potash type.

Care: Keep alstroemeria moist, well fed, and well sunned. Remove faded flowers and dead leaves.

Storage: Leave bulb in the pot in a cool, shady, dry place.

Propagation: Divide roots in the fall or early spring when they are very overcrowded; set clumps in pots just big enough to hold them. Handle gently, as these roots are quite brittle and do not like being disturbed unless absolutely necessary.

Remarks: The long-stemmed clusters of these small, colorful, lily-like flowers are charming, but the bulb is not one of the easiest for pot culture.

GENUS: *Anthurium*
FAMILY: Araceae (Arum)

Flamingo flower, flamingo lily, pigtail flower. Native to Colombia and other South and Central American jungles. Like its relatives the calla lily and spathiphyllum, anthurium bears an inflorescence composed of a spathe that appears to be a large petal with a spike, or spadix, in front of it, bearing the tiny true flowers. The spathe is usually bright orange-red or scarlet; the spadix is the same color or, in some forms, cream or yellow. The spadix is curlier than in most members of the arum family, earning anthurium the nickname "pigtail flower," a rough translation from the Greek *anthos,* meaning flower, and *oura,* meaning tail. Leaves are dark green, lance-shaped, and rather leathery in texture, 3 to 4 inches long in young plants and 8 to 10 inches in mature ones. *A. scherzerianum* is the most familiar variety for home culture. *A. andreanum* is larger and less readily obtainable. *A. crystallinum,* the crystal anthurium, has insignifi-

Anthurium scherzerianum

cant flowers but magnificent foliage. Its huge leaves, up to 2 feet long and a foot wide, are deep, glowing green with silvery-white midrib and veins. Very high humidity is essential; this is not a plant for the average home.

Light: Indoors and outdoors: bright, but no direct sun. This jungle plant likes medium light.

Soil: A highly organic mix of good potting soil, peat or sphagnum moss, sand or perlite, and a sprinkle of dried manure. Fir bark is also recommended as a component of the soil.

Moisture: Water liberally and keep moist at all times, only slightly less so when plant is not in flower. Mist frequently. High humidity is vital. Supply humidity tray.

Fertilizer: Dilute liquid feeding every two weeks in active growth period. A contented plant will flower almost continuously; keep it well fed.

Care: As anthurium grows, crowns develop with side shoots that send aerial roots down to the soil. To protect these roots and keep them moist, wrap damp sphagnum moss around them and keep it moist. A small plant from a greenhouse in a 3- or 4-inch pot may need repotting if it becomes very overcrowded. The most common variety, *A. scherzerianum*, rarely needs more than a 5- or 6-inch pot. Warm temperatures are fine, but dry air and burning rays of sun are lethal.

Propagation: A very potbound, overcrowded plant may be divided in spring. Remove offsets (side shoots with leaves and roots) and plant them close to the surface in shallow pots in rich, organic, porous soil. Handle carefully; they are very delicate. Keep them warm, well misted, and in medium light. When well established with new leaves, move into brighter light. Mist frequently.

Remarks: These exotic flowers have a long life both on the plant and in cut displays. To ensure flowering, keep anthurium humid, moist, warm, regularly fed, and in good light. Admittedly, this may be a difficult task in the average home. Be on the lookout for new dwarf varieties with pink or rose-colored flowers.

GENUS: *Aphelandra*
FAMILY: Acanthaceae (Acanthus)

Zebra plant, saffron spike. Native to Brazil. Like cyclamen, poinsettia, and certain other flowering plants, aphelandra is usually sold in full bloom. Like them, too, it is often thrown away when flowering is over. While reblooming is not guaranteed, it can be done, with pampering. The commonly available form, *A. squarrosa* 'Louisae', has 8- to 10-inch shiny green leaves with pronounced white veins and midrib. In summer, flower spikes appear, consisting of overlapping, orange-tipped yellow bracts with small yellow flowers. The bract lasts for several weeks. *A. aurantiaca* 'Fiery Spike' has bright reddish-orange blooms.

Aphelandra

Light: Indoors and outdoors: bright or filtered.

Soil: Peaty Basic Soil Mix, page 28. Enough sand or perlite to provide good drainage.

Moisture: Water liberally and keep moist. Soil must not dry out. Give high humidity and warmth. Mist and pebble tray are helpful.

Fertilizer: This plant is hungrier than most. Feed it dilute liquid plant food weekly, except in winter rest, October to early spring.

Care: After flowering is over, cut off flower spike and shorten stem by a few inches to encourage branching. Keep cool, 55° to 60° F in winter rest. Maintain good light. Keep slightly moist in winter. In early spring, prune back hard for a compact, bushy shape. Repot if roots fill pot, in rich, fresh soil. Light misting encourages new growth.

Propagation: Tip cuttings, or prunings, in moist rooting mix in spring.

Remarks: The zebra plant is decorative and bears striking flowers. It is, however, rather difficult to keep in good health and to rebloom. The soil must be kept evenly moist and the air warm and humid; the light, bright and the nourishment, generous. Coddle your aphelandra and you may see it bloom again. A tip: A severe spring pruning may result in more than one stem and thus more flowers.

GENUS: *Asparagus*
FAMILY: Liliaceae (Lily)

Asparagus fern. Native to dry regions of South Africa. A tuberous root. This "fern" is not a fern at all, but somewhat resembles one because of its fernlike foliage. *A. densiflorus* 'Sprengeri' is the most popular container plant variety in the genus *Asparagus,* which includes the edible kind. Arching, wiry stems up to 3 feet long bear bundles of bright green, tiny needlelike leaves that give a feathery appearance. Small pink, fragrant flowers are produced in fall, followed by red berries.

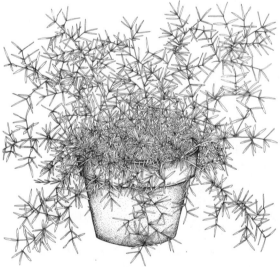

Asparagus densiflorus '**Sprengeri**'

Light: Indoors: bright or filtered, some full sun. Outdoors: part or filtered shade.

Soil: Basic Soil Mix, page 28.

Moisture: Water plentifully and keep slightly moist.

Fertilizer: Dilute liquid fertilizer every two to three weeks during spring and summer; light applications every two or three months at other times.

Care: No special demands. The asparagus fern is quite tolerant of variations in light, temperature, watering, and so on, providing they are not extreme. It grows quickly, however, and has big greedy roots that seek ample nutrients and space. Repotting into large pots may be necessary yearly until largest convenient size is reached; then topdress.

Propagation: When the roots of an overcrowded plant break the surface of the soil—and possibly the pot—it's time to divide. Take the plant out of the pot and cut down the foliage to the soil level. Take care, as the stems are unpleasantly prickly. With a sharp knife, cut apart the thick tuberous roots into clumps. Replant each in good, fresh soil, allowing about 2 inches of space from surface to pot rim, as the strong roots tend to push soil upward.

Remarks: An old favorite, asparagus fern remains a popular hanging basket choice for its lacy, billowy, trailing foliage. A large specimen looks smashing displayed atop a pedestal or mantelpiece.

GENUS: *Aspidistra*
FAMILY: Liliaceae (Lily)

Cast iron plant. Native to China and Japan. A rhizome. A common fixture of the cold, dark, and drafty Victorian parlor replete with gas fumes that were the coup de grâce to most plants, aspidistra's name of cast iron plant was well deserved. This is a tough plant, but the glossy, arching, broad, dark green leaves of *A. elatior* can be quite handsome, given a minimum of care. *A.e.* 'Variegata' has leaves striped white or cream-colored. This is a very attractive and tolerant cultivar.

Light: Indoors and outdoors: low light is tolerated, but aspidistra will grow faster and better in medium light.

Soil: Basic Soil Mix, page 28.

Aspidistra elatior

Moisture: Moderate. Let soil get rather dry before next watering.

Fertilizer: Dilute liquid fertilizer every two to three weeks.

Care: No demands. Repot infrequently; potbound, it flourishes.

Propagation: Divide the clump of rhizomes in the spring when the pot becomes very over-crowded. Each piece of root must have a few leaves. Several pieces may be planted in fresh soil in one pot.

Remarks: Along with the snake plant, the spider plant, and the Chinese evergreen, the cast iron plant is tolerant of a good deal of neglect. It can endure dry air, dry soil, chilly drafts, poor light, and lack of nutrients with remarkable stoicism. It is said that only overwatering will kill an aspidistra. But given good treatment, it is a fine-looking foliage plant and an ideal choice for difficult places; it may even produce small purple flowers at soil level.

GENUS: *Begonia*
FAMILY: Begoniaceae (Begonia)

Native to the Andes mountains and other tropical and subtropical regions. This vast family of plants includes thousands of species and varieties and their innumerable hybrids. The three main groups consist of the fibrous-rooted, which includes many tall varieties and hairy-leaved varieties as well as the familiar wax begonia; the rhizomatous, comprised mainly of plants with large, distinctively marked and colored foliage such as the Rex begonias; and the tuberous, prized for their large, beautiful flowers. A fourth group, the semi-tuberous, are grown as gift plants and include the fairly recent Rieger hybrids and other hybrids that bloom in great profusion in winter, but are rather difficult to maintain and rebloom. The two groups that are grown most successfully indoors and out are the fibrous-rooted, specifically the wax begonia, and the tuberous, both upright and hanging basket types, which may be started indoors, then brought outdoors for frost-free growth and bloom.

Begonia semperflorens-cultorum. Wax begonia. Fibrous-rooted. Small, bushy, and busy, wax begonias have a very secure place in container planting as well as in garden beds almost everywhere. Grown primarily for their multitude of single or double blossoms in shades of red, pink, rose, and white, they are a charming sight either by themselves or grouped with summer-blooming flowers such as trailing blue lobelia, sweet white alyssum, geraniums, and

Begonia semperflorens-cultorum

others in containers or window boxes on the terrace or deck. Leaves may be all green or variegated green and white, and those of a handsome bronzy-red make a particularly nice contrast to nearby green foliage.

Light: Indoors: bright; some full sun. Outdoors: same but tolerates filtered light or part shade. More flowers are produced in good light.

Soil: Peaty Basic Soil Mix, page 28.

Moisture: Water plentifully, then let soil dry somewhat before watering again. Begonias like humidity. Don't spray the foliage, however, as powdery mildew may develop.

Fertilizer: Dilute liquid fertilizer every two or three weeks outdoors; less indoors during winter when active growth diminishes.

Care: Cut down leggy stems, and pinch growing tips often to induce branching and a full, bushy look. This means more flowers, even if a few must be sacrificed. Prunings can be propagated. Start nipping back when plants are only 4 or 5 inches high. Leaves with white spots should be promptly removed. This condition is powdery mildew, caused by dampness and poor air circulation. If it continues to spread, you may have to discard the plant before the disease infects others. But first, you may wish to isolate it and try a fungicide.

Propagation: Wax begonias root readily in water. Group several well-rooted cuttings in a 4- or 5-inch pot, one alone in a 3-inch pot, or intersperse them in a container with other plants. They are easily grown at any time from trimmings of older plants.

Remarks: The ubiquitous wax begonia is small, useful, floriferous, and almost completely care-free. They are pretty and showy in a group, and they combine well with many other container plants outdoors. An interesting combination that worked well for me was a dense group of bronzy-red-leaved pink begonias around the stem of a ti plant with leaves mostly deep rose-red in color. Back indoors in a sunny spot, the begonias continued to flower all winter long. They go well with impatiens, geraniums, wandering Jew, iresine, coleus, sweet alyssum, and many summer-flowering annuals in containers outdoors.

Begonia tuberhybrida. Tuberous begonia. This is a showy aristocrat among flowering plants. The large flowers may be single or double, and come in shades of red, pink, rose, orange,

Begonia tuberhybrida
pendula

yellow, salmon, and white. Different forms resemble the shape of a rose, camellia, or carnation, and the petals may be ruffled, flared, or frilled. They bloom all summer until mid- to late fall outdoors, and then go dormant. Properly wintered over indoors, they will bloom again.

Light: Indoors: bright or filtered. Outdoors: filtered, some light shade.

Soil: Peaty Basic Soil Mix, page 28, rich, organic, and porous. Add a dash of bonemeal and dried manure.

Moisture: Water moderately and carefully. If the soil becomes waterlogged, the stems may rot. Allow soil to dry slightly before next watering. Try to avoid wetting the leaves. A pebble tray indoors will add humidity.

Fertilizer: Dilute liquid fertilizer every two to three weeks. Give high phosphorus-potash formula as buds begin to appear.

Care: In the fall, the leaves turn yellow and flowering tapers off. Reduce watering, cease fertilizing, and when foliage dies down, remove the stems. Lift the tubers and shake off the soil from the roots. Let them dry for a few days and then store them in dry peat, sand, perlite, or vermiculite in a cool, dark place, preferably with a temperature of 55° to 60° F. In late February or early March, take a look to see whether little pink growth buds are poking up. Any tubers that are soft or mushy must be discarded. Small tubers that developed on large ones may be detached for propagating separately. If a great many stems grow and crowd each other, it is a wise precaution to sacrifice a few early on to avoid a tangled thicket and the likelihood of diminished flowering. Pinch back some young stems before flower buds appear. For more and larger flowers, it is best to have only a few stems. Male and female flowers appear on the same plant, and since the male flowers are usually double and larger, if a really huge blossom is desired, the female flowers may be pinched off

Begonia tuberhybrida

before fully open. The male is usually in the center, the single-petalled smaller females to each side. If this sounds too sexist, just let them all bloom. In any event, tuberous begonias bloom better outdoors than indoors, with good air circulation and dappled sunlight or part shade. Set all plants outdoors when night temperatures reach 50° F, sheltered from wind and direct sun. You can expect that dormant tubers started into growth in March will be in flower by mid- to late June.

Repotting and Propagation: When the pink shoots appear, set the tubers shallowly in moist peat, with shoots above the surface, in a warm, bright spot. Keep moist, not wet. In a few weeks, the growth will be a couple of inches high and the tubers can be transferred to individual 4- or 5-inch pots. Large tubers may be divided into sections for replanting, provided that there is a growth bud on each section. As a precaution against rot, dust the cut end with a fungicide such as sulfur dust. Later in the season when a plant has grown quite large, it may require transplanting into a larger pot. Give it rich, organic, well-drained soil with a considerable proportion of humus and enough sand or perlite for a loose, porous texture. Successful rooting of tuberous begonia cuttings is chancy; they are susceptible to mildew, rot from waterlogging, and leaf drop and wilt from underwatering. Stick to the tubers for propagation.

B. tuberhybrida pendula. Hanging basket tuberous begonia. Dazzling cascades of bloom in a wide range of colors make this summer-flowering basket plant a stellar attraction on the terrace or hanging from a tree branch or window box. Plant three to five tubers in a 6- or 8-inch pot or basket, more in a larger container. Place them in filtered or light shade, never in full sun, and sheltered from wind. Pinch out young stems to encourage branching and lush growth. Because of the open exposure of a hanging basket, more frequent attention to watering and fertilizing needs should be given. Mist lightly if the weather is hot and dry. Most growing and care instructions are the same as for the tuberous begonias. For more details on care and preparation of hanging baskets, see Hanging Baskets, p. 74.

B. hiemalis. This semi-tuberous group with roots that are fibrous rather than bulbous includes the Rieger and Cheimantha (Lorraine) hybrids. These winter-flowering begonias are often called Christmas begonias because they are usually available in November and December, loaded with big, beautiful, single or double blooms. Colors are red, rose, orange, and yellow. Large foliage may be green or red. They make glorious gift plants, blooming abundantly for two or three months. When they stop, they are not very attractive. Most people pitch them out at this point, but they can be made to bloom again. Cut them down severely, water sparsely, keep them cool, and wait until spring. Then, new growth, new pot, new rich, humus-y soil, and regular care as above. Or, after blooming ends, cut down stems, lift the plant, shake off dirt from roots, trim back long roots, and repot as above. New growth will emerge and the plant will flower again in about three months. Always repot in the next largest pot, just big enough to accommodate the roots.

GENUS: *Brassaia*
FAMILY: Araliaceae (Ginseng)

Brassaia actinophylla (Schefflera actinophylla). Umbrella tree, Australian or Queensland umbrella tree, octopus tree. Native to Australia and New Zealand. Still commonly called schefflera, this is a shrubby plant that in its native habitat grows to tree size, up to 30 or 40 feet. Sold usually 2- to 3-feet high in pots, it can be kept below 6 feet if properly restrained. A young plant bears leaves with several leaflets, and as the plant grows the number of leaflets increases up to ten or more. This is an imposing accent plant. *B.a. compacta* is a smaller, more compact form.

Brassaia actinophylla

Light: Indoors: bright, filtered light; no direct sun. Outdoors: filtered or medium shade.

Soil: Basic Soil Mix, page 28.

Moisture: Water well, let soil get somewhat dry before next watering. Occasional misting is appreciated.

Fertilizer: Infrequent; two or three times yearly is sufficient, but only in the growing season.

Care: Repot in early spring if the pot is very overcrowded. Topdress when maximum convenient pot size is reached. Schefflera is a strong, swift grower. If you don't want it to hit the ceiling, you must control its growth by keeping it potbound in a smaller pot than a mature plant would like—that is, a 10-inch pot at most. Also for growth control, prune it back (this will make it bushier as well), let the soil get quite dry before watering, and give little fertilizer.

Propagation: By air layering. (See page 45.)

Remarks: This generous-sized, glossy-leaved plant can be an important foliage feature in a large room, office, lobby, or other area where it has plenty of space.

GENUS: *Caladium*
FAMILY: Araceae (Arum)

C. hortulanum hybrids. Fancy-leaved caladium. Angel wings, elephant's ears. Native to tropical America, West Indies. A tuber. The leaves of these tropical plants are shaped somewhat like arrowheads or hearts and are tissue-paper thin. The numerous hybrids are magnificently colored in combinations of green and white; rose and green; pink, rose, and white; pink, rose, and green; red and green, and other combinations that are sometimes marbled, splattered, or veined. Leaves may be over a foot long; miniature forms are available. An arum-type flower, which resembles a jack-in-the-pulpit, may be produced. A spathe, or petal-like bract, arises from and partly encloses a spadix or spike that bears the tiny true flowers. They are not particularly attractive, however, and as they draw strength away from the foliage, they may well be cut off.

Light: Indoors and outdoors: filtered shade or light shade. Direct sun damages delicate leaves.

Soil: Peaty, organic, well-drained. A dash of cow manure.

Moisture: Water plentifully and keep moist. A tropical jungle plant, caladium needs moisture, humidity, and warmth. Mist for humidity.

Fertilizer: Dilute liquid fertilizer every two to three weeks.

Care: In early spring, set tubers about an inch deep in damp peat or peat-sand mix. Dormant tubers can be divided at this time, providing there is a growth bud on each section. After pink growth buds appear and grow a couple of inches tall, transfer each tuber to a 5-inch pot in recommended soil, or plant two or three in a 6- or 8-inch pot. Use shallow pots as these tubers are shallow-rooted. Bring into good light and warmth and start regular watering. Set pots outdoors when nights are mild, over 60° F, in a sheltered spot and out of direct sun. In late summer when leaves begin to die, reduce watering and stop fertilizing. Remove dead leaves and bring the plants indoors before any danger of frost.

Storage: Tubers may be left in the pot in dry soil, or removed and stored in dry peat or perlite in a cool but not cold place, first shaking off soil clinging to tubers and roots and removing

Caladium hortulanum

dead stems or leaves. If desired, label them as to color. In a few months, pink noses should be again poking up; look for them in late winter or early spring. If tubers are mushy or rotten, discard them.

Propagation: Large tubers produce offsets, or small tubers, during winter storage. These can be detached and potted separately or with other tubers. If spring arrives and the tubers, large or small, have not produced pink growth buds, plant them anyway in shallow pots with the recommended soil. You may be in for a pleasant surprise. Even very small tuber offsets will probably spring to glorious life.

Remarks: When the leaves die down, these lovely plants are too often discarded. This is a pity, for the tubers are easy to store and can be resurrected for many years of enjoyment of their sensationally colorful and decorative foliage. If you want a pretty miniature form, look for 'Little Miss Muffet,' with lime-green leaves and dark red speckles. 'White Queen' is a particularly handsome large-leaved form with white and green leaves veined in crimson. 'Frieda Hemple' is stunning; deep, rich red edged in green.

GENUS: *Calathea*
FAMILY: Marantaceae (Arrowroot)

Native to tropical South America and Africa. The numerous species of this tropical jungle plant are outstanding for their strikingly patterned foliage. One of the handsomest is *C. makoyana,* the peacock plant, or cathedral windows. Leaves 10 to 12 inches long have dark green patches on light green, with purplish-brown markings on a pink or maroon underside. *C. insignis,* the rattlesnake plant, bears olive green markings on a light green topside, and has a reddish-purple reverse. *C. ornata* is dark green above, with maroon or purplish-red below. It has pale, narrow white or pink stripes. The variety *C.o.* 'Roseo-lineata' has more markedly pink stripes (which get paler in older leaves) and is more attractive. *C. zebrina,* the zebra plant, has 10- to 15-inch velvety leaves with light green stripes on a rich, deep green, with a reddish-purple underside. Stems of most forms are also reddish-purple. Some forms bear their leaves upright, others in a more horizontal fashion and tend to fold upward and

Calathea makoyana

inward at night like their relative maranta, with which they are often confused and for which they are often mislabeled.

Light:	Indoors and outdoors: medium to filtered. Direct sun will damage the foliage.
Soil:	Peaty Basic Soil Mix (page 28), loose, fibrous; add fine-ground tree bark, leaf mold.
Moisture:	Water plentifully and keep consistently moist, but not wet. Calathea needs high humidity. Keep it well misted and on a pebble tray.
Fertilizer:	Biweekly dilute liquid fertilizer.
Care:	Keep calathea moist, misted, and warm. Other plants nearby and a jar of water help keep the atmosphere humid.
Propagation:	In spring, if the pot is very overcrowded, remove the plant, divide and replant sections of roots with several leaves attached. If the roots have not filled the pot, remove some old soil and replant calathea in the same pot with fresh, rich soil.
Remarks:	Calathea, like maranta, reacts very unfavorably to dry air, sudden fluctuations in temperature, strong sunlight, and dry soil. If you can keep it well misted, moist, humid, and warm, this tropical forest plant will be a gorgeous addition to your foliage plant collection. It should be comfortable outdoors in a shady spot in a mild climate. Growing a jungle plant in a pot is a challenge, but that's what makes container gardening exciting.

GENUS: *Ceropegia*
FAMILY: Asclepiadaceae (Milkweed)

C. woodii is the only species that is a popular, easy-to-grow container plant. Called string-of-hearts, rosary vine, hearts entangled, or hearts-on-a-string, *C. woodii* is native to South Africa. A tuber and succulent, it is a most appealing plant, best displayed in a hanging basket. Very narrow purple vines dangle several feet, bearing pairs of small heart-shaped leaves mottled green and white on the upper side, purple on the underside. The vines can be trained to climb but they look much better trailing. Little tubers appear at intervals along the vines. In late summer, tiny odd-shaped pink or purple flowers are produced.

Light:	Indoors and outdoors: bright, filtered; some full sun.
Soil:	Porous and rich; half potting soil, half sand, a bit of bonemeal.

Moisture: Water well, then let soil get quite dry between waterings. In winter rest, give water sparingly. Soil should be almost dry.

Fertilizer: Dilute liquid fertilizer monthly to mature plants only.

Care: No special demands. Give plenty of light. Repot infrequently.

Propagation: Remove small tubers from the vines and set them on top of damp potting mix with sand sprinkled on top. Water sparsely and keep out of sun. After new growth appears and roots are established, pot in recommended soil and move to a sunny spot. Water well and treat as a mature plant. Several of these young plants can be transferred to a small, shallow hanging basket.

Remarks: This charming trailing succulent is an intriguing addition to the plant collection.

Ceropegia woodii

GENUS: *Chlorophytum*
FAMILY: Liliaceae (Lily)

Spider plant, ribbon plant, airplane plant. Native to South African tropics and other tropical regions. A tuberous root, or rhizome. *C. comosum* 'Vittatum' is the common favorite, and it is very common. Walk down any street and you will be sure to see a shabby spider broiling away against the window of the shoe repair shop or real estate office. Somehow, it clings to life, and doubtless that is why it is so popular. The spider has narrow, arching, green, strappy leaves with a white or cream stripe down the center. Long, thin, pale yellow stems dangle and produce tiny white star-shaped flowers and spidery plantlets, some with roots, at their ends.

Light: Indoors and outdoors: bright or filtered. Direct sun scorches the leaves.

Soil: Basic Soil Mix, page 28.

Moisture: Water well, keep moist. Misting is desirable.

Fertilizer: Dilute liquid fertilizer every two or three weeks.

Care: The minimum. Although spiders prefer cool, humid conditions, they are very tolerant of a warm, dry environment. Their thick roots store water, so they can get along without regular watering for quite a while. Dry leaves pull out easily. Snip off brown leaf tips.

Propagation: Spiders eagerly reproduce themselves. The miniature plants at the ends of stems may be pressed firmly into the surface of nearby small pots of soil or pegged to it and kept moist. When the plantlet sends up new leaves and is well rooted, sever the stem to the mother plant. A large plant may be divided in spring when stems and roots fill the pot to overflowing.

Remarks: Spiders are easy to grow and easy to neglect, and usually look it. But given sufficient light, water, and nutrients, they can be very decorative and display cascades of rather cunning plantlets.

Chlorophytum comosum 'Vittatum'

GENUS: *Cissus*
FAMILY: Vitaceae (Grape)

Related to the grape vine, the several species of cissus are popular, easy, and beautiful plants that accommodate themselves to most conditions indoors and out. They will climb or dangle. *C. antarctica.* Kangaroo vine or kangaroo ivy. Native of Australia. A fast grower, the kangaroo vine may have been so named because it grows in leaps and bounds. It has toothed, shiny, green leaves on short, reddish-brown leafstalks. Given support, its tendrils will cling and its stems will grow to

Cissus rhombifolia

the ceiling if not controlled. *C. a.* 'Minima', a dwarf, grows more slowly and is more compact.

C. rhombifolia. Grape ivy, treebine. Native of West Indies and tropical America. The leaf of this species is composed of three notched, glossy leaflets resembling a grape leaf and bears a reddish-brown fuzz on its underside. Like the kangaroo vine, it can trail or climb, and grows eagerly to great lengths if allowed. *C.r.* 'Ellen Danika' has larger, rounder leaflets lobed somewhat like oak leaves and is a more compact form.

C. striata. This miniature grape ivy has five tiny leaflets to a leaf and is particularly nice on a table or hanging in a small basket. It can grow very long if not nipped back.

Light:	Indoors and outdoors: bright, filtered, or medium light.
Soil:	Basic Soil Mix, page 28.
Moisture:	Water well, then let soil get somewhat dry before next watering. Keep barely moist during winter rest. Mist occasionally.
Fertilizer:	Dilute liquid fertilizer every two to three weeks.
Care:	No special demands. Excessively dry air may invite the dreaded red spider mite and brown leaves or leaf drop. Otherwise, cissus is extremely tolerant. Its rampant growth habit must be controlled unless you want it to grow freely on a fence, wall, or railing. Prune it back hard in early spring, and nip back terminal shoots any time. Cissus can be trained to cling with its curly tendrils to a trellis, hoop, or sticks in its pot.
Propagation:	Like the true ivies, cissus will root in water, or in damp rooting mix. It's simpler to pop trimmings in a jar of water.
Remarks:	Of the two species, the grape ivy is somewhat the more tolerant of less than ideal conditions; but both are very adaptable, easy to grow, and highly attractive as climbing or hanging plants. When it's time to bring an outdoor container back in the house, you may need major surgery to disengage a cissus from a nearby railing to which it has become deeply attached. If this happens, you will have plenty of stem cuttings to root.

GENUS: *Citrus*
FAMILY: Rutaceae (Rue)

Orange, lemon, lime, mandarin, kumquat. Native to many warm climates and tropical regions. With their glossy, dark green foliage and delicately scented, dainty white flowers, citrus are very attractive container plants even without their fruit. A number of dwarf varieties that are 2 to 5 feet in height are ideal for container growing. Citrus are particular about the conditions they need in order to produce flowers and fruit and to maintain good health in the house. They are quite insistent on spending the summer outdoors. Take care when handling, as some kinds have spines.

Recommended dwarf varieties for indoor-outdoor container growing:

Orange, Mandarin, Kumquat

C. mitis. Calamondin orange. One of the most popular dwarf citrus. Many-branched, it grows 2 to 4 feet tall and flowers in summer and intermittently at other times. Fruits are produced in November and December and will stay on the plant all winter. This variety is desirable for its very fragrant flowers and ornamental value; its small, kumquat-like, bright orange, very tart fruits are not valued for their edibility. Flowers and fruit, which often appear at the same time, may be produced on a plant only a foot tall in a 5- or 6-inch pot.

C. taitensis. Otaheite orange. One of the best citrus for pots, Otaheite bears extremely fragrant white, pink-tinged, long-lasting flowers, and yellow or orange plum-sized fruits in December. Like the Calamondin, they are tart and limey. This species is usually for sale at Christmastime and often bears bloom and fruit at the same time. It has spines.

Citrus mitis

'Dancy', a popular Mandarin orange sometimes called "Christmas tangerine," bears small fruits in December.

'Satsuma' Mandarin orange bears sweet, seedless fruit with a thin rind.

'Nagami' kumquat has bright orange, olive-sized fruit that ripens in early summer. It fruits best in warmer areas.

Washington navel, a sweet, juicy type, fruits in mid-winter.

Lime

'Bearss' or Persian seedless lime has exceedingly fragrant flowers. It's the favored variety to grow well in cool areas. This is a small tree (2 feet high or less) with full-sized fruit.

Lemon

C. limon 'Meyer' or Meyer lemon is a highly edible lemon that has a pleasant tart flavor. Improved Meyer lemon has a smaller, more golden-yellow, juicier fruit and is more cold-resistant. Both are quite hardy and are good choices for containers.

C. limon 'Ponderosa', called American Wonder lemon, is one of the easiest citrus for container growing. The large lemons, up to 5 inches long and 4 or so inches in diameter, are bright orange-yellow and very sour. Beware of spines.

Containers:	Sturdy clay pots with good drainage are best, at least until the tree grows quite large. Plastic, which is not porous, is not advised. After a few years, the tree will graduate to a wood box, preferably naturally rot-resistant redwood or cedar. It is still recommended that you paint the inside with a preservative containing copper sulfate to prevent the possibility of rot. Do not use creosote, which is toxic to plants. Before the maximum convenient size is reached, the plant will move on every year or two to a larger container, one that is just large enough to comfortably accommodate the roots. For indoor-outdoor portability, the larger, heavier containers should be set on a dolly. In frost-free regions, of course, the trees can remain outdoors all year round.
Light:	Give citrus as much direct sun as possible. When you first take your tree outside, expose it to the sun gradually over a few weeks before giving it full sun. Before making the return trip, reverse the procedure, gradually withdrawing the tree from full sun. Indoors again, it will need the best light possible. One cause of leaf and flower drop is insufficient light.
Soil:	Basic Soil Mix (page 28), with rich organic elements added when repotting or topdressing; decomposed cow manure, bonemeal, leaf mold, or humus are recommended. Some growers prefer shredded sphagnum moss to peat moss for a looser, more fibrous mix. Sand is preferable to perlite.
Moisture:	Citrus need careful watering. Water plentifully and let the soil get somewhat dry between waterings, but never let it dry out or allow roots to languish soggily; either way, loss of leaves and flowers or premature fruit drop will likely result. The dry climate of most houses is not conducive to citrus health. Spray frequently and provide a humidity tray. Water kept in a receptacle nearby will supply additional humidity as it evaporates.
Fertilizer:	Dilute liquid fertilizer every two to three weeks. Give occasional high-potash formula. Many growers like to feed their citrus organic substances such as fish emulsion or liquefied seaweed, adding bonemeal, dried cow manure, or well-decomposed compost when repotting or topdressing. Citrus are heavy feeders.
Care:	Citrus trees tend to grow rather symmetrically, and pruning may be minimal. Awkward-growing or out-of-shape branches may be pruned any time. To keep

trees dwarf, prune more vigorously in spring and remove low, unwanted watersprouts that shoot upward. After five or six years, a hard root prune may be needed at repotting time to help control growth and keep plants more compact. When this is done, shorten any leggy tops and tips of branches. Mulching the surface of the soil all year round reduces evaporation and helps keep roots cool and moist; use stones, gravel, peat, wood chips, bark chips, or a combination.

In northern and eastern climates, bring citrus inside early in September. Although the weather may continue to be mild, an untimely cold snap or frost could arrive at any time and give your precious tree the coup de grâce. Citrus like temperatures on the cool side, however, and during their winter rest period a temperature of 50° F is ideal. A protected sunporch or cool plant room is ideal for these conditions; a cool cellar where artificial lighting can be provided is also suitable. Even at rest, citrus need bright light and high humidity.

Pollination: Citrus need to be pollinated to set fruit. Outdoors, bees and other insects will take care of pollination. Indoors, you can transfer pollen on a small brush, or even with your fingertip, from one flower to another.

Citrus from Seed: Seeds can be planted shallowly in moist rooting mix and kept damp, dim, and warm. When shoots appear in four or five weeks, give good light. Small plants may be potted in good soil and given lots of sun. These juveniles grow slowly and take many years to flower and bear fruit, if they do so at all; but they make pretty foliage plants and they are fun for children to start and care for.

Remarks: Not to put too fine a point on it, growing indoor-outdoor citrus is not simple. Success can be yours if you can provide an abundance of sunlight, careful watering, high humidity, rich yet well-drained soil, abundant fertilizer, a sun-filled summer outdoors in a spot that gives protection from wind and violent storms, and a well-lit winter in a cool place. If despite all your tender care your citrus refuses to set fruit, take pleasure in its attractive shiny foliage and charming, fragrant white flowers. In mild climate regions, of course, citrus trees in containers can spend a lot more time outdoors, and present fewer problems.

GENUS: *Clerodendrum*
FAMILY: Verbenaceae (Vervain)

Bleeding heart vine, glory bower. Native to West Africa. *C. thompsoniae* is a husky, twining plant with large, glossy, dark green, heart-shaped leaves. Scarlet flowers surrounded by clusters of white calyxes are unusually attractive, and appear from spring to early fall. This plant can trail out of a hanging basket, climb on a trellis or stakes, or be kept fairly compact by relentless pruning. Hardy in warm climates.

Light: Indoors and outdoors: plenty of bright light; some full sun.

Soil: Basic Soil Mix (page 28); add a bit of bonemeal.

Moisture: Water plentifully, keep soil moist. Provide high humidity with misting and pebble tray. Water very sparingly in winter.

Fertilizer: Dilute liquid fertilizer every two to three weeks.

Care: Pinch back growing tips during active growth period. After flowering is finished in autumn, cut down some crowded older stems and prune entire plant vigorously. Keep cool during winter rest, or semi-dormancy; around 55° F is best. During this time, the plant may lose some leaves. Repot in late winter. Lush growth requires renewed soil and nutrients yearly. Replace the plant in the same pot with fresh soil after shaking off old soil from roots, unless roots and plant have outgrown their pot and require a pot one size larger. When new growth appears, move the pot to a warm, bright spot and give all old stems a hard pruning. Spray new shoots to stimulate growth, but pinch them back soon to encourage branching and production of flowers and to keep the plant from growing rangy.

Propagation: Tip cuttings in moist rooting mix, in spring.

Remarks: Clerodendrum will sulk if its needs are not met. It must have good light, plenty of moisture, humidity, and warmth when actively growing, and cool temperatures and drier soil when at rest. Mindful of its needs, you will be rewarded with a long season of glorious bloom. This is a spectacular basket plant, but keep the clippers handy.

Clerodendrum thompsoniae

GENUS: *Clivia*
FAMILY: Amaryllidaceae (Amaryllis)

Kaffir lily. Native to South Africa. A bulb. Only one species, *C. miniata*, is suitable for container culture. Its lustrous, dark green, straplike, arching leaves, 1½ to 2 feet long, are handsome all year round. The spectacular orange trumpet-shaped flowers with yellow throats are produced in umbels of ten to twenty on stalks 1½ to 2 feet high in early spring. A mature plant can be 3 feet or more wide. Budded or flowering clivias are expensive; if you buy a small juvenile instead, don't expect it to bloom for three to four years.

Light: Indoors: bright and sunny, no direct sun, from January to October. Outdoors: filtered sun and light shade.

Soil: Basic Soil Mix (page 28) plus a dash of bonemeal and dried manure. Add a bit of extra sand for good drainage. Soil must be rich, organic, and porous.

Moisture: Ample water in spring and summer. Let soil get quite dry from October to January. As flower stalks appear, increase watering. Mist for humidity.

Fertilizer: Dilute liquid feeding every two weeks, early spring to fall.

Care: Clivia should have cool temperatures, 50° to 55° F if possible, during its 6- to 8-week winter rest. In late winter when flower stalks appear, move it to a warm, bright spot, and when nights are over 50° F and days are mild, the plant can be set outdoors in filtered shade. After flowers wither, red berries appear. Remove them before they sap too much of the plant's energy, and pull out dead flower stalks. Repot after winter rest only if roots have filled the pot to bursting and even appear on the surface of the soil. They are quite capable of doing this, as they are thick and very strong. Up to this point, however, do not disturb, as clivia flowers best when potbound. When largest convenient size is reached, topdress with a rich mix. Don't neglect feeding these hungry roots.

Propagation: Small new plants or offsets, produced at the base of the parent, may be cut off with some roots and leaves at repotting time, using a sharp knife. Be sure the offset has several good-sized leaves. A large, mature plant can be pulled apart or cut carefully into sections with plenty of roots and leaves on each and even with attached offsets. Offsets left on the parent will eventually flower, and crowd the pot. Not until then is it wise to divide the plant and repot the sections. Give rich, organic, well-drained soil. The pot should be only large enough to comfortably house the roots. A newly

Clivia miniata

divided plant and its divisions require a shaded location, liberal watering, and humidity to help them get well established. Frequent misting encourages new growth. It will be several years before divided sections and offsets come into flower. Small, young plants from the greenhouse will also take several years to flower.

Remarks: Clivia's big, glossy foliage and dazzling display of bloom make it a dramatic focal point inside the home or outside. Cool night temperatures in the fall outdoors stimulate bud formation, but be on the alert for a drop in temperature or hint of frost, and hustle the plant back into the house. Clivia is not at all a difficult plant to grow, and it flowers more profusely as years go by. It is sometimes available in shades of red or pink, as well as orange.

GENUS: *Codiaeum*
FAMILY: Euphorbiaceae (Spurge)

Croton. Joseph's coat. Native to Malaysia, Australia, and the Pacific islands. *C. variegatum pictum* is the species that has given rise to a great number of varieties and cultivars. These woody-stemmed, shrubby, branching plants offer an amazing diversity of leaf shapes and colors. Leaves may resemble a rippled ribbon, a corkscrew, or an oak leaf and may be oval, lobed, notched, or lance-shaped. Of various sizes, the leaves are variegated in wild mixtures of green, red, bronze, purple, crimson, rose, cream, yellow, and gold. They are fast growers, and a young plant a foot high may reach 4 feet in as many years, and 2 feet or more in width, with several side branches. Happy in mild climates everywhere, they thrive indoors in a sunny spot.

Codiaeum variegatum pictum

Light: Indoors and outdoors: several hours of direct sun; good bright light.

Soil: Basic Soil Mix, page 28.

Moisture: Water plentifully and keep moist. Mist for humidity.

Fertilizer: Biweekly dilute liquid feeding spring to fall.

Care: Croton needs sun, warmth, moisture, humidity, and plenty of space. If a 12- or 14-inch pot is the maximum convenient size, topdress yearly with rich, fresh soil. Croton needs no pruning, but a plant that has become inconveniently tall or wide may be cut back. New side shoots will appear. Euphorbias, like crown of thorns and poinsettia, exude latex, a milky liquid, when cut. Apply water or powdered charcoal to the cut end to stop the flow. Turn the pot frequently to expose foliage evenly to sunlight. Wash large leaves.

Propagation: Tip cuttings or air layering.

Remarks: Crotons offer a truly lavish variety of unusual leaf forms and brilliant color combinations. They are easy to grow and are long-lived. Indoors at a sunny window or outdoors on a deck or patio, they are a spectacular accent. A tall plant may need to be staked.

GENUS: *Coleus*
FAMILY: Labiatae (Mint)

Flame nettle, painted nettle. Native to many warm regions. *C. blumei* is the only species commonly grown as a container plant, and is one of the most familiar, colorful, and versatile of all indoor-outdoor plants. The numerous hybrids display a glowing variety of rounded, toothed, or frilled leaves in mixtures of red, copper, orange, yellow, cream, plum, green, and chartreuse. Colors appear as spots, splashes, stripes, or edgings. Spikes of small, light blue, insignificant flowers rise on mature plants. These are best removed before they draw strength away from foliage production. *C. pumilus* is the trailing form, ideal for hanging baskets and available in various colors. I find the rose-green-white combination particularly pleasing.

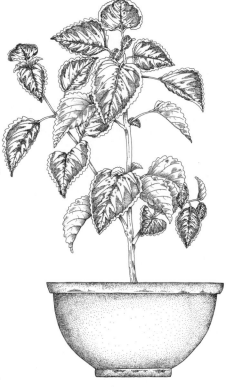

Coleus blumei

Light: Indoors: bright with some direct sun. Outdoors: bright, filtered, or semi-shade.

Soil: Basic Soil Mix, page 28.

Moisture: Water plentifully and keep moist. Coleus is a big drinker.

Fertilizer: Dilute liquid fertilizer every two to three weeks.

Care: Coleus is a fast grower and will get tall and ungainly if not controlled by frequent nipping of growing tips and stems. Pinch and pinch again, to keep a plant bushy and compact. Turn pots frequently for even exposure to sun.

Propagation: Cuttings and prunings root with alacrity in water.

Remarks: Coleus is so easily propagated that you can have a continuous supply all year round. These lively, colorful plants combine beautifully with many other plants in containers on terrace or deck and in window boxes with part sun and are especially nice with trailing green-purple-silver zebrina. Eventually it grows too lanky; take cuttings for a new generation. Children enjoy growing coleus.

GENUS: *Cordyline*
FAMILY: Agavaceae (Agave)

Ti plant, good luck plant, flaming dragon tree, tree-of-kings. Native to Polynesia, Hawaii, and Australia. In its native habitats, the ti plant may grow to be a 6-foot shrub whose large leaves are used for making hula skirts and sandals, thatching roofs, wrapping fish, and as plates for food and fodder for cows. It was once believed that a ti plant hedge could ward off evil spirits. *C. terminalis* in a pot grows to a height of 2 or 3 feet and bears lance-shaped leaves a foot or more long in shades of red, rose, copper, and green. Ti plant resembles dracaena, to which it is closely related; but most are far more colorful. *C.t.* 'Firebrand' has vivid rose-red and bronze tones with some

Cordyline terminalis

green. *C.t.* 'Red Edge' has smaller, narrower leaves with rose-red edges and streaks. *C.t.* 'Tricolor' adds cream, pink, and red to green on a broad leaf.

Light: Indoors and outdoors: good bright light with some full sun. Avoid intense rays of the midday sun.

Soil: Basic Soil Mix, page 28.

Moisture: Water generously and keep moist. Mist for humidity.

Fertilizer: Dilute liquid fertilizer every two to three weeks.

Care: No special demands. Lower leaves turn brown on a mature plant and may be picked off. Snip off brown tips on leaves with a scissors. A tall cane, or stem, with a bare lower part can be cut down to within a few inches of the base. Side shoots and basal growth will develop. Repot or topdress in spring.

Propagation: Leafy tips root readily in water. Cane cuttings, each with one or two growth nodes, will root in moist peat or sand.

Remarks: I find cordyline easy to grow, easy to propagate, and easy to love. The glowing, deep rose, broad-leaved forms are particularly handsome and dramatic inside the house, by themselves or in a group of green foliage plants, or in the outdoor living area in summer.

GENUS: *Crassula*
FAMILY: Crassulaceae (Orpine)

Jade plant. Native to South Africa. A succulent. Of all the varieties in the crassula genus, jade plants are those most commonly found as container plants. They adapt well to temperature variations and dry air, they are quite patient if occasionally neglected, and they reproduce with ease. *C. argentea,* the jade tree, has a stout, woody trunk and many curving branches with smooth, fleshy, glossy, dark green leaves that may have a red edge if they get abundant sunlight. *C. arborescens,* the Chinese jade or silver jade, has rounder, more gray-green leaves with red edges and dots and a more symmetrical habit of growth. Both forms are often reluctant to flower indoors, and you cannot expect them to do so before they become large, mature plants a foot or so in height and several years old. A sunny summer outdoors may help. The clusters of tiny, star-shaped, fragrant pink or white flowers may appear in late fall or winter, or sometimes in spring.

Crassula argentea

Light: Indoors and outdoors: full sun half a day; good bright light consistently.

Soil: Basic Soil Mix (page 28), with an extra bit of sand for good drainage.

Moisture: Water plentifully and let soil get rather dry before next watering. Succulents store water, and jades hate sitting with wet feet. In winter, the plants can be allowed to go quite dry before watering.

Fertilizer: Dilute liquid fertilizer monthly.

Care: The tough and tolerant jade can survive in the same pot for years. Repot in spring only when it is too large or top-heavy for its container. Topdress after largest suitable pot size is reached. Prune long branches for a more shapely plant. New shoots sprout near cut end.

Propagation: Jades reproduce themselves enthusiastically. A cutting or a pruning stuck in moist soil or in water is quick to develop roots. A leaf fallen on any soil will take root and become a new plantlet. You can't keep a good jade down.

Remarks: You can depend on jades to thrive almost anywhere, given good light and moderation in watering. Long-lived and dependable, they will provide you with a plethora of little ones all clamoring for their place in the sun. These offspring also make nice gift plants.

GENUS: *Crossandra*
FAMILY: Acanthaceae (Acanthus)

Firecracker flower. Native to the East Indies and India. *C. infundibuliformis* is a tropical beauty that grows to about a foot tall with glossy gardenia-like leaves. Short spikes bear overlapping bracts with salmon-pink or coral-orange flowers, each with a small yellow eye. Bloom, which begins in spring, is continuous until autumn, and even a very young plant is eager to start flowering. Blossoms open in clusters of 2 or 3, and due to their luscious color they make a dazzling display. Needful of a warm and humid environment, crossandra is not among the easiest plants to grow.

Crossandra

Light: Indoors: filtered to bright; some full sun. Outdoors: medium to filtered light; no direct sun.

Soil: Peaty Basic Soil Mix, page 28.

Moisture: Water liberally and keep moist. Never let the soil dry out. Since crossandra must have high humidity, spray daily and give pebble tray or double pot. Being near other plants helps to raise humidity.

Fertilizer: Light dilute liquid fertilizer every two to three weeks, none in winter rest. However, crossandra may decide to flower intermittently all year round if conditions are to its liking, in which case continue fertilizing.

Care: This rather small plant can remain in a 4- to 5-inch pot indefinitely. Shrubby by nature, it requires little pinching or pruning. Remove spent flower spikes and keep moist and warm.

Propagation: Tip cuttings in moist rooting mix.

Remarks: Other than its native tropical habitat or a greenhouse, crossandra demands a warm, moist, and humid environment. If you can provide for its needs, it will reward you with richly colored clusters of blooms.

GENUS: *Cyclamen*
FAMILY: Primulaceae (Primrose)

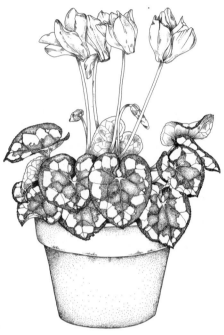

Cyclamen persicum

C. persicum, the florist's cyclamen. Shooting star, butterfly wings. Native to Mediterranean regions and nearby European and Asian areas. A tuber. Cyclamen is a captivating ornamental plant with heart-shaped green leaves marbled in silvery-white. Rising 10 to 12 inches above them are flower stalks bearing flowers in shades of pink, lavender, rose, red, magenta, white, and yellow. Miniatures half the height with smaller, fragrant flowers are improved in their adaptability to temperature variations and other conditions of container culture. Still, all cyclamens are tender plants and have specific demands for a healthy life and the pos- sibility of reblooming. Too often, as bloom wanes, the plant is tossed out. With careful nur- turing, it will bloom for two or three months, and can survive to bloom again. Cycla- men are usually available at the florist or greenhouse in full or part bloom in late autumn or early winter. Choose one that has a good many unopened buds, and watch those lovely butterfly wings unfurl.

Light: Indoors and outdoors: bright, but no direct sun.

Soil: Rich, peaty basic with a bit of bonemeal or dehydrated manure.

Moisture: Water well and keep moist. Don't let the soil get dry until the dormant period begins. The tuber, which projects above the surface of the soil, should not have water poured directly on it, so as to avoid the possibility of rot. To ensure this, water cyclamen from below. Let the plant drink from a deep saucer for about fifteen minutes, then remove any remaining water. Provide high humidity with pebble tray or double potting, and mist the leaves.

Fertilizer: Dilute liquid fertilizer every two to three weeks.

Care: Keep cyclamen in a cool, well-ventilated spot away from heat or drafts. Cool is the key word—really cool—low 50s at night and no more than 65° F in the daytime. Hot, dry air is the kiss of death to this plant. When outdoor temperatures are 55° to 60° F at night, you may set the cyclamen in a sheltered, lightly shaded place. Remove dead flowers and stalks after flowering ends in spring. As the leaves gradually yellow in summer, reduce watering and omit fertilizing. When the leaves wither, cease watering as the plant is now dormant, and should be left in a cool, shady spot outdoors, or a cool, dark spot indoors. In early fall, when new growth begins to emerge, repot if the plant's roots are very overcrowded. Gently remove the old soil from the roots and repot the plant in rich, fresh soil in the next larger pot. Spray often to encourage new shoots. Bring indoors well before frost and give regular watering and care. An important note: The cyclamen mite can be devastating if not controlled immediately. Indications are curled, twisted leaves, buds that won't open, malformed flowers. Remove and destroy affected parts. Isolate the plant. Last resort: a spray specific for the purpose. A severely infested plant must be destroyed. See Pests and Problems, page 57.

Propagation: The home gardener may not be able to accomplish this task successfully, given the cyclamen's exacting nature. I suggest that you buy a nice new plant if you want more.

Remarks: Cyclamen is a pretty plant with enchanting flowers that you can enjoy for several months, and possibly again in another season, if you can meet its finicky requirements. As a winter bloomer, it's an ideal gift plant as long as the recipient keeps it cool, moist, and bright.

GENUS: *Dieffenbachia*
FAMILY: Araceae (Arum)

Dumb cane. Native to tropical South and Central America. If any of the sap from a cut stem or leaf gets into the mouth, a painful burning sensation and possible numbness and temporary paralysis of the tongue will result, hence the common name. Prevention is in washing hands thoroughly after taking cuttings or removing yellowed leaves. Easy to care for, dieffenbachia is a favorite container plant. *D. amoena* has white veins or markings and *D. maculata,* or *D. picta,* has even more white splashes. Other forms have cream or yellow markings. All species have stout stems and large, oval-shaped leaves up to a foot long, somewhat pointed at the ends. In rare instances, a mature plant will exhibit a typical white or creamy arum-family flower.

Light: Indoors and outdoors: bright, filtered, or medium.

Soil: Basic Soil Mix, page 28.

Moisture: Water well and let soil become slightly dry before next watering. Low humidity is tolerated.

Fertilizer: Dilute liquid feeding biweekly when in active growth, monthly in winter.

Care: No special demands. Wipe off dusty leaves. Remove older, lower leaves that turn yellow and die.

Propagation: When a dieffenbachia grows too tall and ungainly—and it will—cut it down near to the base. The leafy crown will root in water and look very attractive there for a long time. The long bare stem will yield several sections with one or two nodes, or growth buds, on each. Lay them on moist rooting mix or sandy soil, enclose them in plastic, and wait for new shoots to rise. Vigorous new growth will also sprout from the stump of the old plant.

Remarks: Dieffenbachia is an old reliable: a handsome, large plant needing little in the way of care. Moderation in watering, light, and fertilizing suits it well.

Dieffenbachia amoena

GENUS: *Dracaena*
FAMILY: Agavaceae (Agave)

Native to tropical Africa. These popular plants are reliable standbys for almost any spot, as they are quite adaptable to dry air and fairly low light conditions. There is great variety in the size and color of the various species, but most can grow to a height of 4 or 5 feet, albeit very, very slowly.

D. deremensis 'Warneckii' has stiff, pointed green leaves with two white stripes. *D.d.* 'Janet Craig' has broad, dark green, glossy leaves and is particularly dense and handsome. *D. fragrans* 'Massangeana', the corn plant, bears large, shiny, arching dark green leaves with a broad yellow-green center stripe and narrow yellowish stripes. It may, but rarely does, produce fragrant yellow flowers. *D. marginata*, the dragon tree, bears a cluster of narrow, red-edged leaves atop a straight, bare stem. One of the easiest forms to grow, it is also one of the tallest, but it grows very slowly. *D.m.* 'Tricolor', striped green, rose, and cream, is a very pretty cultivar. To encourage side branching, the topknot of leaves with a section of stem may be cut off.

D. surculosa or *D. godseffiana*, the gold-dust dracaena, grows only 1 to 2 feet tall and has small,
dark green leaves, splashed with cream or
creamy-yellow, held horizontally on thin stems.
It's the different dracaena. Look for its cultivar
'Florida Beauty' whose leaves have more yellow or creamy-white than green. The Belgian
evergreen, *D. sanderana*, has narrow green and
white striped leaves.

Dracaena fragrans 'Massangeana'

Light:	Indoors: bright, filtered to medium. No full sun, no dark corners. The variegated forms need good light to maintain their color. Outdoors: filtered light or light shade.
Soil:	Basic Soil Mix, page 28.
Moisture:	Water well. Dracaena prefers soil kept slightly moist, but it will tolerate drier conditions.
Fertilizer:	Dilute liquid fertilizer every two to three weeks.
Care:	Dracaena is one of the best-natured foliage plants, and has no special demands. Snip off occasional brown leaf tips and remove lower leaves that occasionally turn brown or dry. Repot this slow grower infrequently. Top-dress when in largest convenient size pot.
Propagation:	Tip or stem cuttings in moist rooting mix, enclosed in plastic bag. Tip cuttings are best taken from young plants. Stem segments from older plants must have a growth bud or nodule on each segment. Air layering may be used on large, thick stems.
Remarks:	Dracaenas are handsome, often striking, and mostly colorful plants, particularly desirable for their tolerance of average and even less than average conditions. Large, tall specimens are dramatic decorative accents. Dracaenas are among the long-lived old reliables.

GENUS: *Eucharis grandiflora*
FAMILY: Amaryllidaceae (Amaryllis)

Eucharis grandiflora. Also known as *Eucharis amazonica*. Amazon Lily. Native to
Colombian Andes, and Amazon region. A bulb. Deriving its name from the Greek
'eu,' good, and "charis," an attraction, eucharis is indeed a strikingly handsome

flowering bulb. Broad, evergreen, glossy, deep-green leaves are 8 to 12 inches long. A cluster of three to six blossoms 4 inches across may appear two or three times yearly. Startlingly daffodil-like with white petals around a greenish-yellow center, they are borne atop a 1- to 2-foot stem. The fragrance is extremely sweet, strong, and somewhat lemony.

Light: Indoors and outdoors: bright, filtered; no direct sun.

Soil: Peaty Basic Soil Mix (page 28). Add a bit of sand for drainage and a sprinkle of dried manure.

Moisture: Water plentifully and keep moist during active growing period. See details on water under Care. This tropical forest plant requires humidity and warmth. Mist daily indoors, and continue outdoors as well in dry weather. Humidity tray helps.

Fertilizer: Dilute liquid fertilizer every two weeks in active growth. When flower stalks appear, feed weekly with low nitrogen fertilizer such as 10-30-20.

Care: Plant three or four bulbs in a shallow 8- to 10-inch pot or bulb pan with the tips exposed. Saturate the soil. Do not water again until the shoots appear. During this period, keep the pot in low temperatures and maintain high humidity. Normally, the Amazon lily enjoys high temperatures, even in the eighties or over, but to induce bloom, temperatures must be reduced to 55° to 60° F or even less, if possible. When growth appears in a few weeks, water well and resume regular schedule. In two or three months, the bulbs will flower. After the blooms wither, the Amazon lily takes a rest. Give a scant amount of water only when the ever-green foliage shows signs of wilting. Another method of inducing bloom is said to produce two crops of flowers annually. It endorses fertilizing year round and keeping the soil constantly moist. It is probable, however, that in following this route, you will get no more than one crop of flowers each year.

Eucharis grandiflora

Propagation: Take offsets, or bulblets, from around the parent bulb when you repot a very potbound plant. Bear in mind that this is a very touchy bulb that seriously resents root disturbance. Therefore, unless the pot seems impossibly over-crowded and leaves and flowers show signs of dwindling vigor, do not attempt these procedures. If you must do so, wait until a rest period after flowers have bloomed, and handle roots and foliage most tenderly. Pot in rich, well-drained soil.

Remarks: The Amazon lily is a flower of extraordinary beauty and is worth a bit of pam-pering. It is not a difficult bulb to grow. Even if you are not able to give it the highs and lows of temperature as outlined earlier, you will surely get one and possibly two crops of elegant, fragrant blooms. Like freesia, it is a long-lasting cut flower and its perfume pervades a room.

GENUS: *Euphorbia*
FAMILY: Euphorbiaceae (Spurge)

Euphorbia milii Crown of thorns. Native to Madagascar. A succulent. This popular shrub can grow 2 to 3 feet tall and is equipped with sharp thorns on its sturdy stems and branches. Two- to three-inch oval, thick leaves eventually turn yellow and drop off near bases of stems. New leaves are produced at ends of stems. Like its relative the poinsettia, crown of thorns' "flowers" are bracts, enclosing tiny, yellow, actual flowers. These bracts are usually crim-son, but are also obtainable in yellow or rose. The flowers are nestled within a pair of the rounded, petal-like bracts that grow in clusters at the stem ends. Bright and cheery, these blooms have a long flowering season, often spring through fall, and may continue to appear intermittently all winter long. After the crop withers and falls, the plant takes a rest, and if conditions are right, new buds will soon

Euphorbia milii

appear. Even young plants just a few inches high will flower. Look for dwarf form, *E.m.* 'Bojeri'.

Light: Indoors and outdoors: as much sun as possible.

Soil: Light Basic Soil Mix (page 28) or half potting soil, half sand/perlite, with a dash of bonemeal or dried manure.

Moisture: Water well and let soil get rather dry before next watering.

Fertilizer: Dilute liquid fertilizer every two to three weeks. Feed high-potash formula occasionally to boost flowering. Give light feeding all winter if plant continues to bloom.

Care: No special demands other than plenty of sun.

Propagation: Not for the faint of heart. Take tip cuttings in spring. The cut ends exude latex, a milky substance that can be irritating and sometimes poisonous. Water applied to the cut ends will staunch the flow. Let the cuttings dry for a day, then insert into slightly moist sand or perlite. Place pots in good light and keep barely moist. If the rooting medium is too wet, the cuttings will rot. If all goes well, roots and new leaves will develop within six to eight weeks. (This gives you time to recover from the wounds the thorns inflicted upon you.) Finally, transfer the young plants to the regular soil mixture. Wouldn't you just rather buy a new plant?

Remarks: Propagation aside, and careful handling kept in mind, crown of thorns with its spiny, curving stems and bright, jolly little flowers that keep on coming has long been a favorite and fascinating potted plant. Keep it out of reach of children and pets.

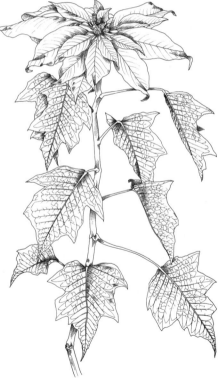

Euphorbia pulcherrima

Euphorbia pulcherrima
Poinsettia. Native to Mexico. It all began when Joel Poinsett, first U.S. Ambassador to Mexico, became enchanted with the red-flowered plant that grew wild in that country and bloomed in December. An amateur botanist, he brought some back to his greenhouse in Greenville, South Carolina. He propagated them and gave some away. Soon the plant named after him had captured the attention of growers, and then potted-plant collectors, across the country. Many new varieties in shades of red, pink, white, mottled pink and white, red with pink dots, pale yellow, and gold have been developed, as well as doubles and dwarfs. To keep the naturally tall shrubs compact and short-stemmed, growers apply growth-inhibiting hormones. The "flowers" are actually brightly colored modified leaves, or bracts,

surrounding the small, green true flower buds. Poinsettia, like Christmas cactus, kalanchoe, and others, is a photoperiodic plant, requiring a period of long nights and short days in order to set buds. Instructions for making a poinsettia bloom for a second winter follow.

Light: Indoors and outdoors: bright with some full sun. See flowering instructions for further light requirements.

Soil: Basic Soil Mix (page 28). When repotting, add a dash of bonemeal and dried manure.

Moisture: Water plentifully while in bloom, letting soil dry slightly but not completely before next watering. A plant stressed by too little watering will shed its leaves, but take care to avoid soggy soil.

Fertilizer: Weekly dilute liquid fertilizer in active growth.

Care: Poinsettias can continue blooming for two to three months under the right conditions: plenty of bright light, ample water, fairly cool temperatures, light feeding, and an absence of hot or cold blasts of air.

Reblooming: Untold thousands of poinsettias are thrown out every winter after blooming. They can be made to bloom again, but it takes patience and strict adherence to a challenging ritual that begins right after flowering ends in late winter. At that point, the plant goes dormant. Remove dry bracts and leaves; cut back the stems to a couple of inches from the base. Repot with fresh soil and organic amendments. Keep in fairly bright light. Water thoroughly. New sprouts will appear. By late spring, branches will need trimming back to promote more side branching. When the weather becomes mild, set the pot outdoors in part shade and gradually move it to brighter light, then to full sun. The branches will need more pruning once or twice during summer. In early September, bring the plant back inside and give it as much bright light as possible, with moderate amounts of water and very little fertilizer. Around the first day of fall, September 21, begin the short-day treatment.

In order to set buds, the poinsettia must have fourteen hours of uninterrupted darkness—say, 6:00 P.M. to 8:00 A.M.—in a dark room or a closet or under a tent of black plastic. During the ten hours of bright daylight, continue moderate watering and light feeding, and rotate the plant so that it gets light from all sides. In early or mid-November, after about eight weeks of short days, reestablish the poinsettia in full light with direct sunlight. Expect to see it bloom in December, although it may bloom later. If it stubbornly refuses to bloom, it may have had too much or too little water, not quite enough nutrients, or exposure to gusts of hot or cold air. The main cause of failure is, alas, the minute or two of light that reached the plant from a table lamp or street lamp when it was supposed to be in total darkness. Too much darkness can upset it as well—even one morning of delayed release into the light.

Ferns

FAMILY: Polypodiaceae (Polypody)

Ferns, one of the oldest forms of vegetation and one of the most diverse, belong to many different genera, and can be found in almost all parts of the world. Together with other ancient kinds of vegetable and animal life that flourished, died, and were buried millennia ago, they were slowly transformed into fossil fuel, or coal. Thousands of species still thrive today in tropical, subtropical, and temperate areas. The species native to warm regions and tropical forests adapt best to container plant conditions. The ones presented here are among those both most likely to succeed in containers indoors and out and most readily obtainable. As different from one another as they may be, they still have a number of characteristics and requirements in common.

Ferns do not flower. They reproduce by spores, which can be seen as little brown dots or lines on the lower surface or on the edges of their fronds (their leaf stalks and foliage). New fronds open from tight coils, giving them the appearance and nickname of "fiddleheads." The fern fronds have blades with leaflike segments called pinnae. Fronds and pinnae in different species vary greatly in appearance. Some don't even look like ferns. In the wild, they grow in porous, richly organic matter. Some are epiphytes that grow in trees, drawing nourishment from bits of organic debris that have lodged in crevices to which their roots cling, and from moisture in the air. Others are terrestrial, growing in leafmold on the ground under trees. In containers, they require rich yet light, well-drained soil, part or filtered shade, liberal amounts of water, and high humidity. They will not thrive in dark corners or waterlogged soil, nor will they tolerate strong sunlight. Indoors, north or east exposures suit them best, and outdoors, shaded, sheltered spots on terrace or balcony are necessary. Fern roots breathe better in clay pots.

Adiantum

The maidenhair ferns are one of the most delicate and dainty species of fern. Wiry, hairlike black stems bear fan-shaped fronds of bright green leaflets. Give filtered to bright light, some partial shade, and provide high humidity with frequent misting and pebble tray. Don't drench the soil and then let it dry out; water it moderately and keep the soil slightly moist but not soggy. Repot only when roots crowd the pot. The creeping rhizome may be separated into pieces with a frond or two attached, and repotted. The following recommended varieties are native to tropical America.

A. capillus-veneris, Venus fern or southern maidenhair, grows to about a foot tall. *A. raddianum,* the delta maidenhair, is larger, denser, and somewhat easier to grow than the Venus. *A. tenerum* may grow up to 3 feet tall. Its long, graceful fronds have many finely cut pinnae, some of which are pinkish when young. *A. hispidulum,* the Australian maidenhair, grows to a height of about a foot and has an unusual appearance—its fronds are divided into sections resembling outstretched fingers or a starfish, with rather leathery leaflets in pairs.

Asplenium

The most common of the epiphytic ferns is *A. nidus,* the bird's nest fern. With upright, smooth, broad, shiny, bright green fronds growing in a rosette shape, it continues to grow as a single cluster with no offsets. *A. bulbiferum,* the mother fern, or hen-and-chicken fern, has feathery fronds that resemble carrot tops. *A. daucifolium* is similar, though darker green and more finely divided. Both forms bear small brown bulbils on the fronds from which tiny fernlets grow. Detach them carefully, place on moist rooting mix, enclose in plastic in medium light, and when sprouts appear, give better light. In a few weeks, transplant fernlets into pots with rich peaty soil.

Cyrtomium

C. falcatum, holly fern. This rather unfernlike fern has leaves that resemble holly leaves; they are glossy, leathery, and sharply pointed and are held on upright stems. A furry rhizome covers the lower part of the leafstalks. Holly fern tolerates lower light and lower humidity and is a bit tougher than most ferns, but it still benefits from misting and a pebble tray in a warm, dry room. Move into a larger pot only when roots fill the pot. Divide in spring. Segments of the rhizome with feeder roots and a frond or two attached may be planted separately and shallowly, just below the surface of the soil. This species prefers a more organic soil than most, with a greater proportion of leafmold and humus-enriched potting soil.

Davallia

D. fejeensis, squirrel's foot or rabbit's foot fern, is one of the most popular species. A rather small fern, it has delicate, lacy fronds 6 to 10 inches long on thin, wiry stems. This epiphyte has unusual rhizomes that crawl along the surface of the soil and often creep over the sides of the pot, looking uncannily like the brown, furry feet of squirrels or little rabbits. Medium light, moderate watering, and light misting suit the squirrel's foot. It is more tolerant of dry air than some other species. Repot in spring when rhizomes cover the surface of the soil, and propagate rhizome sections with fronds by placing them firmly in moist rooting mix. When new fronds emerge and the rhizome seems well rooted, transfer to

Davallia fejeensis

small pots with recommended soil. These surface-growing rhizomes are shallow-rooted and thrive best in shallow pots. Rabbit's foot ferns make superlative hanging basket plants.

Nephrolepsis

Sword fern, Boston fern. This popular fern is big, fast-growing, quite adaptable, and easy to grow. Its large, graceful fronds up to 3 feet long were commonly on display in Victorian parlors. Out of favor for a while but now back in style, *N. exaltata* 'Bostoniensis' the Boston fern, may be the most popular container-grown fern. *N.e.* 'Dallasii', the Dallas fern, is shorter, more compact, and more tolerant of low light and dry air. There are many other cultivars of the Boston fern, including 'Fluffy Ruffles,' a densely growing upright form. The southern

Nephrolepsis exaltata **'Bostoniensis'**

sword fern, *N. cordifolia,* has bright green, erect, 2- to 3-foot fronds. All these kinds quickly outgrow small pots and may need larger pots every spring until the maximum convenient size is reached. Before that happens, you may wish to propagate the large fern by division. Use the younger, outer parts rather than the more tired, older, central ones. These individually rooted crowns, or sections, should be kept warm, shaded, and humid with frequent spraying. Runners on the surface of the soil bearing little fernlets at their tips may also be cut off and propagated in the same way as the rabbit's foot fernlets. Boston fern and its various forms will become thickly packed masses of decorative foliage. They are liable to grow quite huge and will need plenty of space. They look splendid in a handsome ornamental container on a pedestal, or in a large hanging basket.

Pellea

Button fern. *P. rotundifolia* is a fern that doesn't look like a fern. Its fronds, no more than a foot long, grow upright at first, then arch downward, bearing round, dark green, leathery pinnae, or leaflets, closely spaced. *P. viridis,* called green cliffbrake, is another popular variety, with longer fronds and more feathery leaflets on stems that darken and turn black as they mature. Button ferns are very shallow-rooted and should be planted in small, shallow pots or half-pots, where they remain for a long time. Repotting when a plant becomes very overcrowded, or dividing the rhizome into segments with roots and fronds attached for potting individually, may be done in spring. Use rich, organic soil as recommended.

Pteris

Table fern. The prettiest and most popular variety is *P. cretica* 'Albolineata', the white ribbon brake, a small fern with a creamy white stripe down the center of each dark green leaflet. Water generously and keep moist and misted—it's a thirsty fern. Rhizome may be cut into segments and repotted, but this fern does not propagate well except by spores. It's best to let it age gracefully and move it into a larger size pot. Spores produce numerous tiny fernlets, which may take root in the pot and can be removed and potted.

The following guidelines pertain to all of the above-mentioned fern species.

Light: Indoors and outdoors: filtered, dappled, part shade, some bright. No direct sun.

Soil: For terrestrials, Peaty Basic Soil Mix (page 28) with a bit of extra humus or leafmold, a dash of dried manure or bonemeal. For epiphytes, a more fibrous, open, growing medium containing little soil; mainly fibrous peat or sphagnum moss with bark chips, leaf mold, osmunda fiber (a growing medium for other epiphytes), and a good scattering of dried manure or bonemeal.

Moisture: Water thoroughly and let dry slightly before next watering. Never allow the soil to dry out; dried fern fronds will not make a comeback. Soggy soil must also be avoided and a plant should not be allowed to sit in water. Ferns rarely have a total rest period, but need less water in winter. High humidity is desirable at all times. Mist daily and indulge with humidity tray. Hot, dry air will kill these tropical or forest plants. Outdoors, mist if the weather is hot and dry.

Fertilizer: Give a light nitrogen-rich dilute liquid feeding weekly to encourage lush foliage growth, spring through fall; in winter, feed every three to four weeks, as ferns don't go totally dormant.

Care: Most ferns are shallow-rooted and thrive in shallow pots or half-pots where roots and rhizomes can spread out. Repot only when roots and/or rhizomes fill the pot, and then into a pot only one size larger. When the fern has filled a pot of maximum convenient size, it may be time for a root trim before returning it to the same pot with fresh soil. If you want more of this fern, divide it and replant sections instead (see Propagation). A caveat: The roots of some ferns may cling to the inner sides of a clay pot and must be carefully detached.

Propagation: Ferns are rhizomes. The fleshy roots grow underground in some species and above ground in others. To propagate the former by division, the plant must be removed from the pot and the large rhizome just below the surface cut into sections, with feeder roots and growing tops on each piece. Repot individually in fresh soil in small pots. To grow a new fern from a surface rhizome, cut off a 2- or 3-inch piece of the creeping tip of the rhizome, with a frond attached, and place it on damp rooting mix. Secure the tip in place with a bent hairpin, bit of wire, or even a shard of pottery laid lightly on top. All newly propagated rhizomes should start life in a warm, dim spot, and be kept humid under a plastic bag or tent. New fronds will appear within a few weeks, and the rooted cutting or runner can be uncovered and treated to more light and water. Soon it may be transferred to a small pot with rich soil. Some ferns (see *Asplenium*) have bulbils with tiny fernlets on their fronds, which may be detached and placed on a moist rooting mix. Some runners, or surface rhizomes, take root inside the rim of their pot and produce their own fernlets.

Remarks: With their infinite variety of delicate, lacy, or odd-shaped foliage and graceful habits, ferns have a wild and woodsy charm that is delightful to see in a hanging basket or a container on a pedestal, shelf, or table. Mist, and mist again; keep moist and humid.

GENUS: *Ficus*
FAMILY: Moraceae (Mulberry)

Fig. Native to tropical and subtropical regions. Figs are among the old reliables that, given a modicum of good treatment, are durable, handsome, and imposing container plants. Save for the trailing varieties, figs are large plants or small trees that need space and may hit the ceiling, eventually, if not decapitated en route.

Ficus benjamina. Weeping fig, weeping Chinese banyan. This fig grows to be a small tree up to 6 feet tall with gracefully drooping branches; a pretty specimen for indoor landscaping. A summer outdoors is welcomed.

F. lyrata. Fiddleleaf fig. These leaves are shiny, leathery, rippled, dark green, and very large, up to 15 inches long by 8 inches wide. They are violin-shaped, hence the name.

Ficus benjamina

F. elastica. The familiar old standby, the rubber plant, or India-rubber tree. Thick, leathery, glossy, dark green leaves emerge from a red sheath that soon drops away. Improved forms include the favorite *F.e.* 'Decora' with a bronzy hue, and a number of variegated forms with cream, pink, and yellow markings. Give them plenty of light and some direct sun to keep the colors bright.

F. carica. The edible fig does not fruit indoors. This is the fig tree with the famed leaves so visible in painting, sculpture, and the decorative arts.

F. pumila. Creeping or climbing fig. This is a small, many-branched, creeping or vining plant with small, heart-shaped leaves. Nice in a hanging basket or on a shelf. It needs a peatier soil and more moisture than its large relatives. *F.p.* 'Variegata' has white spots.

F. sagittata. Another trailer, with larger, lance-shaped leaves.

F.s. 'Variegata' has cream markings. The variegated trailing, creeping forms need more light than the green species.

Ficus elastica

Light: Indoors and outdoors: medium or filtered to bright. Variegated forms need more sun than green ones. None will flourish in dim or poor light.

Soil: Basic Soil Mix, page 28.

Moisture: Water well and let soil become rather dry before next watering. It's better to err on the dry side; soggy soil is very harmful. Creeping or trailing forms, however, can take more moisture.

Fertilizer: Once a month with dilute liquid fertilizer.

Care: Don't rush repotting. Figs are quite happy in pots that seem a size too small for them. Wait until roots appear through the drainage hole, and then make sure that the roots have filled the pot before you repot. When largest convenient size pot is reached, topdress yearly with fresh soil. Control height by cutting off a section of the top, and be prepared for a milky flow from the cut, which can be staunched with powdered charcoal or ashes. The plant, which is almost always single-stemmed, will now branch out. Avoid drafts, abrupt changes in position, or overwatering, any of which may cause leaf drop.

Propagation: Trailing, creeping figs root readily from tip cuttings in moist rooting mix. All others must be air-layered.

Remarks: Figs are quite foolproof to grow and are considered highly desirable for interior decorating in areas where they have plenty of space, or where an impressive accent is desired. Particularly attractive are the graceful weeping fig and the sturdy variegated rubber plants. Low humidity and moderate watering are all well tolerated.

GENUS: *Fittonia*
FAMILY: Acanthaceae (Acanthus)

Mosaic plant, nerve plant, painted net leaf.
Native to the coasts of Colombia, Peru, and
Ecuador. These low-growing, creeping, tropical
rain forest plants like moisture and warmth.
F. verschaffeltii has red veins on olive green, oval
leaves up to 3 inches long. *F.v. argyroneura* has
silvery-white veins on smaller, lighter green
leaves, and has a dwarf form, 'Nana'. The red-
veined form is very handsome. Erect, terminal,
light green bracts up to 8 inches long bear tiny
yellow flowers. They appear intermittently
throughout the year and remain for quite a
while before drying up and dropping off.

Fittonia verschaffeltii

Light:	Indoors: moderate to bright. Some direct sun. Outdoors: filtered or light shade.
Soil:	Peaty Basic Soil Mix, page 28.
Moisture:	Water generously and keep moist. Fittonia is a heavy drinker. Mist and pebble tray are desirable.
Fertilizer:	Dilute liquid fertilizer every two to three weeks or less frequently.
Care:	As in its native jungle, fittonia revels in a warm and humid atmosphere. It will get limp and droopy if the soil is allowed to dry out, but a thorough watering will quickly restore it. Check soil frequently for dryness. Trim back overlong stems that have lost some leaves near the base. New growth will soon sprout from sides and base.
Propagation:	Tip cuttings root willingly in water.
Remarks:	Fittonia has an ill-deserved reputation for being somewhat difficult to grow. Aside from sulking—rightfully—if it doesn't get sufficient water, this plant is easy to grow and propagate. The carmine-veined fittonia makes a particularly beautiful display anywhere that it can spread out or trail from a pot or basket, indoors or out. Group several plants together in a pot for maximum effect. This is one of my favorite decorative foliage plants.

GENUS: *Freesia*
FAMILY: Iridaceae (Iris)

Native to South Africa. A corm. This charming, dainty flower is intensely fragrant. Two-
inch trumpet-shaped blooms are lined up
almost at right angles on slender stems. *F. arm-
strongii* is pink with an orange throat. *F. alba* is
white, and *F. refracta* is light yellow to greenish-
yellow with purplish-brown markings. Numerous hybrids come in shades of cream, red,
orange, copper, purple, and lilac; most have
tones of more than one color. Some have contrasting veins, and some have double blooms.

Freesia refracta

Light:	Indoors: bright, some direct sun. Outdoors: sunny, filtered sun.
Soil:	Basic Soil Mix (page 28) with extra sand or perlite for porosity and a bit of dried manure.
Moisture:	Water newly planted bulbs well, then scantily until growth appears. Then increase watering and keep moist. Taper off when leaves begin to yellow and die. Keep dry during rest period.
Fertilizer:	Weekly dilute liquid fertilizer when flower stems appear and until foliage yellows.
Care:	The small corms are planted in groups of six or eight, pointed ends up, an inch or less deep in a 6-inch pot in late summer or early fall for midwinter bloom. Cool outdoor nights help to stimulate strong growth. For early spring bloom, plant from October to December, and for midsummer bloom, plant in spring. Keep cool and shaded, water as indicated previously. When growth appears, give more light gradually, then full sun. Water liberally. Delicate stems may need the support of sticks or twigs, and string around the outside. Freesia likes cool nights, but if you have moved it outdoors, be on the alert for a chill or frost. A mulch of damp peat is helpful in conserving moisture.
Storage:	Remove dried foliage. Leave corms in the pot, dry, dark, and cool, or lift corms, shake off soil, store in peat or perlite.
Propagation:	Cormlets may be removed from dormant corm and potted.
Remarks:	Give these tender bulbs bright days, cool nights, and cool, dry, shady dormant time. Freesia is somewhat difficult to rebloom.

GENUS: *Fuchsia*
FAMILY: Onagraceae (Evening-primrose)

Sometimes called lady's eardrops. Native to
tropical America. Grown most successfully in
cool coastal climates of the East and West
Coasts where they can get the moist, even foggy,
air they enjoy. Fuchsias are plants of great variety.
On the West Coast, some are grown as shrubs that grow
from 3 to 10 feet tall. Most often seen in hanging baskets,
fuchsia hybrids come in elegant cascading types. The taller,
larger-leaved shrubby varieties usually bear the larger flowers; the
lower-growing, smaller-leaved kinds are suitable for baskets. Flowers,

Fuchsia

which may be single, double, or more than double, come in lovely combinations of pink, rose, red, lavender-blue, purple, white, and, of course, fuchsia.

Light:	Indoors and outdoors: filtered sun; partial or light shade (no direct sun).
Soil:	Rich, organic, well-drained. If you buy a plant in a light soilless medium, repot in good potting soil with added humus.
Moisture:	Water liberally. Fuchsia should always be moist. Never let it dry out. In hot climate or hot summer, spray frequently.
Fertilizer:	Dilute liquid fertilizer every ten days to two weeks. Fuchsias are always hungry. Add bonemeal and a bit of dried manure to plantings.
Care:	Pinch out growing tips of young plants to induce side-branching for profuse flowering. Place three or four plants in a hanging basket. In fall, gradually decrease watering, then keep barely moist. To overwinter a plant, cut it back by half and give it medium light in a cool place, around 60° F or less if possible. Indoors, the plant will lose all its leaves, but don't despair; if it remains cool and doesn't dry out completely, it probably will send up new growth in spring. Then, repot in rich, fresh soil, feed and water well, and cut back to about 3 to 4 inches.
Propagation:	Tip cuttings in spring or fall in damp peat/sand, peat/perlite, or sand alone.
Remarks:	Fuchsia is a gorgeous flowering basket plant, shrub, or standard. In frost-free West Coast regions, where it is happiest, it is evergreen. Elsewhere, it needs some pampering. If you cannot keep it moist and misted in summer, and very cool and barely moist in winter indoors, I suggest you enjoy its beautiful blooms and buy new ones each spring. See *Lantana* for growing fuchsia as a standard.

GENUS: *Gardenia*
FAMILY: Rubiaceae (Madder)

Called Cape jasmine, but not related to jasmines. Native to Japan, China, and tropical regions. *G. jasminoides* and its varieties, the most popular of which is the double *G.j.* 'Veitchii', is the species grown as a potted plant. In the south United States, it is considered a shrub and grows up to 6 feet tall in gardens; confined in a pot, it usually doesn't exceed 2 feet in height. Glossy, dark green, leathery leaves make it an attractive container plant. Getting gardenia to bloom is the tricky part, and a cause for celebration by gardeners who see the buds unfurl into pure white flowers that waft an intensely sweet perfume.

Gardenia jasminoides

Light: Indoors: half a day minimum of full sun. Outdoors: bright or filtered sun, part shade. See specifics under Care.

Soil: Peaty Basic Soil Mix (page 28) or equal parts peat and good potting soil with a generous sprinkle of dried manure and some sand for drainage. Special acid-type packaged potting soil for these acid-loving plants may be used instead.

Moisture: Water generously and keep soil moist; never let it dry out. Plants may be bottom-watered by placing the pot in a bowl of tepid water until the surface of the soil is moist. Provide humidity tray and mist the plant daily. Avoid wetting petals; they may discolor.

Temperature: A drop of 10° F at night is essential to the formation of buds. Generally, 72° F during the day and 62° F at night is suitable. In colder areas where gardenias are grown to bloom during the winter months, bud drop is likely to occur if temperatures at night are higher than this, so watch the thermostat. This temperature range is quite comfortable for people as well as finicky gardenias.

Fertilizer: Give an acid-type fertilizer, which has iron, once a month from March to September. In an area where the water is alkaline, add about a teaspoonful of iron chelate or iron sulfate to a quart of water; use this every other month. When the gardenia is budding and in flower, from fall to spring, give high phosphorus-potash fertilizer to encourage bloom. Chlorosis, or yellowing of leaves, means lack of iron in soil that is not acidic enough for gardenias.

Care: Prune back long stems in spring for a more compact shape. Examine the drain hole and the surface of the soil for protruding roots, which would indicate a need for a larger pot with fresh soil. If in doubt, remove plant carefully and inspect the root mass. Repot only when it crowds the pot, as gardenias object strenuously to being disturbed and flower best when slightly potbound. When repotting or topdressing, add peaty, rich, organic, well-drained soil and mist frequently for vigorous growth.

When nights are mild, gardenias may be moved outdoors to a sheltered spot that gets bright or filtered sun, preferably in the morning, and no hot midday sun. Continue spraying. Before any possibility of frost, shift pots back indoors to a bright, sunny spot and spray frequently to help plants readjust to house temperatures and dry air. Some leaf drop is likely to occur.

Liberal misting of a newly purchased plant will also help it to adjust. Bear in mind that a new plant has been accustomed to the very humid atmosphere of a greenhouse and may go into shock in the Mojave Desert-like environment of its new home, where the humidity may be 50 percent or more lower.

Propagation: Take tip cuttings in early spring. Dip them in hormone rooting powder before inserting them in a peaty rooting mix. Cover with plastic bag and keep in a fairly cool spot in filtered light. When firmly rooted in a month or more, transfer to pots with the recommended potting soil. Spray young shoots frequently.

Remarks: Gardenias have lots of excuses for dropping their buds and letting their leaves turn yellow: The air is too dry or too warm, there's a draft, the soil isn't consistently moist, the night temperature is too warm indoors or suddenly too cool outdoors, the sunlight is too strong or there isn't enough of it. If it isn't one crisis, it's another, and you can't always pinpoint the cause. Cater tenderly to your gardenia, and with a little bit of luck, those beautiful white flowers and heady fragrance will be your well-earned reward. If buds always drop and you get no flowers, either live with your gardenia as a foliage plant, or conclude that something in your environment is antipathetical to gardenias, and direct your energies to other flowering plants. You are not alone.

GENUS: *Gynura*
FAMILY: Compositae (Daisy)

Purple passion, velvet plant. Native to Java. Popular for its distinctive foliage, purple passion has notched leaves covered on both sides with velvety purple hairs with an iridescent sheen. Stems are also purple and hairy. Small, insignificant orange-yellow flowers have a unpleasant scent and may be removed while in bud. *G. aurantiaca* is the upright form, although it may flop if not controlled by pruning, and *G. sarmentosa* is the trailing form.

Light: Indoors and outdoors: bright, with some full sun to promote most vivid color.

Soil:	Basic Soil Mix, page 28.
Moisture:	Water well, keep slightly moist. Pebble tray is fine, but avoid water or spray on leaves, as they may scorch in direct sun.
Fertilizer:	Light dilute liquid fertilizer once a month is sufficient.
Care:	Purple passion grows leggy and must be pinched back when young and pinched again several times to maintain a full, bushy plant. Pinch less if you want it to trail. If the leaves become more green than purple, the plant needs to be moved to a sunnier location. Warmth is also desirable.

Gynura sarmentosa

Propagation:	Tip cuttings root easily in water.
Remarks:	The unique violet color, enhanced by plenty of sunlight, makes the purple passion a great attraction when several young ones are grouped together in a pot, or in a hanging basket with green-leaved plants for a special effect. Since it propagates so readily, start fresh new plants often from stem tips, and don't bother to save the old straggly plants.

GENUS: *Hedera*
FAMILY: Araliaceae (Ginseng)

Ivy. Native to North Africa and Europe. *H. helix,* English ivy, the species most suitable for container culture, has a great many varieties. The variation in shape, size, and color is amazing. The most decorative ones combine green with white, cream, ivory, grey, yellow, or gold. Among the hundreds of attractive forms are: *H.h.* 'Glacier' whose small gray and green leaves are bordered in white; *H.h.* 'Needlepoint' with tiny, sharply pointed leaves; 'Manda's Crested' with rippled, pointed, star-shaped green leaves and rosy margins; 'Jubilee', variegated green, gray, and white; 'Goldenheart' or 'Gold Heart' with bright splotches of yellow in the center of a small green leaf; and others such as 'Gold Dust' and 'California Gold' that have more yellow than green, with a gilded look. A different species, *H. canariensis,* Canary or Algerian ivy, grows taller and has larger leaves. *H.c.* 'Variegata', also called 'Gloire de Marengo', has handsome silvery-gray markings and creamy margins. All these and many more have aerial roots that sprout from the stems and eagerly grab and cling to anything nearby. If you want them to climb, place a small trellis or some sticks in the pot and tie the stems upward. Allowed to trail, they are quite graceful, and blend well with many other plants.

Light: Indoors and outdoors: bright or filtered sun. Some full sun is fine for variegated forms.

Soil: Basic Soil Mix, page 28.

Moisture: Water well and let soil dry slightly between waterings. High humidity is essential to avoid the insidious spider mite. Mist daily and provide humidity tray. Dunk the entire plant once a week in tepid water laced with a bit of detergent or Safer's Insecticidal Spray if mites are suspected.

Fertilizer: Dilute liquid fertilizer once a month is sufficient.

Hedera helix

Care: Keep ivies moist and cool and give good light. They adapt well, however, to less ideal conditions, except for extremes of heat and dry air. Nip back overlong stems to force side-branching and a bushier appearance. If variegated forms are losing color, move them to a sunnier spot. Ivies love summering outdoors.

Propagation: Stem prunings root readily in water.

Remarks: Years ago when rooms were not as well heated and air not as dry as today, ivies flourished as container plants with very little care. Today, they are most grateful when you provide humidity and, at least at night, lower temperatures. Ivies look particularly attractive in hanging baskets, on pedestals, or in urns, where they can trail effectively. They are useful to mantle the surface of a large planter and to drape themselves down over the sides. Small varieties combine nicely with other foliage and flowering plants in a mixed planting. A fresh-air vacation does wonders for ivy. Avoid direct sun outdoors, but all variegated forms will do well in a bright, sunny location and are good choices for spilling out of a window box or large planter box between begonias, impatiens, geraniums, sweet alyssum, and flowering annuals of many kinds.

GENUS: *Hibiscus*
FAMILY: Malvaceae (Mallow)

Rose-of-China, Chinese hibiscus, China rose. Native to China and tropical areas of Asia. A flowering tropical shrub. *H. rosa-sinensis* is a shrubby plant with handsome, dark green, toothed-edge foliage on woody branches. The huge, gorgeous flowers, 4 to 5 inches across, may be double or single, with flat, scalloped, ruffled, or fringed petals, in shades of red, pink, yellow, apricot-orange, lavender, and white. Although each flower lasts for little more than a day, a contented plant will produce them in profusion and almost continuously from spring to fall, sometimes longer. Hibiscus can grow 8 to 10 feet tall, and needs rigorous pruning to keep it to a manageable size (about 3 feet). *H. r-s* 'Cooperi' is a much more compact dwarf form, notable for its beautiful pink, red, white, and green foliage and its bright red flowers. Look for new hybrids with spectacular color range, some multicolored, capable of staying open up to three days.

Hibiscus

Light: Indoors and outdoors: bright light, some direct sun.

Soil: Basic Soil Mix, page 28.

Moisture: Water generously and keep lightly moist. Give less water in winter.

Fertilizer: Dilute liquid fertilizer monthly. A large plant needs more nutrients; feed biweekly in active growth. Give high phosphorus-potash fertilizer to encourage flowering.

Care: In spring, hibiscus needs a drastic pruning. Cut branches down to 4 or 5 inches, leaving two or three growth nodes. New shoots will soon appear. Hibiscus is a vigorous grower and needs frequent repotting. When it is no longer practicable to move it into a still-larger container, and roots are emerging from the drainage hole, lift the plant, give it a root trim and replace it with fresh soil in the same pot. Thereafter, you will have to topdress it annually. When pruning roots, prune back some top growth as well.

Hibiscus revels in a summer outdoors, where its blossoms will be a dazzling attraction on deck or patio. Accustom a plant to bright sun gradually so that the leaves don't scorch. In early fall, be on the alert for a cold spell or frost; this is a heat-loving plant. When it's time to return it to the house, you may realize that it has grown prodigiously. If you're looking at a 4- or 5-foot shrub that needs more space than you can spare, you may need to reduce the height and width somewhat. This is a painful procedure because the plant is still blooming. Trim as little as possible, as the hibiscus is about to enter its slow-growth period anyway. Stop fertilizing and reduce watering. Cooler night temperatures are desirable; 55° to 60° F is ideal.

Propagation: Tip cuttings in spring in moist rooting mix.

Remarks: Hibiscus is an easy care plant with a long life span. It needs no coddling, just plenty of sun, water, nourishment, and space, but it requires a firm hand with the clippers. Buy a young, small plant and watch it grow. Recently I moved a husky five-year-old into a 10-inch pot, where I hope it will remain content for several years. The root ball was immense and needed a resolute hand for pruning. Watch for roots coming through the drainage hole. This robust shrub, which can live for many years, eventually needs the largest pot you can give it, or a tub. In warm climates, it can remain outdoors all year and may bloom nonstop. In cold regions indoors, it may continue to produce flowers intermittently during the winter; keep feeding. Hibiscus may be grown as a standard. See *Lantana*.

GENUS: *Hippeastrum*
FAMILY: Amaryllidaceae (Amaryllis)

Amaryllis. Native of tropical America. A bulb. This large bulb produces big, bold and beautiful flowers year after year with a minimum of care. The fat flower bud, already formed in the bulb, arises on a thick, tall stalk that grows to 2 feet or more with amazing speed four to six weeks after planting or reviving from dormancy. Long, straplike, arching leaves follow or accompany the bud, and often a second bud arises. The flowers are huge—6 to 8 inches across—and there may be anywhere from three to six on a stem. Colors are shades of red, pink, rose, orange, coral, and white, and many have contrasting streaks or borders. Also look for new bright yellow. The most and largest flowers are obtained from the largest bulbs, which are about 6 inches in diameter.

Hippeastrum

Light: Indoors and outdoors: full or bright sun from planting to flowering. When buds open indoors, less bright light is desirable to prolong blooming time.

Soil: Basic Soil Mix, page 28. Enrich with a bit of dried manure or bonemeal.

Moisture: Many bulbs come with a large, dry root mass and benefit by a good soak in tepid water for half a day or more before being potted. When planted, drench thoroughly. If you are using a clay pot, make sure that it is well soaked beforehand or it will draw water from the soil. Do not water again until the first sign of growth emerges, and then commence regular watering. This is a large, thirsty plant. Taper off in late summer, but as long as foliage remains green, do not withhold water.

Fertilizer: The flower buds are in the bulb, and as buds and leaves emerge, fertilizing is not needed. When bloom begins, start light liquid fertilizing and continue after flowering ends and until leaves turn yellow. This helps the bulb to store nutrients for next season's bloom.

Care: After flowers fade, cut down flowers and stalks but retain the foliage, which remains green and nourishes the bulb. The plant should continue to receive good light, and may remain outdoors until the leaves turn yellow, then brown and dry. The dormant period is beginning. Remove dead leaves and store the bulb in the pot in a dark, dry, rather cool place. After two or three months, bring it into the sunlight and topdress, adding a dash of dehydrated manure. If the bulb and roots appear to have outgrown the pot, lift the bulb, shake off old soil, trim tangled and overlong roots, and repot in the next larger size pot. Water copiously, place in full sun, and do not water again until new growth, either bud or leaf, arises. Usually, the bud comes first.

Propagation: At time of repotting, remove good-sized bulblets, or offsets, and plant separately. Leave small bulblets on parent bulb.

Choosing, Planting, and Perpetuating an Amaryllis Bulb: Amaryllis are often sold prepotted in small plastic pots. I prefer to choose an unpotted bulb so that I can pick a large, healthy bulb without mushy spots or other damage. It should be labelled as to color and named cultivar. Some labels show the flower in color. I add to the label my planting date and, later, the date of bloom, for future reference. For a 5- or 6-inch bulb, a sturdy 8-inch clay pot is needed. After soaking the roots well, plant the bulb with a generous third above the surface of the soil, leaving 1 to 1½ inches between the bulb and the sides of the pot. Before filling in all the soil, insert a 2-foot stake to which you will later tie the flower stalk as it becomes heavy with its crown of big blooms. Press the soil firmly around the roots and the stake. Water thoroughly and give care as described previously. When growth appears, turn the pot now and then to give even exposure to light.

What to Do When Nothing Happens: Now and then a bulb just sits there and refuses to budge out of its dormancy. This usually results from a too-short rest period. If it's your own bulb that bloomed last season, perhaps you didn't let it hibernate long enough. If it's a newly purchased bulb, it is likely that the grower didn't give it sufficient resting time, cut off too many roots, or removed leaves that were still green. Once you have watered the bulb well and placed it in the sunlight after its dormant period, there's no going back. Patience is now required. Don't let the soil dry out or the roots will suffer. Keep the pot sun-drenched and warm. Your amaryllis will almost certainly send up one or two flower stalks and some leaves—eventually. You may have to wait eight to ten weeks, but for sheer size, color, and drama, these flamboyant flowers are worth the wait.

Remarks: Amaryllis are a stellar accent any time of year, but I find them particularly rewarding in the dull days of midwinter. They are full of surprises as to just when they decide to bloom, how many flowers will appear on a stalk, when the second fat bud will arise, and so on. Very rarely, and just when you are getting tired of sunning and watering those big green leaves after the flowering has ended, a bulb will produce a third flower bud. That's exciting! Rarer still, a bulb will send up a fourth bud, as was the case with my 'Mona Lisa', a delicious coral-pink, which first bloomed in mid-December, and, amazingly, bore a fourth bud with four flowers in mid-May!

GENUS: *Hoya*
FAMILY: Asclepiadaceae (Milkweed)

Wax plant. Native to Australia. Thick, waxy green or green and white leaves are borne on stems that can dangle or be trained to climb on a trellis or hoop. Long-lasting round clusters of small, fragrant, creamy-white, waxy flowers with pink star-shaped centers are produced in summer on small spurs or stubs on the stems. These spurs must not be removed as they will give rise to future flowers. *Hoya carnosa* is the most common form, with green leaves. *H.c.* 'Variegata' adds pink edges to green and white leaves and has perhaps the most beautiful foliage of all the hoyas. *H.c.* 'Krinkle Kurl', the Hindu rope plant, has curly, thick, rather tortured-looking green and white

Hoya carnosa

leaves closely spaced. *H. bella* is a miniature form with small, pointed leaves and very fragrant flowers with violet centers; it likes more moisture than the other forms. *H. australis* bears red-centered flowers in the fall. It is more difficult to bring into bloom than other forms.

Light: Indoors and outdoors: half day full sun needed to set flower buds. Good bright light is needed at all times.

Soil: Basic Soil Mix (page 28) with some extra sand or perlite for good drainage.

Moisture: Water well, then let the soil get somewhat dry before watering again. Don't let soil get soggy. Decrease watering after the flowers fade, and in winter, give only enough to keep the soil from drying out completely. This also applies to plants that have not produced flowers.

Fertilizer: Low-nitrogen formula to stimulate bud and flower production during active growth period only, every two or three weeks.

Care: Hoya flowers best when potbound. Once buds are set, don't change the plant's position. Pruning is rarely needed, and trimming might remove some of the spurs that produce the flowers. Sparse watering in winter helps to induce flowering, but do not allow the plant to become so dry that the leaves begin to shrivel. Repot only when the pot is very overcrowded, every two or three years. High humidity is very important to this heat-tolerant tropical rain forest plant.

Propagation: Stem cuttings in moist rooting mix or in water.

Remarks: A young plant will take several years to reach the flowering stage. Only a fairly large and mature plant will flower, and then only if it has optimum conditions. Perhaps this year my four-year-old will bloom; but if not, the lovely, fragrant, jewel-like flower clusters are worth another year's wait. Be patient with your hoya.

GENUS: *Hypoestes*
FAMILY: Acanthaceae (Acanthus)

Freckle face, polka dot plant, pink dot plant, flamingo plant, measles plant, baby's tears. Native of Malagasy. One glance tells you the reason for these descriptive common names. *H. phyllostachya* (formerly known as *H. sanguinolenta*), the one species grown in pot culture, has 1- to 2-inch-long pointed leaves splashed and splattered with glowing pink spots. Look for *H.p.* 'Splash', which has the biggest and brightest pink markings. Pale lavender flowers may appear, but they are insignificant and are best removed to conserve the plant's energy for foliage production.

Light: Indoors and outdoors: plenty of bright light and some direct sun.

Soil: Basic Soil Mix, page 28.

Moisture: Water liberally and keep moist.

Fertilizer: Dilute liquid fertilizer every two to three weeks.

Care: Freckle faces grow quickly and need frequent pruning of their thin stems to create a bushy effect. Plentiful side growth soon needs pinching back, too. These plants look best low and dense, no taller than 8 inches. Less is even better.

Propagation: Tip cuttings and prunings root eagerly in water.

Remarks: Enhanced by enough bright light, the vivid pink dots and splashes of color on the leaves make this plant an unusual attraction. Grow several rooted cuttings in a shallow pot. If the light is insufficient, the color will fade and green will predominate. Provide front-row sunshine or a sunny windowsill, and freckles will return. Youngsters find this plant fascinating and fun to grow.

Hypoestes phyllostachya

GENUS: *Impatiens*
FAMILY: Balsaminaceae (Balsam)

Busy Lucy, Busy Lizzie, patience plant. Native to Southeast Africa. This popular, dependable flowering plant starts to bloom when only a few inches tall and rarely exceeds a foot in height. Banks of impatiens line driveways and border paths and billow out of pots, window boxes, and hanging baskets. Only frost, total neglect, or hungry deer can make it stop blooming. *I. wallerana* has innumerable hybrids in shades of red, pink, rose, salmon, lavender, orange, white, and some bicolors. New Guinea hybrids are sturdier plants that don't need pruning. They have larger, showier

Impatiens wallerana

flowers in a wide color range, but not as many blooms as common impatiens. Leaves are longer and variegated, green with yellow or green with rose. They are at their best in full sun. Indoors in winter, they remain huskier and often live longer than the common impatiens, and they do not get as straggly.

Light: Indoors: bright, some sun. Outdoors: filtered light or part shade.

Soil: Basic Soil Mix, page 28.

Moisture: Water well and keep moist. Mist daily to ward off spider mite.

Fertilizer: Light dilute low-nitrogen fertilizer biweekly.

Care: Impatiens is undemanding. It tends to grow leggy, with blooms only at the ends of long stems. This can be controlled if you start pinching the stems back on a young plant, and pinch again if need be, to produce a bushy plant and profuse flowering. Repot only when roots fill the pot. For a hanging basket, let some stems sprawl.

Propagation: Tip cuttings, with buds or flowers removed, root enthusiastically in water any time of the year.

Remarks: Because they are easily obtainable and inexpensive, impatiens are often left to die outdoors at summer's end. Why not enjoy these pretty little flowering plants all winter long, especially since they are so easy to propagate? Winter prunings can be grown for another season of blooming plants. Give young ones plenty of water and sun.

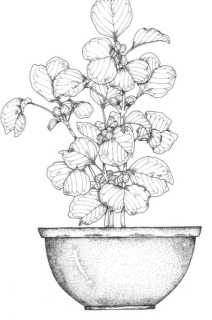

GENUS: *Iresine*
FAMILY: Amaranthaceae (Amaranth)

Bloodleaf, beefsteak plant. Native to Brazil. These small sun lovers, *I. herbstii,* are prized for their purplish-red or wine-red foliage with pink midrib and veins, and red stems. A less common cultivar, *I.h.* 'Aureoreticulata', has coloring that is more green and yellow than red, but it too has red stems.

Light: Indoors and outdoors: bright light with several hours of full sun.

Soil: Basic Soil Mix, page 28.

Moisture: Water plentifully and keep moist. Pebble tray is welcomed.

Iresine herbstii

Fertilizer: Dilute liquid fertilizer every two to three weeks.

Care: Pinch young bloodleaf unmercifully before it grows tall and lanky, and as it grows, pinch some more, to promote bushiness.

Propagation: Tip cuttings root eagerly in water. Use the pinchings.

Remarks: As with the purple passion plant, iresine's claim to fame lies in its intense and glowing color. It's easy to grow and to propagate. Place several young plants in a small pot and enjoy the sun-drenched ruby and pink foliage. Toss out old, straggly plants after you take the stem tips for propagation. In a sunny window box or other outdoor container, iresine adds a bright, bold note to an all-green or variegated foliage group or flowering plants and annuals. Beware infelicitous combinations with true red, orange, and coral.

GENUS: *Ixia*
FAMILY: Iridaceae (Iris)

African corn lily. Native of South Africa. A small corm. Star-shaped flowers are borne in clusters on slender stems above narrow-bladed leaves in spring. The foliage dies down in mid-summer. *I. paniculata* has ivory-white flowers. *I. maculata* bears bright yellow or orange blooms. A host of hybrids offers red, pink, mauve, golden yellow, and white blooms, most with small purple or brown centers. The lighter-colored blossoms are fragrant.

Light: Indoors and outdoors: full sun.

Soil: Basic Soil Mix (page 28) with extra sand or perlite for good drainage.

Ixia

Moisture: After growth is up, keep moist until foliage begins to yellow, then reduce watering. Stop altogether when leaves die.

Fertilizer: Biweekly liquid dilute feeding, weekly as buds begin to open and roots fill the pot. Cease feeding at dormancy.

Care: Set corms shallowly, like freesia, about an inch deep, five or six corms to a 5- or 6-inch pot. Plant in fall. Use a shallow pot or bulb pan as these are shallow-rooted plants. Water well and place in a cool, shady spot. Don't let the soil dry out, but be careful not to overwater. When shoots appear, give bright light, and then full sun. Mist new shoots for healthy growth. Later, they may need staking.

Storage: After the foliage withers, the corms go dormant. Leave them in the pot and place in a dry, cool, dark spot, or lift and store dry.

Propagation: Cormlets form at the base of the corm and may be detached and planted in cool autumn weather. They may not produce blooms for two or three years.

Remarks: Ixia closes its petals in shade, so give it plenty of sun. They grow best with cool night temperatures. One of the less common and less robust bulbs, they produce dainty, charming flowers in a lovely, soft color range.

GENUS: *Justicia*
FAMILY: Acanthaceae (Acanthus)

Justicia brandegeana. Formerly called *Beleropone guttata.* Shrimp plant. Native to Mexico and tropical America. As a long-flowering potted plant, the shrimp plant has few equals. In early spring, small overlapping chartreuse bracts appear. As they grow to a length of 3 to 5 inches, they turn a rosy-copper color with some yellow tones. Another form, 'Yellow Queen', is all yellow. From the bracts hang little narrow white flowers with purple markings. The full-grown, curving bract is positively shrimp-like! Flowering may be continuous for eight to ten months, and the "shrimps" last a long time before drying up and falling off.

Justicia brandegeana

Light: Indoors and outdoors: good bright light with some direct sun.

Soil: Basic Soil Mix, page 28.

Moisture: Water plentifully. Let soil dry slightly before next watering, but do not allow it to dry out.

Fertilizer: Dilute liquid fertilizer every two to three weeks.

Care: No special demands except sun. In order to have a bushy plant with abundant blooms, it is necessary to pinch back growing tips when the plant is young and soon pinch some more, as the shrimp is a fast grower. Stems tend to grow tall and gawky. After flowering has ended, cut down stems relentlessly to 2 or 3 inches from the base. The plant will soon produce new growth, and keep right on growing all winter long. Keep nipping away at stems longer than 4 to 5 inches.

Propagation: Tip cuttings root readily in water.

Remarks: This durable and prolific bloomer is one of my favorites. I deplore its spindly lack of charm before flowering, but I forgive it everything when the shrimps appear and grow big and ruddy. A group of these plants basking in the sun on the patio or by steps or door has a sensational effect all summer and fall.

GENUS: *Kalanchoe*
FAMILY: Crassulaceae (Orpine)

Native of Madagascar and Africa. A succulent. Kalanchoe is a small, decorative container plant that normally blooms in spring but is often forced into bloom by growers for sale at Christmastime. The most common variety is *K. blossfeldiana;* it grows to a height of 8 to 10 inches and has thick, glossy, bright green 1- to 2-inch leaves occasionally edged in red. The scarlet-flowered form called 'Flaming Katy' may be the most popular, but pretty shades of pink and rose, as well as yellow, orange, and white, are refreshing additions to a movable garden. The dense flower clusters, rising well above the foliage, are long lasting. Another variety, *K. tomentosa*, has chunky, gray-green leaves with rusty-brown toothed edges covered with

Kalanchoe blossfeldiana

silvery-white hairs, growing in a rosette form. It rarely flowers, but makes an unusual and attractive foliage plant. One common name, panda plant, doesn't seem to make much sense, but the other common name, pussy ears, is delightfully appropriate. Another interesting form with the rather forbidding name of *K. fedtschenkoi* 'Marginata' bears roundish, slightly scalloped, bluish-gray leaves with white margins. A leaf placed on the soil will produce tiny white, pink-tinged plantlets all along its borders, which develop rootlets—a curious and intriguing phenomenon. A cultivar, 'Aurora Borealis', adds pink to the borders of leaves if given sufficient light. Another form, 'Aurora Borealis Rosea', has predominantly dusty-rose-colored leaves.

Light: Indoors and outdoors: full sun except in rest period.

Soil: Basic Soil Mix (page 28) with some sand or perlite added for porosity and a bit of bonemeal or dehydrated manure.

Moisture: Moderate. Let soil dry out well between waterings. Succulent leaves store water and will become unhealthy if overwatered.

Fertilizer: Dilute liquid fertilizer every two to three weeks spring to fall. None in rest or short-day period (see Care).

Care: "Gift plant" kalanchoes, often forced into bloom for a December display, normally bloom in spring. After bloom ends, cut off faded blooms, cease fertilizing, and water only enough to keep the soil from drying out completely. Let the plant rest in bright or filtered light. To get another crop of flowers, it must receive the short-day treatment. As with other succulents (see *Euphorbia pulcherrima,* the poinsettia) a short day and a long, dark night of fourteen or fifteen hours for about eight weeks, followed by full sun and regular care, bring reflowering. If you want blooms by Christmastime, start this procedure in early fall (mid-September). If not forced, the plant may bloom normally the following spring without the short-day treatment.

Propagation: Tip cuttings in water or leaf cuttings with a bit of stem attached in moist rooting mix. A leaf with plantlets may be gently pressed on the moist mix, or sand. Tiny plantlets will take root. Keep warm, bright, and damp.

Remarks: Kalanchoes in bloom are cheery and charming and make excellent gift plants. Out of bloom, the common variety *K. blossfeldiana* is not much to look at and is often discarded. It's always worth a try to bring a plant back into bloom again, although it is not always easy. The other forms are attractive as foliage plants. The 'Auroras' are highly decorative.

GENUS: *Lantana*
FAMILY: Verbenaceae (Verbena)

Yellow sage, mountain sage. Native to South and Central America. Of the many shrubs in this genus, only one, *L. camara,* is suitable for containers indoors and out. In the wild, it grows several feet high, but in a pot it can be tamed to a foot in height by judicious pruning. When not in bloom, the small, fuzzy leaves are not much to look at, but lantana is a lovely sight when in flower, and it has a long season of bloom, from spring well into fall. The round flower clusters, about an inch or so in diameter, are crammed with tiny buds that open from the outside of the circle. The first florets to open are yellow, then orange and red or a combination of pink and lilac appear. A trailing form, *L. montevidensis,* has cascades of rosy-lavender flowers and makes an elegant hanging basket plant. Leaves and flowers of all forms are fragrant.

Lantana camara

Light: Indoors and outdoors: bright light, some full sun.

Soil: Basic Soil Mix, page 28.

Moisture: Water thoroughly, let dry somewhat between waterings.

Fertilizer: Dilute liquid fertilizer every two to three weeks. When blooming, give low-nitrogen formula.

Care: For prolific bloom, pinch back growing tips in late winter and again in spring before buds form. Summer the plant outdoors and remove spent flowers for continuous bloom. When bloom season is over, cut down branches to 5 or 6 inches from the base. It will need less water during the rest period, but keep the plant in good light. New growth will soon appear. Repot when roots emerge from drainage hole.

Propagation: Tip cuttings without buds or flowers taken in summer or early spring root readily in moist rooting mix or in water. You can also grow a new plant from a short growing tip. Give it a touch of rooting hormone and insert it into the soil where the parent is growing. Keep it moist.

Remarks: A bushy lantana loaded with bright, colorful, globular blooms is a pretty sight on the terrace or deck, or cascading from a hanging basket. I find the pungent, lemony fragrance of foliage and flowers delightful. Outdoors, this scent draws butterflies, an added bonus. Occasionally it draws an unwelcome visitor: white fly. Control at once with insecticidal spray and hose spray (see Pests and Problems, page 57).

How to Grow a Lantana Tree or Standard: Lantana lends itself well to being grown as a standard which will live for many years. Start with a vigorous young plant in a 4- or 5-inch pot. Remove most of the side branches, leaving only the four to six nearest the top. Insert a small, narrow stake and tie the stem to it. Fertilize it well and give plenty of sun. As it grows, it will need a larger, sturdy clay pot and a taller stake. When the stem is about a foot high, cut back on the terminal bud, or tip, which forces fuller side growth. These new side branches should be nipped back to about 5 inches. They will branch out some more and must be pinched again. The plant will attempt to sprout little side growths on the trunk; rub these off with your finger. Over two to three years, the lantana will develop a bushy, rounded mound of foliage at the top that will flower profusely from spring to late fall. Remove spent flowers. Prune before spring flowering and again after flowering ends. Summer it outdoors. After its winter rest it will need a rich topdressing or a transfer to a larger pot. It will eventually reach a height of 3 to 4 feet, and the roots will need more room. Keep it well fertilized and watered except during winter, when it should not be pushed; it deserves a rest. Always provide good bright light. Other flowering plants that can be trained successfully as standards are geranium, fuchsia, and hibiscus. These little flowering trees are big, beautiful eyecatchers.

GENUS: *Lily*
FAMILY: Lilium (Lily)

Lilies have lent a stylish beauty to gardens for centuries, and they are absolutely elegant in containers in any outdoor living area as well. Of the hundreds of species, the Asiatic hybrids are the most suitable for pot culture because they do not grow as tall, generally 2½ to 3 feet or slightly higher, as most of the other kinds. The array of colors from cool, pale pastels to warm, vibrant tones is dazzling, and the seductive fragrances are an added bonus. Bloom time is from late spring to midsummer, depending on the variety. Lilies develop offsets and multiply quite rapidly, but the bulblets take several years before they are of blooming size.

Light: Indoors and outdoors: bright, some full sun, some light shade. It's an old axiom that lilies should have their heads in the sun and their feet in the shade. This is easier to accomplish in the perennial border than in containers. To help soil and roots keep cool, mulch the surface with peat, pebbles, wood or stone chips, gravel, bits of twigs or shards, and pine needles. Try to avoid midday glare and heat.

Soil: Lilies need rich, light, well-drained soil. To Peaty Basic Soil Mix (page 28) add some extra sand or perlite and a dash of bonemeal or dried cow manure.

Moisture: Water new shoots plentifully and keep the soil moist. Spray lightly for added humidity. Outdoors, be watchful for dry soil in warm, sunny weather. Roots must not dry out. Taper off watering as leaves turn yellow and wither, but don't stop altogether. Even in dormancy, roots must be kept slightly moist. See Storage.

Fertilizer: Dilute liquid fertilizer weekly in active growth. When buds appear, give low-nitrogen fertilizer, higher in phosphorus and potash. Stop when foliage dies.

By this time, the bulb has stored the nutrients it will use for next season's growth and bloom.

Care: Use an 8- or 10-inch sturdy clay pot for planting, as lilies have big root systems. For optimum drainage, place a handful of gravel or pebbles on the bottom of the pot over the drainage-hole shard. Add soil and set in bulb so that its top is about 3 to 4 inches below the surface of the soil; stem-rooting lilies, including the Asiatics, need this depth. Insert a $2\frac{1}{2}$- to 3-foot stake, add remainder of soil, and firm down. Water well. Keep the soil moderately moist until shoots appear, then give good light and ample water. Bring the pot outdoors when night temperatures become mild, and move it gradually into bright sunlight. Morning sun, which is bright but not too strong, is the best.

Lilium candidum

Storage: After the flowers fade, cut them off, but retain leaves and stems, which nourish the bulb for next season's bloom. Continue watering and fertilizing until leaves wither and die. Set the pot in a cool, dim, or dark spot such as a protected sunporch, unheated cellar, or attic, where the bulb will not freeze. Over winter, the lily will be dormant, but must not be allowed to dry out completely, as the roots remain alive and need to be kept slightly moist. Several pots clustered together may be surrounded with damp peat or sphagnum moss, or may be covered or mulched for added protection. You must remember to peek and poke now and then to check the soil for dryness, and if necessary, add a little water. If the roots dry out altogether, the plant may die.

Propagation: Small bulbs or bulblets develop around the base of the bulb and may be detached in late winter or early spring for propagation. They may also be left on the mother bulb to increase in size and await potting for another year. It takes at least three years for bulblets to reach blooming size. Take care not to break off tiny bulblets or new growth when you explore the soil. When topdressing, spoon up an inch or two of the old soil before adding a rich, organic, loose mixture of fresh soil. Repot when roots and bulblets fill the pot.

Remarks: Even more thrilling than the first year's bloom is the reappearance of new growth, buds, and flowers the second time around and perhaps more times after that. Good soil and nutrients, sunshine and water, and proper storage from fall to spring with slight amounts of moisture given in dormancy will do the trick. A threat to young growth in spring is very heavy spring rains. Move the outdoor containers to a sheltered spot so that the roots don't get hopelessly waterlogged. Put them right back in the sun when the storm is over.

Special Notes: *Lilium longiflorum,* the Easter lily, commonly forced for spring bloom, cannot be forced a second year, but if planted out in the garden, it will bloom again the next year. The beloved *L. candidum,* the Madonna lily, whose pure white trumpets are highly fragrant, grows 3 to 4 feet tall and blooms in early summer. A recommended cultivar is 'Cascade'. Plant only an inch deep; these are not stem-rooting. Excellent choices for container growing include 'Enchantment', an Asiatic, glowing orange-red, that grows 3 to 4 feet tall; and 'Stargazer', an Oriental, crimson with white margins, that grows 2 to 3 feet tall. Taller lilies such as the magnificent *L. regale,* white with a yellow throat, and *L. speciosum rubrum,* deep rose and white, may be container-grown but will require large, deep pots and tall stakes to accommodate heavy root growth and to withstand windy weather.

GENUS: *Maranta*
FAMILY: Marantaceae (Arrowroot)

M. leuconeura, the prayer plant, is native to Brazil. A low-growing tropical forest plant rarely over a foot tall, it has many forms, all with spectacular foliage. *M.l. erythroneura* may be the most popular and colorful, with dark green blotches on lighter green, 5- to 6-inch oval leaves. Light green markings line the midrib, and both rib and lateral veins are rose-red. The underside of the leaf is purplish-red. This is a real beauty. Another form, *M.l.* 'Kerchoviana', the rabbit's foot or rabbit's tracks plant, has light gray-green leaves with brown or green blotches and a grey-green reverse. *M.l.* 'Massangeana' has deep green leaves with a silvery-white center rib and markings and a burgundy reverse. Closely related to calathea, one is often mistaken or mislabeled for the other. Both species are grown in the same way. Rarely, narrow spikes of insignificant lavender flowers appear.

Maranta leuconeura erythroneura

Light: Indoors: filtered, indirect, or medium. Outdoors: partial to full shade. Direct sun scorches the foliage.

Soil: Peaty Basic Soil Mix, page 28.

Moisture: Water plentifully and keep moist. For the extra humidity that these plants crave, mist frequently and provide pebble tray or double pot.

Fertilizer: Dilute liquid fertilizer every two to three weeks.

Care: Keep maranta moist, humid, warm, and out of drafts and direct sun.

Propagation: When roots crowd the pot, remove the plant in spring and divide clumps with a few leaves attached to each portion of root. Repot in rich, organic soil. Stem cuttings should have the leafstalk sheath, seen at the bottom of the stalk, taken off before placing them in rooting mix. As marantas are shallow-rooted plants, they should be grown in shallow pots or half-pots.

Remarks: The prayer plant folds up its leaves when darkness falls and opens them in the light. What it prays for is uncertain, but if the leaves stay closed in the day-time, you can be sure it is praying for better light. Try moving the plant to a slightly brighter spot. Curling, droopy leaves will warn you if it is too bright. Marantas have outstandingly beautiful foliage and are not difficult to grow if their needs are met. An extra spritz a day with the mister helps to keep them happy. Tip: Add some damp sphagnum moss to the surface of the soil around the base of the stems to help retain moisture.

Genus: *Nematanthus*
Family: Gesneriaceae (Gesneriad)

Goldfish plant, candy corn plant (also known as *Hypocyrta glabra*). Native to Brazil. This trop-ical forest epiphyte is a gesneriad that likes warm and humid conditions. The 1- to 2-foot stems are closely packed with small, glossy green leaves that are succulent in appearance and in their ability to store water. The flowers emerge in the leaf axils all along the stems from spring through fall. Puffy in shape, they are bright yellow as they open, then gradually become vivid orange; with their pursed little red "mouths," they truly resemble goldfish.

Light: Indoors and outdoors: bright or fil-tered; some sun that is not too strong.

Nematanthus

Soil: Peaty Basic Soil Mix (page 28) with a little extra sand for good drainage.

Moisture: Water well and keep slightly moist. This jungle plant appreciates frequent misting and a humidity tray. High humidity plus warm temperatures are very important.

Fertilizer: Dilute liquid fertilizer every two to three weeks. Taper off in fall, but if the plant continues blooming, which it may do, fertilize lightly in winter.

Care: The shallow-rooted goldfish plant is well suited to a shallow pot. Judicious pruning can keep it upright, but it is most attractive as a trailing plant. It flowers most profusely when somewhat potbound. Trim back in early spring to keep a compact shape, if that is desired. Some trimming will result in more sidebranching and flowering. Repotting is not necessary for a few years. Give rich, porous soil.

Propagation: Tip cuttings in moist rooting mix. Keep warm.

Remarks: This shrubby plant with its odd, bright, pouchy, fishmouthed blossoms is an excellent choice for a hanging basket or any place where its stems may cascade. Given optimum conditions, it may bloom almost continuously—a rare delight!

Palms

FAMILY: Palmae (Palm)

Palms, which add so much beauty and charm to warm climate landscapes, make elegant additions to interiors of colder regions, and to their exterior living areas, as well, in summer. Most of the thousands of species grow very tall in their native tropical habitats. Those most popular as potted plants are sold as juveniles, and grow very slowly, taking many years to become outsized. A few are small forms and remain quite small. The varieties that follow are easy to grow and quite adaptable to variations in light and temperature. A big plus for palms is that they don't need a front row in the sunlight that is so often a scarce commodity in many homes.

Chamaerops humilis

Chamaedorea elegans

Formerly *Neanthe bella.* Parlor palm. Native to Central America. This Victorian favorite is still one of the most popular and easy-to-grow choices of palms for containers. One of the smallest, it seldom exceeds 3 feet. A tolerant plant, it stoically endures low to medium light if it must, but does require more water than some other species. The parlor palm has graceful, feathery foliage.

Chamaerops humilis

European fan palm. The only palm native to Europe. Like the parlor palm, it is one of the shorter species and requires more moisture than most other palms. Its narrow, deeply cut leaves arranged in a large fan shape up to 2 feet wide grow to about 4 feet high. This species needs plenty of bright light with some full sun.

Howea

Also called *Kentia* palm. Often sold as sentry palm. Native to Lord Howe Island in the South Pacific. Large, dark green, rather feathery fronds on single stems are very slow growing. This palm will tolerate low to medium light and dry air. *H. belmoreana* bears gracefully curving leaflets on erect leafstalks. *H. forsteriana,* the paradise or Kentia palm, extends its leaflets more horizontally, making it a more widespread form. Both can grow up to 8 feet, but height can be controlled by keeping the plant in a rather tight pot until it becomes very overcrowded; repot only every few years. These palms are the darlings of hotel lobbies, and are excellent, trouble-free choices as dramatic accent plants in a big room. They are handsome, dependable, low-light choices.

Howea belmoreana

Rhapis excelsa

Lady palm, bamboo palm. Native to China. Lady palm is one of the best choices for container growing. Fan-shaped fronds have five to seven segments and grow in bamboo-like clumps very, very slowly, eventually reaching 3 to 5 feet. Lady palm tolerates fairly low light and dry air if it must, but likes to be well watered. Leaflets are broader than in some other forms and the plant has a bushy appearance. *R.e. variegata* is striped yellow and green. Dwarfs in many green and variegated varieties are durable and decorative.

Light: Indoors: good light, no direct sun. Most palms are quite tolerant of low to medium light, where they will survive but not grow vigorously. Outdoors: light or part shade in summer suits them well.

Soil: Peaty Basic Soil Mix, page 28. Add a handful of extra sand for drainage and a sprinkle of bonemeal and dehydrated cow manure.

Moisture: Water thoroughly and keep slightly moist. Palms abhor wet feet, so it's better to err on the dry side. Frequent misting is beneficial, especially for the palms from humid tropical regions; they will also benefit from a humidity tray.

Fertilizer: Dilute liquid feeding monthly, more frequently for large plants in large containers that will not be repotted again.

Care: Palms don't like to have their roots disturbed. Since they don't mind a crowded pot, repot in spring only when the plant becomes extremely pot-bound, every few years. Handle the roots with care, and trim long, tangled ones before repotting. Spray newly potted or repotted plants frequently. When largest convenient pot size is reached, topdress with rich, organic soil. Cut off lower fronds that turn brown and dry, as well as brown tips of fronds.

Propagation: Propagation of palms for the home gardener is difficult and is not recommended.

Remarks: Palms are admired for their tropical grace and exotic, even romantic charm. Yet, because they are survivors, they are often treated shabbily and that is how they become—shabby. Why not make a palm happy and more beautiful? Provide a rich, organic, well-drained soil, some additional nutrients, good light, and sufficient water so that they don't dry out. Treat them to a summer outdoors in a sheltered, semi-shady spot where you can spray them with the garden hose from time to time. A tip: if you must keep a palm indoors in a dim spot, move it into brighter light every now and then for a few days. It will be most appreciative.

GENUS: *Pelargonium*
FAMILY: Geraniaceae (Geranium)

Geranium. Native to South Africa. The versatile geranium thrives almost anywhere and is one of the most popular plants for pot, window box, hanging basket, and other forms of container culture. Bright and colorful in flowers, foliage, or both; some upright, some trailing, some scented, this vast genus is divided into four main groups. These are easygoing plants that thrive with plenty of sunshine and a dry atmosphere.

The Four Groups of Geraniums

P. hortorum hybrids. These common bedding or garden geraniums have plain green leaves or fancy leaves. The fancy-leaved, or zonal geraniums, have two or three colors and borders or markings inside the margins of the leaves in shades of brown, red, gold, cream, or white. They flower from spring to late fall in dense red, coral, pink, white, and salmon clusters. Also look for new dazzling orange. Miniature forms are ideal for windowsills and small spaces indoors or out. Many grow no more than 4 or 5 inches high. Feed sparingly or they will outgrow their dwarfism.

P. domesticum hybrids. These regals, or Lady Washington hybrids, have a different flowering season, from early spring to midsummer. No fancy foliage here, but the blooms are very large and showy in a wide color range. Many are bicolored and some have darker blotches, giving the flowers a "pansy" look. When their bloom time ends in midsummer, the regals take their rest period and need only enough water to keep from drying out. Start moderate watering in early fall and gradually increase to regular levels. Culture otherwise is the same as for the hortorum hybrids.

Pelargonium hortorum

P. peltatum hybrids. The ivy-leaved geranium. This trailing variety has stems that spread and droop 2 to 3 feet. The glossy, bright green, rather fleshy leaves are ivy-shaped. Some are variegated white and green. Bloom time is spring to fall, in a wide range of colors. The ivy-leaved geranium makes a splendid hanging basket. When the leaves die back in autumn, store the plant in its pot in a cool, dark place. When new growth appears in late winter or early spring, bring it back into the light and water well. Give brighter light gradually. Pinch back growing shoots for a fuller plant with more flowers, which will appear in spring.

Scented geraniums. The leaf is the big attraction, not the rather insignificant flowers. All-green foliage in various sizes and attractive shapes offers a variety of delightful scents when lightly pressed or rubbed between the fingers. Take your choice of apple (*P. odoratissimum*), lime (*P. nervosum*), lemon (*P. Lemon crispum*), nutmeg and spice (*P. fragrans,* 'Old Spice'), cinnamon (*P. limoneum*), rose (*P. graveolens*), peppermint (*P. tomentosum*) and other fruity and pungent aromas. These forms don't need as much sun as others do; good bright light, not direct sun, suits them fine. So does a cool, bright window indoors. Scented geraniums make grand gifts especially appreciated by shut-ins, hospital patients, and their visitors.

Light: Indoors and outdoors: full sun at least half a day, good bright light always.

Soil: Basic Soil Mix (page 28); add a dash of bonemeal.

Moisture: Moderate. Let soil get quite dry between waterings. Don't mist, and provide good air circulation, to avoid possibility of mildew.

Fertilizer: Fertilizers higher in potash and phosphorus rather than nitrogen will promote abundant blooms and good leaf color. Apply every two or three weeks from early spring until October.

Care: Geraniums bloom best when slightly potbound. Repot only when roots fill the pot and come out of the drainage hole. Remove the plant, shake off old soil carefully, trim over-long roots, and repot in one size larger pot with fresh soil. If root growth is not excessively thick, the plant can be repotted in the same pot with fresh soil. Do the repotting just before the plant blooms. Cut back top growth to within 4 to 6 inches of the base. Drench, then water sparingly until new growth appears. Pinch growing tips. You may sacrifice a few early buds, but you will get a much bushier plant with a great many more flowers. Do not overwater; stems rot in soggy soil and the plant may die. If the geranium is in a container with other plants, exercise care in watering. Remember too that this plant grows wide with large leaves that may shade out smaller, less vigorous plants. Wax begonias, ivy, coleus, wandering Jew, and trailing blue lobelia, an annual, are good companions in a planter outdoors.

Pelargonium peltatum

Wintering Over Plants That Bloomed Outdoors: Geraniums can be saved for another season in a variety of ways. They can be cut back to 5 or 6 inches from the base and given a rest period in a cool, dark basement; provide them with just enough water to keep the stems from shriveling. This may also be done without cutting them down first. In frost-free springtime, water lightly; when new leaves appear, give fertilizer, light, and sufficient water and set outside. Or, prune plants in fall, place pots in a bright spot by a window and water sparingly until new growth appears. Then give regular care. Repot large, older plants in early spring and take cuttings for propagation before buds start to form. Keep cool;

too much heat in winter prevents bud formation. An overwintering plant by a sunny, cool window may bloom during the winter. Fertilize lightly and prune back leggy growth. New growth sprouts on old, woody stems.

Propagation: Geraniums are easy to propagate. Tip cuttings without buds or flowers will root in water. Or place a cutting in moist rooting mix or sand alone. If the bottom end is allowed to dry and the cutting is dipped in hormone rooting powder, it may take root more quickly. Position it near medium-bright light and keep it warm and lightly moist. In a few weeks, when well rooted and showing new growth, pot the little plant in a 3- or 4-inch pot with basic soil, and provide good light and sufficient water. Do not mist; humidity invites mildew. Cuttings may be taken in summer, fall, or late winter. They should be no more than 3 to 4 inches long, and half that size if taken from the miniature or dwarf forms.

Grooming: To promote the most profuse bloom and to keep geraniums healthy and beautiful, snap off dead flower heads and stems and remove dead, yellow, discolored, or mildewed leaves. For fuller, bushier plants and more flowers, pinch back all forms when young. Pinchings may root quickly if placed in water or planted right back in the pot, and kept damp and lightly shaded.

Remarks: Where summers are hot and humid, particularly in the East, gardeners may find that their geraniums bloom less abundantly. In a hot spell, the ivy-leaved forms and the regals will falter and will not produce many blooms until cool nights return. In cooler weather they will perk up and bloom abundantly, often as late as October, until a cold snap arrives. Pacific Northwest gardeners have cooler summers and the most luxuriant geraniums. But geraniums can be grown almost anywhere and may well be the most popular flowering plant for container culture world-wide. New hybrids are constantly being developed by growers in stunning colors and combinations of colors, many with a higher tolerance of heat or less bright light, some with a more compact, branching habit of growth and more abundant flowers. Look for them in spring and summer in garden centers.

Like lantanas, geraniums may be grown as standards with one center stem and side branches only at the top. See *Lantana* for details. They thrive for many years with loving treatment, which includes plenty of sunlight and nourishment. A scented geranium tree with sweet or spicy fragrance to its leaves is sure to be a much-admired treasure.

GENUS: *Peperomia*
FAMILY: Piperaceae (Pepper)

Native of tropical South and Central America. Of the hundreds of species of these warmth-and-humidity-loving plants, several are very popular and useful as small, attractive container plants. Perhaps the best known is *P. argyreia*, commonly known as the watermelon peperomia. It has dark green, shiny leaves with lengthwise silvery-white stripes that resemble watermelons; the leafstalks are red. *P. obtusifolia* 'Variegata', the baby rubber plant, has smooth, waxy, creamy-white and bright green leaves. *P. caperata* 'Emerald Ripple' has very unusual leaves, rich green and deeply wrinkled with brownish valleys. This is a more compact variety than most other peperomias. There are many other varieties with variegated green and yellow foliage. Most have red leafstalks and bear odd flower spikes in spring that resemble white mouse tails, also on red stalks. They are all low-growing plants that rarely exceed 10 inches in height. Also look for *P. magnoliifolia* 'Rainbow', whose thick, leathery, green and cream leaves have lovely pink borders.

Peperomia caperata

Light:	Indoors: bright or filtered light. Variegated foliage can take more light than green. Outdoors: filtered or dappled sun, light shade.
Soil:	Peaty Basic Soil Mix, page 28.
Moisture:	Moderate. Thick, succulent leaves retain moisture. Let soil get quite dry between waterings; avoid wet feet at all times. Peperomias need humidity, however, so misting and a pebble tray will help.
Fertilizer:	A light feeding once a month is sufficient.
Care:	No special demands. Pinch back growing tips for a bushier plant.
Propagation:	Short tip cuttings in spring in moist rooting mix. You may also be able to root a leaf with some stem attached.
Remarks:	Peperomias are pretty foliage plants for small spaces. In medium light, they will manage nicely with additional light from a 100 or 150 watt incandescent bulb a few feet away for several hours daily.

GENUS: *Philodendron*
FAMILY: Araceae (Arum)

Native of South and Central America and the West Indies. This large family of handsome foliage plants includes a number of vining and non-vining varieties that are easy to grow, dependable, and long-lived. The climbers have aerial roots that in the wild cling to trees and in containers need support. Some of these climbers, and most of the non-vining or self-heading types, are plants with large leaves that may require plenty of space. All need only basic, simple care.

Philodendron oxycardium, also called *Philodendron cordatum.* Most common of all, the heartleaf philodendron will hang or climb almost anywhere and to great lengths. Trim back to keep it controlled.

P. bipennifolium: Fiddle-leaf philodendron. This climber has large leaves, up to 10 inches, that resemble violins.

P. selloum. A big and wide plant, this one has huge, deeply divided or lobed leaves that need a lot of space. It has an attractive tropical look. Keep it potbound to discourage it from growing too fast too soon.

P. erubescens. A large-leaved climber with interesting coloration. New leaves are pinkish, gradually turning coppery-green with red undersides. Stems are reddish, too. Look for *P.e.* 'Royal Queen'.

P. radiatum or *dubium.* A climber with leaves that are heart-shaped and deeply lobed.

P. wendlandii. This variety grows in a rosette of immense bright green leaves that is pleasingly symmetrical from all sides.

P. 'Burgundy', a hybrid, has foot-long arrow shaped leaves that are green above and deep burgundy-red below, with red leafstalks and red stems. It's beautiful and, fortunately, a slow grower.

P. bipinnatifidum. This variety doesn't grow as tall (to about 4 feet) as some others but has immense leaves, over a foot long and as wide. The leaves are sharply and deeply cut. This

Philodendron '**Burgundy**'

impressive, tropical-looking specimen is a fine choice for a poorly lit spot. Give it plenty of space.

Light: Indoors: filtered, indirect, medium. Outdoors: semi-shade or shade.

Soil: Peaty Basic Soil Mix (page 28); add a dash of dried manure.

Moisture: Ample water. keep moist. Mist for extra humidity.

Fertilizer: Light liquid feeding, monthly; less to control large size.

Care: Philodendrons are undemanding—it's part of their charm. Light is not a priority. Extra humidity is not vital, albeit enjoyed. Ordinary indoor temperatures are acceptable; anything above freezing is tolerated, and so is occasional neglect in the form of lack of water, fertilizer, or soil enrichment. A climber, of course, needs something to climb on. Some can be purchased already attached to a slab of bark. For others, insert a stout stick or pole deeply into the pot and wrap thickly with sphagnum moss. Tie it firmly with string all the way up, dampen and keep moist. As the plant grows and needs a larger pot, it may also need a taller support. Initially, aerial roots will be encouraged to dig in if the stem is tied to the dampened mossy support or moist bark. As a philodendron grows older, you may notice that the leaves are getting smaller. This could indicate that you are taking advantage of its good nature. Try giving water and fertilizer more regularly

Philodendron cordatum

and check to see if the roots have completely filled the pot. Repotting may be needed. If leaves and stems are pale and droopy, it may need a bit more light. Like all large-leaved plants, foliage should get an occasional wash.

Propagation: Place tip and stem cuttings in water, where they may live for a long time and look very decorative; or, pot rooted cuttings for new plants.

Remarks: The vast variety and ease of growth and maintenance offered by the philodendrons make them attractive and useful to every container plant gardener. To control large size, keep the big ones slightly dry, cool, hungry, and potbound.

GENUS: *Pilea*
FAMILY: Urticaceae (Nettle)

Native to tropical southeast Asia. This small, easy-to-grow plant has a great many species and varieties, most of them upright, not over 10 to 12 inches tall, and some trailing. They all like warmth and humidity. Most of them bear clusters of tiny, unremarkable, white or pinkish flowers. *P. cadierei*, the aluminum plant or watermelon pilea, has silvery markings like aluminum paint on puckered green leaves. *P.c.* 'Minima' grows to only about 6 inches and has very small leaves. *P. involucrata*, the Pan-American friendship plant or Panamiga, is a showy plant whose corrugated leaves appear coppery-green above and reddish-purple below when grown in bright light. In less light, foliage is greener and less colorful. Other Panamigas have silver stripes and dots on olive-green leaves. One particularly handsome form,

Pilea cadierei

P. mollis, known as 'Moon Valley', has very deeply quilted, rich green leaves with bronzy valleys. The center portion of the leaf takes on a bronze tint as well. This one is a beauty with an interesting texture. The creeping or hanging pileas, *P. depressa*, Creeping Jenny, and *P. nummulariifolia*, Creeping Charlie, have tiny leaves and make nice basket plants of small size.

Light: Indoors: bright or filtered. Outdoors: filtered, dappled sun, part shade.

Soil: Peaty Basic Soil Mix, page 28. Shallow pots are best for these small root systems.

Moisture: Moderate. Let soil get almost dry before next watering. Pilea abhors soggy soil but craves humidity. Give pebble tray, and mist.

Fertilizer: Dilute liquid fertilizer every two to three weeks.

Care: No special demands. Nip back growing tips for a bushier plant. As it ages, pilea loses lower leaves. Stems that have become rather bare and straggly may be cut back to their base in early spring. A 3- to 4-inch pot generally is sufficiently large for a single plant.

Propagation: Place tip cuttings in moist rooting mix or in water.

Remarks: Like peperomia, pilea is an easy, compact, attractive foliage plant well suited to small spaces and a good mixer with other small plants in a bowl or group planting. This is not a plant that grows old gracefully, however. I suggest that you don't try to keep old, bare-legged specimens going; make fresh starts with vigorous young plants propagated from tip cuttings.

GENUS: *Plectranthus*
FAMILY: Labiatae (Mint)

Plectranthus australis

Swedish ivy. Candle plant. Native to South Africa and Australia. This is a popular, undemanding trailing plant. *P. oertendahlii* has round, slightly scalloped, green leaves with silvery-white veins. *P. australis* has darker green leaves and a more upright, less sprawling habit of growth. Both produce spikes of insignificant, pale pinkish or lavender flowers that resemble those of their close relative, coleus, which may be pinched off in order to conserve energy for the foliage.

Light: Indoors and outdoors: bright or filtered; some shade outdoors is tolerated.

Soil: Basic Soil Mix, page 28.

Moisture: Water plentifully and keep moist.

Fertilizer: Dilute liquid fertilizer every two to three weeks.

Care: No special demands. Pinch back growing tips frequently for denser growth. Long, dangling, older stems lose leaves near the base. Prune back hard and new leaves will soon appear.

Propagation: Tip cuttings root easily in water as well as rooting mix, and may even be tucked back into the soil of their pot. Nodes of stems lying on the soil often take root there.

Remarks: Swedish ivy is a fast-growing, easy-care plant, desirable for its lush display in a pot or hanging basket indoors and out. Since it is so easy to propagate, I suggest you get rid of old, straggly specimens that have lost many leaves and start a fresh container of lively rooted cuttings.

GENUS: *Rhipsalidopsis*
FAMILY: Cactaceae (Cactus)

Easter cactus. *R. gaertneri*, formerly called *Schlumbergera gaertneri*. This species of epiphytic jungle cactus has stems of narrow, slightly notched segments, and bears one to three scarlet flowers at the stem ends and also between the segments. The stems droop as they grow, and a mature plant is a splendid candidate for a hanging basket. *R. rosea* has smaller stem segments with pink flowers. Hybrids of both forms have pink, rose, or red flowers, and begin to bloom when still quite small. Flowers appear in early spring.

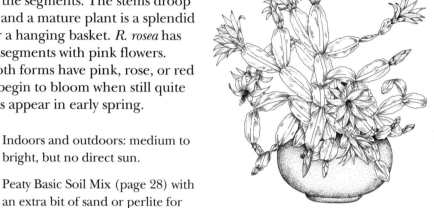

Rhipsalidopsis gaertneri

Light: Indoors and outdoors: medium to bright, but no direct sun.

Soil: Peaty Basic Soil Mix (page 28) with an extra bit of sand or perlite for porosity.

Moisture: Water plentifully and keep moist from late winter or early spring until flowering ends. Reduce watering while plant takes a rest in summer. When new growth appears, resume moderate watering. Mist for humidity; this is a jungle, not a desert, cactus.

Fertilizer: Starting in late winter, give biweekly high-potash formula feeding to encourage bud formation. Stop when plenty of buds appear and open. After flowering, feed all-purpose formula once a month.

Care and Reblooming: These cacti require the same treatment as the Christmas and Thanksgiving cacti (see *Schlumbergera*, page 188). The schedule of flowering is different, as the Easter cactus blooms in spring. Like the other species, the Easter cactus will form buds if it continues to spend time outdoors as the weather cools down. In a frost-free climate this would be autumn and early winter. Alternatively, follow the short-day treatment as described on page 189 but start it a couple of months later to initiate March or April blooming.

Propagation: Detach stem segments; let dry for a day. Insert one end upright into moist potting soil. Easy to propagate.

Remarks: These beautiful flowers show off best in a hanging basket.

GENUS: *Sansevieria*
FAMILY: Agavaceae (Agave)

Snake plant. Also called mother-in-law tongue, devil's tongue, lucky plant. A succulent. Native to West Africa and India. With that collection of common names, this has got to be one tough plant. Snake plant is indeed almost indestructible, enduring extremes of temperature, lack of light, and other indignities with great forbearance. *S. trifasciata*, the most common form, has marbled light and dark green stiff, sword-shaped leaves. *S.t.* 'Laurentii' adds yellow edges. Both can grow to a height of 2 feet or more. The bird's nest snake plant, *S.t.* 'Hahnii', has short broad leaves that grow in a rosette shape. Prettiest of all is *S.t.* 'Golden Hahnii' with broad golden-yellow borders. These small rosette forms fit nicely on windowsills. A spike of small, yellowish-white, fragrant flowers appears occasionally.

Sansevieria trifasciata

Light: Indoors and outdoors: bright light and some sun is preferred, but medium to low light is tolerated. Colorful 'Golden Hahnii', however, needs sun.

Soil: Basic Soil Mix (page 28) with some sand or perlite added for drainage.

Moisture: Moderate. Let soil dry somewhat between waterings.

Fertilizer: Dilute liquid fertilizer monthly.

Care: No demands. Snake plant rarely needs repotting. Wait until it grows too large for its pot, or until it cracks the pot open.

Propagation: Remove an overcrowded snake from its pot and with a sharp knife, cut through clusters of roots and leaves. Replant each segment separately. Horizontal slices of a leaf will take root in moist sand or rooting mix, but must be planted the way they grew on the leaf. They remember which end is up.

Remarks: Often a neglected dust-gatherer in a dim corner, the snake stubbornly survives and may even flower. Given better light, a drink, and a nourishing snack now and then, it can be a handsome and long-lived dramatic accent.

GENUS: *Saxifraga*
FAMILY: Saxifragaceae (Saxifrage)

S. stolonifera is the one species in the saxifrage genus that is commonly grown indoors. Called strawberry begonia, strawberry geranium, roving sailor, and mother-of-thousands, it is none of those—although the latter nickname comes closest in view of the numerous progeny a single plant can produce. Native to China and Japan, this is a small, low-growing plant 6 to 8 inches tall, whose roundish, lightly scalloped, hairy, gray-green leaves with silvery-white veins and wine red reverse emerge on red stems in a rosette form. Narrow red threadlike runners grow out from the center and develop plantlets at their ends. Either they root themselves within the pot on the surface of the soil, or creep over the edge of the pot and dangle. This looks very cute and makes the mother an ideal candidate for a hanging basket. *S.s.* 'Tricolor' adds rosy pink to green and cream, and is most colorful in a sunny spot; however, it is not as easy to grow or as prolific. Saxifraga bears small white flowers on spikes in summer.

Light: Indoors: bright or filtered light. Outdoors: filtered light or part shade. The variegated form needs brighter light and some direct sun indoors and out.

Soil: Peaty Basic Soil Mix, page 28.

Moisture: Water plentifully and keep moist. Mist and provide pebble tray.

Fertilizer: Light liquid feeding once a month in growing season.

Care: No special demands.

Propagation: The numerous slender red stolons, or runners, that the strawberry begonia sends out, like those of the strawberry plant, are looking for a place to root the tiny plantlets that develop at their tips. You can let them dangle and look decorative, or set them firmly in little pots with good soil near the mother plant and let them take root. In a short time, the babies can make it on their own and you can cut the umbilical cords. Keep moist and give good light. Soon these youngsters will send out their own stolons and begin a new generation of saxifragas. Often the runners take root and produce new plants within the confines of the pot rather than creep over the rim.

Saxifraga stolonifera

These too may be lifted and potted. A runner may also find its way on to the surface of any nearby potted plant and root itself happily there.

Remarks: This small, pretty, appealing plant looks charming in a hanging basket or anywhere its runners can venture forth. Clearly, you will soon have saxifragas to give away. This plant is fun for children to grow.

GENUS: *Schlumbergera*
FAMILY: Cactaceae (Cactus)

These two varieties of succulent cactus are epiphytes, native to tropical forests rather than
deserts, growing in bits of debris and organic
matter in the crevices of branches. They thrive
with plenty of moisture and warmth. The
plants are not much to look at, but they
deserve coddling for their dazzling blooms.

Schlumbergera truncata

S. truncata, also called *Zygocactus truncatus.*
Thanksgiving cactus, claw or crab cactus. The
stems are formed of sharply notched, flat segments, with hooked or claw-like projections at
the end of the segment. Vivid rose-red flowers,
singly or in pairs, appear at terminal points and are long-lasting. They usually
appear around Thanksgiving but may open earlier or later. Various hybrids have
pink, violet, salmon, and white flowers.

S. bridgesii. Christmas cactus. These stem segments are slightly notched, almost
smooth. The flowers may be red, pink, yellow, coral, or white. New colors include
two-toned pink and bicolor red and white. Growers promote heavy flowering in
time for the Christmas season. Flowering may begin earlier or later for the home
gardener trying to induce bloom for mid-December.

Light:	Indoors: good bright light, some full sun. Outdoors: also bright light, but avoid blaze of noon.
Soil:	Peaty Basic Soil Mix (page 28) with a bit of extra sand or perlite for porosity.
Moisture:	Ample watering. Keep soil moist while actively growing and flowering. Decrease watering after flowering, while the plant takes a rest; increase again in spring when new growth appears. Misting is appreciated. These jungle plants like humidity.
Fertilizer:	The big attraction here is the flowers, so to boost bud formation start in early spring with a biweekly low-nitrogen, high phosphorus-potash formula such as 10-30-20 or 10-15-15. Stop when the plant blooms.
Care:	Schlumbergeras don't have large root systems. Even quite large plants are comfortable for years in 5- or 6-inch pots. Remove an older plant from its pot in early spring if it appears to have outgrown the pot. If the roots are not overly crowded, replace some soil with a fresh mixture and replant the cactus in the same pot. If the roots have filled the pot and are crowded, move the

plant into the next larger size pot with good fresh soil and a sprinkle of bone-meal. Mist to stimulate new growth.

Propagation: In late winter or early spring, detach one to three stem segments and let them dry for a few hours. Insert one end—two or three segments may be left joined together—into the recommended potting soil in a small pot, or place several segments in a larger pot. They take root readily but grow slowly. Water in moderation; soggy soil invites rot.

How to Induce Flowering: In early to mid-September, Thanksgiving and Christmas cacti are getting ready to form buds. The amount of light they receive is crucial. Begin the short-day treatment. Place the plants in a dark place—a box, closet, or under black plastic—for fourteen or fifteen uninterrupted hours, preferably where the temperature is cool. Bring them into the light for the remaining hours of daylight, say, from 8:00 A.M. to 5:00 or 6:00 P.M. Do this for eight to ten weeks, by which time buds should be visible. Bring the plants back into full light. During the short-day period, watering and fertilizing should not be neglected. Be especially careful not to overwater or let the soil get dried out. Handle these cacti gently and keep away from blasts of heat or cold air. The buds are extremely sensitive and might drop off. You can also initiate bud formation with a less urgent schedule. Plants happily summering outdoors can remain there even after summer is over and the other plants have been returned to the house. Cool temperatures will coax buds to form. Nights can get quite nippy, but short of a killing frost these cacti don't seem to mind at all, and they can soak up the sun all day. They may bud and flower even earlier and as profusely or more so than plants kept indoors, shunted about in the short-day period. The actual hours of light and dark are roughly equal to each other, but it's the cool, even chilly, late summer and early autumn nights that do the trick. If you don't have an

Schlumbergera bridgesii

outdoor area in which to leave your plants, you might try putting the cacti close to a cold window, keeping lights in that room off in the evenings and night. No guarantees. Occasionally a cactus will surprise you by producing buds without any special attention at all.

GENUS: *Scindapsus*
FAMILY: Araceae (Arum)

Devil's ivy, pothos. Native to Malaysia and East Asia. A close relative of philodendron, the heartleaf form of which it resembles, pothos is similarly a tolerant vining or hanging plant that is very useful in less than ideal environments. A traveler, it needs nipping back to keep it within reasonable bounds. Shiny, rather fleshy, heart-shaped leaves may be all green or attractively variegated. *S. aureus* 'Golden Queen' has stems and leaves that are more yellow than green. *S.a.* 'Marble Queen' has variegated white or cream and green stems and leaves. *S.a.* 'Tricolor' combines cream and yellow with two shades of green. *S. pictus* 'Argyraeus', the silver pothos, has silvery-white markings on gray-green leaves.

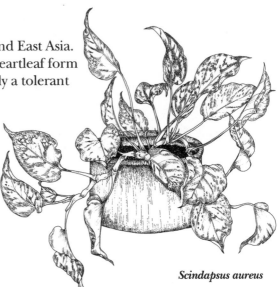

Scindapsus aureus

Light:	Indoors and outdoors: bright, indirect, filtered light or part shade. Colors tend to revert to green when the plant is in dim or poor light. Avoid direct sun.
Soil:	Basic Soil Mix, page 28.
Moisture:	Soak thoroughly, but let soil become rather dry before next watering.
Fertilizer:	Once a month is sufficient, but pothos thrives on less.
Care:	No special demands. Pothos, like vining philodendron, can easily be trained to grow on a slab of bark or moist sphagnum-wrapped pole into which it can sink its aerial roots. It's a fine trailing plant for a basket or pot on a shelf or table. Prune back overlong stems for a bushier, fuller look. Repot over-crowded plant in the next larger pot.
Propagation:	Again, like the vining philodendron or another related arum, syngonium, tip and stem cuttings root readily in water and can live contentedly in water for a long period of time.
Remarks:	Pothos is an easy-care, adaptable foliage plant that climbs or hangs attractively almost anywhere; just be careful to avoid blazing sunlight.

GENUS: *Sedum*
FAMILY: Crassulaceae (Orpine)

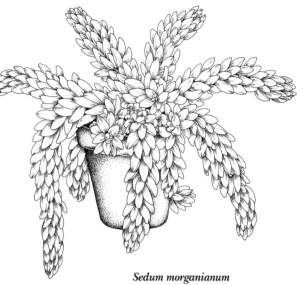

Sedum morganianum

Sedum morganianum. Donkey's tail, burro's tail, lamb's tail. Native to Mexico. The hundreds of sedums of infinite variety in shape and size are all succulents with thick leaves that can store water. The donkey's tail is a fascinating species that is easy to grow, propagate, and care for. It grows in trailing ropes of short, plump, gray-green, over-lapping leaves with a cylindrical or spindle shape ½- to 1-inch long. These are covered with a powdery bluish sheen called "bloom." In full sunlight, the leaves take on a handsome red tint. Donkey's tail "tails" can hang 4 feet or more and are highly decorative indoors and out, suspended from a basket. Terminal clusters of rose-pink flowers may appear in summer, but are rarely produced indoors. *S.m.* 'Burrito' is a miniature form.

Light: Indoors: full sun, as much as possible. Outdoors: full sun, but some filtered shade acceptable.

Soil: Half good potting soil or Basic Soil Mix (page 28) and half sand. The soil should drain well and not be moisture-retentive. Add a bit of bonemeal.

Moisture: Water thoroughly and let dry almost completely between waterings. In winter rest, give water infrequently; keep quite dry.

Fertilizer: Feed liquid dilute fertilizer lightly two or three times from early spring to early fall.

Care: This decorative hanging basket sedum has few demands. Provide plenty of sun all year and cool temperatures in winter rest.

Propagation: Burro's tail is very easy to propagate. Small stem cuttings stripped of lower leaves and allowed to dry for a day will take root in damp sand or rooting mix. A single fat leaf inserted into the medium at the end where the leaf is attached to the stem will soon root and grow new tails. Fun to watch!

Remarks: These pale braided trailers are unusual and highly ornamental. Handle gently, as they are delicate and easily broken off. If that *does* happen, just think of all the new baby burro's tails you'll be able to propagate! Fun for children to grow.

GENUS: *Senecio*
FAMILY: Compositae (Daisy)

Senecio rowleyanus. String-of-pearls, string-of-beads. Native to South Africa. In this large genus, the *Compositae,* there are thousands of species and varieties, many of which seem to be unlikely relatives of each other. One of the oddest is the string-of-beads, a trailing succulent. Long, wiry stems festooned with small, round, green beadlike leaves can grow 6 feet or more, if allowed. Each bead has a narrow translucent band around it that you can actually see through if you hold it up to the light. Small white and purple flowers with a spicy scent appear in summer outdoors. The culture of this succulent is similar to that of the burro's tail.

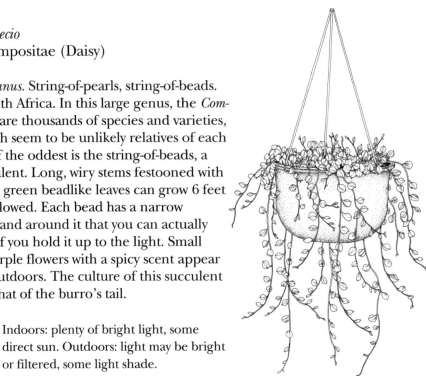

Senecio rowleyanus

Light:	Indoors: plenty of bright light, some direct sun. Outdoors: light may be bright or filtered, some light shade.
Soil:	Sandy Basic Soil Mix (page 28) or half good potting soil, half sand. Add a dash of bonemeal.
Moisture:	Water well and let soil get almost dry between waterings. In winter rest, give only enough water to keep soil from drying out.
Fertilizer:	Feed lightly two or three times from spring to early fall.
Care:	String-of-pearls is an easy plant to grow; it basks in heat, dry air, and good light. No special demands.
Propagation:	Like burro's tail, this succulent propagates with the greatest of ease. Use stem cuttings, or take a single leaf—in this case, a bead—press it into moist sand or rooting mix. Push in the end that was attached to the vine. When young plants are well established, transfer several to a hanging basket or pot where they can dangle as they grow longer.
Remarks:	A unique plant, string-of-beads asks for little care and gets a lot of fascinated stares. It will look its best when the "strings" are gently coaxed to hang down on all sides of the pot. This is another good choice for young gardeners.

GENUS: *Setcreasea*
FAMILY: Commelinaceae (Spiderwort)

Native to Mexico and southern Texas. A trailing plant. *S. pallida* is the one species grown as
an indoor plant, and its commonly found
form is *S.p.* 'Purple Heart'. Lance-shaped
leaves 4 or 5 inches long are purple overlaying
dark green, and altogether purple in full sunlight. Purple stems rise upward, then out and
down, curving 2 or 3 feet, and reaching for
the light. Dainty pink or lavender-pink flowers
open one at a time from clusters of buds in
leaf axils spring through fall, and intermittently at other times.

Setcreasea pallida

Light: Indoors and outdoors: full sun, brightest light for leaf color.

Soil: Basic Soil Mix, page 28.

Moisture: Water thoroughly, then let soil get quite dry before watering again. Purple heart survives admirably in dry air and dry soil.

Fertilizer: Dilute liquid fertilizer monthly is sufficient.

Care: Setcreasea is undemanding. It needs a bit of grooming now and then. Over-long stems may be easily snapped off at any point and any time. Lower leaves on older stems turn brown and may be removed. Repot an overcrowded plant any time, but since large old plants lose much of their charm and are so easy to propagate, it's best to take cuttings and discard the straggly ancients, or cut stems down to their base and let them grow new shoots.

Propagation: Tip and stem pieces, easily broken off, will root in water with surprising speed. Keep the water jar in the sunlight.

Remarks: Purple heart is a tough, long-lived, easy-care plant for pot or basket or any place in the sun where it can stretch out and down. I am very partial to its intense violet-purple leaves, which make such a stunning contrast to green foliage plants, especially outdoors where it gets the brightest light. Leaves that revert to dark green indoors with insufficient light will obligingly turn purple again with plenty of sunshine.

GENUS: *Spathiphyllum*
FAMILY: Araceae (Arum)

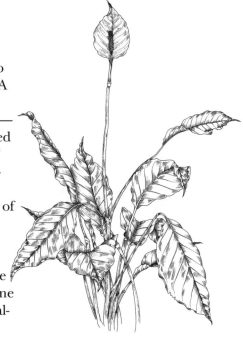

Spathe flower, peace lily, white sails. Native to Colombia and Central America. A rhizome. A thicket of glossy, dark green, lance-shaped leaves rises directly from the soil. The flower—which is called an inflorescence—is composed of two parts: an oval, rather flat white "petal" called a spathe and a creamy or greenish-yellow center spike, or spadix, which bears numerous tiny flowers. These appear on top of a tall stem in spring, summer, and often at other times as well, and have a light, sweet scent. These flowers resemble those of the calla lily in the same family, although they are not as curved or showy. Spathiphyllum is a fine foliage plant even when not in bloom. *S.* 'Wallisii', a foot or less tall, and *S.* 'Clevelandii', taller with larger flowers, are good pot subjects, as is *S.* 'Mauna Loa', which is the tallest of all (up to 3 feet) and has the largest flowers.

Spathiphyllum

Light:	Indoors: medium to filtered or bright light; some shade. Outdoors: light shade.
Soil:	Peaty Basic Soil Mix, page 28.
Moisture:	Water liberally and keep moist. These tropical jungle plants require humidity and warmth. Mist frequently and provide humidity tray.
Fertilizer:	Light dilute liquid fertilizer every two to three weeks from spring to fall.
Care:	No special demands. Spathiphyllum can get along in medium light, but the less light it receives, the less flowers it is likely to produce.
Propagation:	Eventually the pot becomes very crowded and flower production is scanty. The plant needs dividing and repotting. Remove it from the pot and shake off the old soil. If you cannot pull the fleshy rhizomes apart, use the butcher method and slice through the tangled mass with a big, sharp knife. Repot sections with leaves and roots in good organic soil.
Remarks:	Spathiphyllum is a handsome, full, leafy foliage plant with interesting flowers. Keep moist, warm, and in fairly bright light to encourage flower production. The flowers last for many weeks, turning greenish as they age.

GENUS: *Syngonium*
FAMILY: Araceae (Arum)

Formerly known as *Nephthitis*. Arrowhead plant, arrowhead vine. Native to Central America. Resembling some of its relatives, the philodendron, this is an easy-care vining tropical plant. An epiphyte, arrowhead plant prefers a humid atmosphere and can be trained to grow upward on a piece of bark or other support to which its aerial roots can cling. Young leaves are arrow-shaped, and as the plant matures, they gradually evolve into three-lobed, five-lobed, and even up to seven-lobed leaves. The tiny flowers, like others in the arum family, are on a spike with a petallike spathe that ages from light green to a purplish-red. They are rarely seen on an indoor potted plant. *S. podophyllum* is a common variety with light green markings on darker green. *S.p.* 'Emerald Gem' has glossy, crinkly leaves with light green veins on darker green. *S.p.* 'Albolineatum' presents an attractive contrast between silvery-white and dark green, *S.p.* 'Green Gold' between yellow and green. New 'Flutterby' is white and green and is a more compact and bushy form.

Syngonium podophyllum

Light:	Indoors: bright, filtered light. Outdoors: filtered light with some shade.
Soil:	Basic Soil Mix, page 28.
Moisture:	Water well and keep slightly moist. Misting is beneficial.
Fertilizer:	Dilute liquid feeding monthly is sufficient.
Care:	Not a fussy plant, the arrowhead vine adapts well to varying conditions of light and temperature and even occasional lack of moisture. Let it trail or climb. For a bushier plant, cut back long stems.
Propagation:	Tip cuttings root readily in water.
Remarks:	An easygoing old favorite, syngonium is attractive in a hanging basket combined with variegated pothos or heartleaf philodendron or climbing on a mossed pole or slab of bark or wood.

GENUS: *Tolmiea*
FAMILY: Saxifragaceae (Saxifrage)

T. menziesii, the only species of this genus, has many common names: piggy-back plant, pick-a-back plant, youth-on-age, and mother-of-thousands. It is native to mountainous northwest United States, Canada, and Alaska. Bright green, hairy, serrated, heart-shaped leaves grow on 8- to 10-inch stems; its total height is about 12 inches. The novel charm of this small, low-growing plant that hugs the ground under trees in its native habitat is in the production of plantlets where the leaves join the stalk.

Tolmiea menziesii

Light: Indoors: bright, filtered light; no direct sun. Outdoors: filtered or light shade.

Soil: Basic Soil Mix, page 28.

Moisture: Water generously and keep moist. Don't let roots dry out.

Fertilizer: Dilute liquid fertilizer every two to three weeks.

Care: Tolmiea is undemanding, and while it prefers a cool, moist atmosphere, it adapts well to normal house conditions. Repot only when roots and foliage overcrowd the pot. Shallow pots are best for these shallow-rooted plants.

Propagation: New plants are fun and easy to grow. Cut off a leaf with the baby plantlet attached, along with an inch or two of stem. Plant in moist rooting mix with stalk below and leaf with plantlet sitting on the surface. In a short time, the plantlet will take root and be on its own, ready to be moved into a pot with good soil. Tolmiea can also be propagated by affixing a plantlet-bearing leaf to the surface of the rooting mix in a pot next to the parent, still attached to the parent. In a few weeks the baby plantlet, well rooted, can be cut loose. Cuttings can also be rooted in water.

Remarks: Tolmiea is a fast-growing, easy-care plant with refreshing apple-green foliage. It tends to trail as it grows, becoming a fine choice for a hanging basket as well as for a table or stand. This is a nice plant for a child to grow and propagate.

GENUS: *Tradescantia*
FAMILY: Commelinaceae (Spiderwort)

Wandering Jew, inch plant. Native to tropical South and Central America. This fast-growing trailing plant is closely related to and often confused with zebrina, also called wandering Jew. *T. fluminensis* 'Quicksilver' is a commonly seen variety bearing white and green striped leaves with a reddish-purple reverse. *T. blossfel-diana* has dark green leaves with purple undersides. *T.b.* 'Variegata' combines pink with green and cream, and has pink undersides and stems. Small pink and white flowers are borne in spring. Look for 'Rainbow'—pink, white, and green with a pinkish-violet reverse, its small leaves glow prettily in bright sunlight. There are other forms with variegated foliage in shades of green, cream, pink, bronze, purple, and white.

Tradescantia fluminensis

Light:	Indoors and outdoors: bright with some direct sun.
Soil:	Basic Soil Mix, page 28.
Moisture:	Water well and let soil get somewhat dry between waterings.
Fertilizer:	Dilute liquid feeding monthly is sufficient.
Care:	Little is required. Pinch back long, straggling stems. They will sprout out at the side. When older stems lose leaves near the base, they become unsightly and should be cut down close to the base. A potful of these stumps will look terrible for a while, but new shoots will soon appear and the plants will flourish.
Propagation:	As with its relative zebrina, tip and stem cuttings in water will take root with surprising rapidity and can be potted when the roots are an inch long.
Remarks:	These undemanding trailers are often neglected and allowed to become lanky and full of dead leaves. With a little care, they can present a fine cascade of colorful foliage in a hanging basket, window box, or container of flowering New Guinea impatiens or other flowering plants for an attractive outdoor display.

GENUS: *Vallota*
FAMILY: Amaryllidaceae (Amaryllis)

V. speciosa. Scarborough lily. A bulb. Native to South Africa. This bulb in the amaryllis family got its name when a ship was wrecked early in the nineteenth century off the coast of Scarborough, England. The bulbs from the cargo washed ashore and were planted and found to be excellent potted plants. They produce stunning, bright scarlet, trumpet-shaped flowers in tightly packed umbels of from three to ten blooms on 1½- to 2-foot sturdy stems, and straplike, glossy, dark green leaves up to 2 feet long.

Vallota speciosa

Light: Indoors: full sun. Outdoors: filtered or light shade.

Soil: Basic Soil Mix (page 28) with a bit of extra sand and a dash of bonemeal.

Moisture: Saturate soil at planting, then water sparingly. When growth arises, increase watering and keep moist from spring to fall. Reduce after flowering in mid- to late summer and give scant amounts during winter rest from October to March, just enough to keep leaves from wilting.

Fertilizer: Weekly dilute liquid fertilizer from early spring through June. Occasional low-nitrogen formula will promote bloom. Stop feeding after flowering.

Care: Plant vallota in a smallish pot, 5 to 6 inches wide, with the top and neck of the bulb exposed and only about 1½ to 2 inches between the bulb and the sides of the pot. Water thoroughly and place in a sunny spot. Mist new growth often for best results. Scarborough lily blooms best when potbound and can remain in the same pot for several years, with topdressing. The roots are very touchy about being disturbed, so don't transplant unless extremely overcrowded. Cooler temperatures at night are desirable. During winter rest, a constant cool temperature (55° to 60° F) is needed for next season's bloom. Continued bright light is required for the evergreen foliage.

Propagation: In three or four years, the pot will become very crowded with roots and offsets. Parent and bulblets may be moved all together into a larger size pot with fresh soil, or the bulblets can be detached and planted separately in small pots with their tips exposed. The big bulb can be reinstalled with good new soil in the original pot or one a size larger, if that seems necessary. Late spring or early summer is the time for these procedures.

Remarks: Vallota produces strikingly handsome flowers for a sunny window or patio in late summer or early fall when few other bulbs are in bloom. Like many other South African bulbs, it needs bright days, cool nights, and cool temperatures during its resting period in order to flourish happily. Varieties in pink and white are available, but the original brilliant scarlet is the most dramatic.

GENUS: *Veltheimia*
FAMILY: Liliaceae (Lily)

Forest lily. A bulb. Native to South Africa. One of the more unusual bulbs, veltheimia is planted in late summer or early fall and leafs out in late fall. Flowers appear in late winter or early spring. The plant then goes dormant over the summer. *V. capensis* has dark green, rippled leaves up to a foot long. Densely packed, drooping, tubular flowers in clusters on a foot-long stalk are light pink with greenish tips. *V. viridifolia* has longer, brighter green leaves and a taller flower stalk with pinkish-purple, yellow-dotted blooms.

Veltheimia capensis

Light: Indoors and outdoors: full sun at least four hours; bright light otherwise.

Soil: Basic Soil Mix (page 28) with added sand or perlite for good drainage.

Moisture: Moderate. Let soil dry slightly between waterings. In late spring as foliage yellows, reduce water and omit altogether during summer dormancy. Resume watering in late fall when new growth arises.

Fertilizer: High phosphorus-potash formula feeding such as 10-30-20 every three to four weeks during active growth.

Care: Plant veltheimia with its tip above the surface of the soil with 1½ to 2 inches between the bulb and the sides of the pot. Water sparingly until shoots appear. Give plenty of sun, but not heat. Night temperatures should be cool, not over 60° F, if possible. In summer rest or dormant period, heat in addition to sun is welcomed, as in veltheimia's natural habitat. Repot only when offsets fill the pot or when flowers and foliage get skimpier and less vigorous. This plant flourishes best when left undisturbed.

Propagation: When the pot is filled to bursting and the plant must be repotted, take offsets or bulblets, with a couple of leaves attached, and plant them separately in small pots. A mature veltheimia will produce quite a few offsets. They will take about three years to reach the flowering stage.

Remarks: Give veltheimia cool, bright growing conditions and hot, dry summer dormancy, and you will have a distinctive flowering bulb with handsome foliage to grace your collection.

GENUS: *Yucca*
FAMILY: Agavaceae (Agave)

Native to Mexico and the southwest United States. Yuccas are desert plants that can grow extremely tall, but since they are slow growers and inhibited by containers, it takes many years until a potted specimen becomes unwieldy. Buy only young, small ones for the home. Yuccas have thick, woody trunks topped with long, pointed, dark green leaves. They produce splendid spikes of bell-shaped white blossoms, sometimes with a touch of purple. These flowers are delightfully fragrant. The plants rarely bloom if kept indoors all year round.

Yucca aloifolia

Y. aloifolia: Spanish bayonet, dagger plant. The 1- to 2-foot stiff, sword-shaped leaves growing in a rosette form are edged with tiny teeth. Handle with respect. Cultivars have white or yellow stripes or borders, and some sport a red or pink tinge. *Y. gloriosa,* called Roman candle, palm lily, and Spanish dagger, and *Y. filamentosa,* Adam's needle, are two other varieties that have fairly short trunks.

Light: Indoors and outdoors: bright, with plenty of full sun.

Soil: Basic Soil Mix (page 28) with some extra sand or perlite added for good drainage.

Moisture: Moderate. Let soil become quite dry between waterings.

Fertilizer: Dilute liquid fertilizer every two to three weeks during active summer growth period.

Care: These desert plants are more comfortable in dry and heated interiors than most plants. Summer them outdoors in full sun, and you should be rewarded with those sensational flower spikes on mature plants. Use sturdy clay pots or wood tubs when repotting large yuccas.

Propagation: Offsets with several good-sized leaves may be cut off from the parent in the spring and potted in sandy soil.

Remarks: A common sight in west and southwest regions of the country where they may remain in containers outdoors all year round, if so desired, the yucca is a dramatic addition to a plant collection in other areas. My Spanish bayonet finally had to be trucked to a greenhouse when I could no longer get it back into the house, but that was after fifteen years.

GENUS: *Zantedeschia*
FAMILY: Araceae (Arum)

Zantedeschia

Calla lily. Native to South Africa. A rhizome. The elegant calla thrives in a pot, providing it gets watery conditions similar to those in its native boggy home. Bloom time is spring and early summer. *Z. aethiopica,* the common calla, has large, somewhat arrow-shaped dark green leaves a foot or more long and a fragrant white flower, typical of the arum family, consisting of a petallike spathe enclosing a yellow spike, the spadix, that bears the tiny true flowers. *Z.a. minor* is a shorter form with smaller flowers. *Z. rehmannii* has pink or rose flowers and grows to a height of one foot, the shortest of all forms. *Z. elliottiana,* the golden calla, is bright yellow and sports leaves speckled with bright green spots. Hybrid callas are red, lavender, pink, bronze, yellow, and cream. Look for 'Green Goddess', a cultivar of *Z. elliottiana,* for something different and special; it has variegated, large, striking green flowers.

Light: Indoors: bright light, some direct sun. Outdoors: bright or filtered light.

Soil: Basic Soil Mix (page 28) with a sprinkle of dried manure.

Moisture: You will get good results if you waterlog calla during its active growing period and let it get quite dry during summer rest.

Fertilizer: Biweekly dilute liquid fertilizer during active growth; weekly when plant is in bud and flower. Callas are heavy feeders.

Care: Pot rhizomes in early fall, or repot if necessary after a warm, sunny summer outdoors while resting. Place rhizomes 2 to 3 inches deep with tips level with the surface of the soil, one to a 5- or 6-inch pot. Soak thoroughly and set in a cool, dim spot until new growth appears. Then give bright light and slight amounts of water, increasing both generously as the shoots grow taller. Often as many as eight or nine shoots arise. Leaves appear well before buds. Bulbs purchased in spring are getting ready to produce growth; plant at once. Callas like a wet wallow, and you can disregard the cautionary "don't leave a plant sitting in water" for this plant. In fact, it's a good idea to place the pot in a bowl or deep saucer of water with a little fertilizer in it so that the plant can drink to its heart's content. Keep water in the bowl. Cool night temperatures are best until after flowering. Keep in bright light. After leaves yellow and wither, the plant goes dormant. Let it dry out and rest. As new growth starts up in fall, resume regular schedule. If the pot is crowded, separate the tubers for propagation.

Propagation: In fall, when the plant is coming out of dormancy, separate divisions with growing shoots and plant large ones singly in an 8-inch pot; several small shoots or offsets can be planted together in this same size pot. If preferred, start small divisions or offsets singly in 3- or 4-inch pots. Give rich, organic soil; provide care as above. If you wish to keep a very large calla undivided, transfer to a 10- or 12-inch pot.

Remarks: Water and feed callas with a lavish hand, and you will have flowers of great beauty and distinction. They imbibe astounding amounts of water, so make sure there is always plenty to drink in the water bowl, just as you do with your cat or dog.

GENUS: *Zebrina*
FAMILY: Commelinaceae (Spiderwort)

Wandering Jew, inch plant. Native of Mexico. Closely related to tradescantia, which has the same common names. A rapidly growing trailing plant, *Z. pendula* looks graceful in a hanging basket and is foolproof to grow. Its green leaves with two silvery-white stripes have reddish-purple undersides. Both surfaces become more purplish as the plant gets more sun. *Z.p.* 'Quadricolor', one of the handsomest of the variegated forms, has leaves striped in tones of green, cream, pink, and white, with a rosy or purplish reverse. Other forms have attractive bronze, copper, red, and purplish-brown tones.

Light: Indoors and outdoors: bright, with some direct sun.

Soil: Basic Soil Mix, page 28.

Moisture: Moderate. Keep moist. Less in winter. Mist for humidity.

Fertilizer: Dilute liquid feeding once a month.

Care: No special demands. Long stems usually develop dry, brown leaves near their base. Cut stems back for a bushier plant. Hard pruning of a gawky tangle of stems will bring forth ample new growth. Remove brown leaves.

Propagation: Tip cuttings root eagerly in water.

Remarks: Because it is so undemanding and active, zebrina, like its relative tradescantia, is often neglected and gets scraggly and unattractive. When properly pinched back and given plenty of light and regular care, it makes a very decorative and pleasing hanging plant. It roots and grows quickly. From two cuttings rooted in water in winter, potted, nipped back, and nipped back again, I was able to fill an 8-inch hanging basket in spring in time to hang outdoors. Like tradescantia, the other wandering Jew, this is a great plant for children and beginners; easy, fast, and care-free. Both can be used in window boxes and in large pots or tubs to mantle the surface of the soil around a tall plant or trail gracefully over the sides. Inch plants add a nice, cascading touch to pots of upright flowering annuals in summer on patio or deck.

Zebrina pendula

Glossary

Active growth period The period when a plant puts forth new growth. For most plants, this is early spring to fall.

Aerial roots Roots that emerge from stems to grow upward to cling to a surface or downward to grow back into the soil.

Annual A plant that grows, blooms, sets its seeds, and dies in one year or less.

Axil The angle between a leaf and its stem where new growth frequently arises.

Bract A modified leaf growing as part of a flower or around a flower; often very colorful, as in poinsettia.

Cultivar A cultivated variety of a species of plant.

Dormancy A plant is dormant, or in a period of dormancy, when its activity ceases altogether. In semi-dormancy, the top growth dies but the roots remain alive, as in lilies.

Epiphyte A plant that lives in the wild by clinging to a tree, other plant, or rock with its aerial roots, getting nourishment from the air and from decayed matter in the crevice it occupies. Many ferns.

Evergreen Evergreen plants retain their leaves all year, unlike deciduous plants, which lose their leaves after active growth.

Foliar spray A spray that gives nourishment to a plant through its leaves, but does not replace fertilizing into the soil. Foliar spray can be made with water-soluble plant food or a special solution, often with kelp (liquid seaweed), containing nutrients and growth stimulants.

Frond Leaf of a fern or palm with segments called pinnae (singular pinna).

Hardy Able to survive freezing temperatures.

Hormone rooting powder A powdered substance that promotes root production and may hasten establishment of a root system on cuttings. Not considered necessary on soft-stemmed cuttings from most plants. It is most effective on woody-stemmed cuttings.

Hybrid An offspring produced by the crossing, or interbreeding, of two different parents. These may be of two different varieties, or species, or forms of closely related genera, but not of different families. The hybrid bears characteristics of both parents but is different from either one.

Inflorescence The flowering part of a plant.

Node The place or joint on a stem where a bud or leaf is attached.

Offset A young plant that grows at the base of its parent; a shoot or bulblet, often with roots. It can be detached for propagation. If very small, it may be allowed to remain attached and grow larger.

Perennial A plant that lives for two or more years. Those that keep their leaves all year long are referred to as "evergreen."

Potbound A plant is potbound when roots fill all the soil, are emerging through the drainage hole, and/or appear on the surface of the soil. Other indications are reduced growth and vigor or smaller, yellow leaves.

Rest period The period when a plant is more or less inactive, following the period of active growth. Few or no new leaves are produced.

Runner A prostrate stem that produces buds at nodes from which new roots and growth arise.

Spadix The flower spike on which tiny flowers are closely packed, found in Araceae, the arum family.

Spathe The large petal-like bract, or modified leaf, that encloses or partly surrounds the spadix. See spadix.

Standard A plant that can be trained into treelike form, with a crown of foliage on a single trunk. Details given under *Lantana* in The Guide.

Stolon A creeping horizontal stem that may take root at any point where it lies on the surface of the soil.

Succulent A plant, usually from a desert or dry region, with thick or fleshy stems and/or leaves that serve to store water.

Tender Having little or no tolerance for very cold or freezing temperatures.

Terminal The top or uppermost growth, bud, or flower on a stem.

Tip or Stem Cutting A cutting 3 to 5 inches long taken from the end of a stem or branch, and also in some cases from below a growing point or node lower on the stem, for purposes of propagation. It should be without buds or flowers so that no energy is diverted from the root production. See Propagation in The Guide.

Topdressing The replacement with fresh soil of an equal amount of older soil that has been removed from the surface, used on a large plant that is in the maximum convenient size pot.

Variegated Foliage that is colored and/or patterned, not entirely green.

Woody A woody stem is hard and darker in color than soft, tender stems and is more permanent.

Sources for Plants and Supplies

Some firms charge for their catalogs; the cost is usually refunded with your first order.

General Sources of Plants, Bulbs, Growing Aids, Supplies, and Seeds

Antonelli Bros., 2545 Capitola Road, Santa Cruz, CA 95063. Catalog $1. Specializing in tuberous begonia and other bulbs and tubers.

W. Atlee Burpee Co., 300 Park Avenue, Warminster, PA 18974.

Caladium World, P.O. Drawer 629, Sebring, FL 33871. Caladiums and shade-loving bulbs.

Henry Field's, Dept. 87-4487 Oak Street, Shenandoah, IA 51602.

Klehm Nursery, Route 5, Box 197, Penny Road, South Barrington, IL 60010.

Mellinger's, 2370JE Range Road, North Lima, OH 44452.

Milaeger's Gardens, 4838 Douglas Avenue, Racine, WI 53482.

Nature's Garden, Route 1, Box 488, Beaverton, OR 97007. Catalog $1. Plants from the Northwest.

Park Seed, Cokesbury Road, P.O. Box 47, Greenwood, SC 29748.

Shady Oaks Nursery, 700 19th Avenue, NE, Waseca, MN 56093. Catalog $1. Specializing in plants for shade.

John Scheepers, Philipsburg Road, No. 2, Middletown, NY 10940.

Siskiyou Rare Plant Nursery, 2825 Cummings Road, Medford, OR 97501. Catalog $1.

Thompson & Morgan, P.O. Box 1308, Jackson, NJ 08527.

Wayside Gardens, Hodges, SC 29695. Catalog $1.

Sources Specializing in Geraniums

Cook's Geranium Nursery, 712 North Grand, Lyons, KS 67554.

Merry Gardens, Camden, ME 04843. Catalog $2.

Shady Hill Gardens, 835 Walnut, Batavia, IL 60510. Catalog $2. Specializing in ivy, dwarf, and scented geraniums.

Wheeler Farm Gardens, 171 Bartlett Street, Portland, CT 06480. Specializing in European balcony ivy geraniums, zonals.

Sources for Cacti and Succulents

Cactus/Succulent Nursery, 12712 Stockton Boulevard, Galt, CA 95632.

Garden World, 2503 Garfield, Laredo, TX 78043. Catalog $1. Also tropicals.

Henrietta's Nursery, 1345-E N. Brawley, Fresno, CA 93722. Catalog 25 cents.

Highland Succulents, Eureka Star Route-133, Gallopolis, OH 45631. Catalog $3.

Rainbow Gardens, 1444 Taylor Street, Vista, CA 92084. Catalog $2.

Sources for Tropical Plants, Bulbs, and Palms

Davidson-Wilson Greenhouse, Route 2, P.O. Box 168, Ladoga Road, Crawfordville, IN 47933. Catalog $1. Flowering plants, tropicals.

Endangered Species, Box 1830, Tustin, CA 92680. Specializing in sago palm, other cycads, and more.

Fancy Fronds, 1911 Fourth Avenue West, Seattle, WA 98119. Catalog $1. Specializing in ferns.

The Green Escape, 1212 Ohio Avenue, Dept. H, P.O. Box 1417, Palm Harbor, FL 34682. Catalog $6. Hardy, rare, tropicals, palms; help for northern gardeners.

Heliconia & Ginger Gardens, Box 79161, Houston, TX 77279-9161. Tropicals.

Logee's Greenhouses, 55 North Street, Danielson, CT 06239. Catalog $3. Exotic and unusual flowering bulbs, tropicals.

Mary Walker Bulb Co., P.O. Box 256, Omega, GA 31775. Southern specialties.

Oregon Bulb Farms, SE Lusted Road, Sandy, OR 97055. Catalog $2.

Paradise Garden, P.O. Box 2104-B, LaPlace, LA 70069.

Plumeria People, P.O. Box 820014, Houston, TX 77282-0014. Catalog $2. Flowering tropicals, bulbs, growing aids.

Rex Bulb Farms, Box 774, Port Townsend, WA 98368. Catalog $1.

Rhapis Gardens, P.O. Box 287, Gregory, TX 78359. Catalog $1.

TyTy South, Highway 82, TyTy, GA 31795. Unusual bulbs, tropicals.

Sources for Dwarf Citrus Trees

Four Winds Growers, Box 3538, 42186 Palm Avenue, Fremont, CA 94539. Citrus. Leaflet of varieties with instructions for container growing.

Banana Tree, 713 North Hampton Street, Easton, PA 18042. Catalog 25 cents. Citrus, plus.

Burgess Seed & Plant Co., 905 Four Seasons Road, Bloomington, IL 61701. Citrus, plus.

Lifetime Nursery Products, 1866 Sheridan Road, Highland Park, IL 60035. Citrus, plus.

Pacific Tree Farms, 4301 Lynnwood Drive, Chula Vista, CA 92010. Citrus, plus.

Van Bourgondien Bros., Box A, Dept. 4350, Babylon, NY 11702. Citrus, bulbs, plus.

Sources for Tools, Supplies, Containers, and Accessories

The Carolina Gardener, 11746 Route 108, Clarksville, MD 21029. Catalog $2. Specializing in planter boxes and cachepots.

Gardener's Eden, P.O. Box 7307, San Francisco, CA 94120-7307.

Gardener's Supply, 128 Intervale Road, Burlington, VT 05401-2804.

Smith & Hawken, 25 Corte Madera, Mill Valley, CA 94941.

The Plow & Hearth, 560 Main Street, Madison, VA 22727. Catalog $1.

The Kinsman Company, River Road, Point Pleasant, PA 18950.

Hen Feathers, 1000 Black Rock Road, Gladwyne, PA 19035. Planters, statuary, garden ornaments.

Indoor Gardening Supplies, Box 40567, Detroit, MI 48240.

Intracorp, 362 Commonwealth Avenue, Boston, MA 02115. Catalog $3. Planters, statuary, garden ornaments.

Rotocast Plastic Products, 3645 NW 67th Street, Miami, FL 33147. Lightweight plastic planters that look like terra cotta.

Warren Barrel Co., Box 275, Warren, ME 04864. Oak and cedar barrels.

Societies

When writing for information, enclose a legal-size self-addressed stamped envelope.

Indoor Gardening Society of America, 128 West 58th Street, New York, NY 10019.

Indoor Gardening Society of Canada, 16 Edgar Woods Road, Willowdale, Ontario M2H 2Y7.

American Begonia Society, 157 Monument, Rio Del, CA 95562.

American Fuchsia Society, 738-22nd Avenue, San Francisco, CA 94121.

American Hibiscus Society, Drawer 1540, Cocoa Beach, FL 32931.

American Fern Society, Dept. of Botany, University of Tennessee, Knoxville, TN 37916.

American Ivy Society, Box 520, West Carollton, OH 45449.

Cactus and Succulent Society of America, Box 3010, Santa Barbara, CA 93130.

The Cycad Society, 1161 Phyllis Court, Mountain View, CA 94040.

Gardenia Society of America, Box 879, Atwater, CA 95301.

Hoya Society International, Box 54271, Atlanta, GA 30308.

Indoor Citrus and Rare Fruit Society, 176 Coronado Avenue, Los Altos, CA 94022. Newsletter $1.

International Aroid Society, Box 43—1853, South Miami, FL 33143

International Palm Society, Box 368, Lawrence, KS 66044

International Tropical Fern Society, 8720 SW 34th Street, Miami, FL 33165.

The Palm Society, 7229 SW 54th Avenue, Miami, FL 33143.

Suggested Reading

Baumgardt, John Philip. *Hanging Plants for Home, Terrace and Garden*. New York: Simon & Schuster, 1972.

Crockett, James Underwood. *Crockett's Indoor Garden*. Boston: Little, Brown & Co., 1978.

Crockett, James Underwood, and the editors of Time-Life Books. *Foliage House Plants*. The Time-Life Encyclopedia of Gardening. New York: Time, Inc., 1974.

————. *Flowering House Plants*. The Time-Life Encyclopedia of Gardening. New York: Time, Inc., 1971.

Davidson, William. *Exotic Flowering House Plants*. Successful Indoor Gardening Series. Los Angeles: Price Stern Sloan, 1989.

————. *Exotic Foliage House Plants*. Successful Indoor Gardening Series. Los Angeles: Price Stern Sloan, 1989.

DeWolf, Gordon P. Jr., ed. *Taylor's Guide to Houseplants*. Boston: Houghton Mifflin Co., 1987. Revision of Taylor's Encyclopedia of Gardening, Fourth Edition, by Norman Taylor, 1961.

Everett, Thomas H. *New York Botanical Garden Illustrated Encyclopedia of Horticulture*. 10 vols. New York: Garland Publishing, 1980–82.

Faust, Joan Lee. *The New York Times Book of House Plants.* New York: The New York Times Book Co., 1983.

Graham, Victor. *Growing Succulent Plants.* Beaverton, OR: Timber Press, 1987.

Halpin, Anne M. *The Window Box Book.* New York: Simon & Schuster, 1989.

Hessayon, D. G. *The Houseplant Expert.* New York: Sterling, 1990.

Horton, Alvin. *All About Bulbs.* Edited by Michael D. Smith. San Ramon, CA: Ortho Books, 1985.

Huxley, Anthony, gen. ed., and Reader's Digest staff. *Success with House Plants.* Pleasantville, NY: Reader's Digest Association, 1979.

Kramer, Jack. *Easy Plants for Difficult Places.* New York: Walker Publishing Co., 1975.

———. *First Aid for Plants.* New York: New American Library, 1989.

———. *Hanging Baskets Gardens.* New York: Charles Scribner's Sons, 1971.

———. *The New American Emergency Plant Care Guide.* New York: New American Library, 1988.

Liberty H. Bailey Hortorium, Cornell University. *Hortus Third.* New York: Macmillan Co., 1976.

Martin, Tovah. *Once Upon A Windowsill.* Beaverton, OR: Timber Press, 1989.

McDonald, Elvin. *Decorative Gardening in Containers.* New York: Doubleday & Company, 1978.

Reilly, Ann. *Taylor's Pocket Guide to Bulbs for Summer.* Boston: Houghton Mifflin Co., 1989.

Stevenson, Violet. *Indoor Plants.* New York: Arco Publishing, 1980.

Sunset Magazine & Books Editors. *Gardening in Containers.* Menlo Park, CA: Lane Publishing Company, 1975.

———. *Houseplants.* Fourth Edition. Menlo Park, CA: Lane Publishing Co., 1983.

———. *New Western Garden Book.* Menlo Park, CA: Lane Book Co., 1979.

Taloumis, George. *Container Gardening.* New York: Brooklyn Botanic Garden Record, 1989.

————. *House Plants for Five Exposures.* New York: Signet Books, New American Library, 1975.

Yang, Linda. *The Terrace Gardener's Handbook.* Beaverton, OR: Timber Press, 1982.

Index

About the Author

A dedicated and knowledgeable gardener for thirty-five years, Ruth Shaw Ernst tends a vast collection of potted plants indoors and out as the seasons permit at her Scarsdale, New York, home. She writes and lectures on all aspects of indoor and outdoor gardening, is active in the local garden club, and has been a blue-ribbon winner in flower shows. A number of her articles have appeared in *The New York Times* and in other newspapers and magazines. She is also the author of *The Naturalist's Garden*.

OTHER BOOKS OF INTEREST FROM GLOBE PEQUOT PRESS

Garden Smarts

❀

The Wildflower Meadow Book, 2nd edition

❀

Garden Flower Folklore

❀

Wildflower Folklore

❀

The Natural History of Wild Shrubs and Vines

❀

The National Trust Book of Wild Flower Gardening

❀

Classic Garden Plants Series:

*Herbs · Dahlias · Rhododendrons · Fuchsias · Auriculas
Magnolias · Climbing Roses · Modern Garden Roses · Azaleas*

These and other gardening books are available at your bookstore
or direct from the publisher. For a free catalogue write Globe Pequot Press,
Box Q, Chester, CT 06412 or call 1-800-243-0495.
In Connecticut call 1-800-962-0973.